Be a
HERO

WESLEY CAMPBELL
AND STEPHEN COURT

Be a
HERO

*The Battle for Mercy
and Social Justice*

Destiny Image® Publishers, Inc.
P.O. Box 310
Shippensburg, PA 17257-0310

*"Speaking to the Purposes of God for This Generation
and for the Generations to Come"*

ISBN 0-7684-2230-2

For Worldwide Distribution
Printed in the U.S.A.

This book and all other Destiny Image, Revival Press, MercyPlace,
Fresh Bread, Destiny Image Fiction, and Treasure House books are available
at Christian bookstores and distributors worldwide.

1 2 3 4 5 6 7 8 9 10 / 09 08 07 06 05 04

For a U.S. bookstore nearest you, call
1-800-722-6774.

For more information on foreign distributors, call
717-532-3040.

Or reach us on the Internet:
www.destinyimage.com

DEDICATION

With love in the comradeship of this eternal warfare, to Stacey and Danielle.

With humility, to the People people suffering right now under the seven deadly sins.

With hope, to the warriors of the End-Time Hero Army, gearing up for mobilization to win the whole world for Jesus. We salute you!

ACKNOWLEDGEMENTS

God has been churning the contents of this book in us for years now. Preaching it has only stirred up the convictions more. This has been more a burden of necessity than a labor of love, but we are grateful for the legacy of history's hero armies. They stir us on to love and good deeds.

The result of collaboration is better than the sum of its parts. We're excited to work with Destiny Image on this project. We've had input from a handful of comrades: Ralph Bromley, Patrick McDonald, Doug Hammond, and John Norton, heroes all, modeling, spurring on, and helping us tighten things up. You'll read more about Ralph Bromley, the founder of Hope For The Nations, later in this book.

Patrick McDonald is the founder and president of the Viva Network, a Christian leader on the world front of confronting the foes of children at risk. Viva Network was developed in response to that need and today operates in 43 countries, connecting more than 4,000 organizations, helping 157, 000 children. He wrote the Foreword to this book as well as the Epilogue.

Doug Hammond develops Christian community capacity on the front lines in Africa with The Salvation Army. John Norton is both a thinker and a practitioner, advocating for the marginalized as he lives among and evangelizes them.

We recognize that the Holy Spirit, the Hero-maker, is working behind the scenes to make every good page good. We'll take the blame for the rest.

We acknowledge the pioneers of PSN at the 2001 Council of War in Williams Lake, Canada, where the concept of the book and the connection of the authors was made. More!

Praise God!

Wesley Campbell and Stephen Court
July 1, 2004

ENDORSEMENTS

Wesley Campbell and Stephen Court are heroes for showing that mercy and social justice are not optional for the Body of Christ, or for renewal and revival. They are proof of the quality of God's Kingdom on earth, and the measure of our qualification for eternal life in accordance with Matthew 25. In the hands of the Holy Spirit, *Be a Hero* will stir the Church to love and good works through intimate obedience to Jesus, and will fan the flames of revival around the world.

Rolland and Heidi Baker
Authors, *There Is Always Enough*

After thirty-five years of full-time ministry, you develop certain discernment as to the relevance of different men and their ministry. In *Be a Hero* Wesley Campbell and Stephen Court have clearly shown us that although revival starts in the church, the ultimate purpose is for the Body of Christ to share this experience with the rest of the world. Whether it is the inner city of New York, the garbage dumps of Manila or the streets of middle America, I have found that the love of God for mankind transcends culture, race and financial position. We as Christians need to realize that we are chosen to reach the lost and step out in faith. This book will challenge you that "one person can make a difference" and you can "be a hero" to someone less fortunate.

Pastor Bill Wilson
Metro Ministries, Brooklyn, New York

Caution! The reading of this book will leave you with a broken heart. Wesley Campbell and Stephen Court clearly lay out the worldwide scope of abuse, abandonment, and devaluation of the child, all focused on the destruction of a generation of youth. The book, though, provides a message of hope, with a well defined and applicable model of response for those willing to radically follow the One who challenged his disciples to become as a child.

David Boyd
Chancellor, University of the Nations / Kona

I urge you to read this book and let your heart be stirred by things that break God's heart. The children must receive our attention in prayer and compassionate involvement not only because they are much beloved by the Lord, but also because, in His hands, they are the hope of our shattered, despairing world.

John Robb
Chairman, International Prayer Council;
Director of Prayer Mobilization for World Vision International

Be a Hero challenges the complacency of the Western church in the face of injustice and poverty. It shakes up those of us who are content to sit on the sidelines and watch the needless suffering of God's children. Campbell and Court show us that the church has, and can make a difference. Becoming a hero is within us all.

Paul Stephenson
Children At Risk Manager, Tearfund, UK

I believe with all my heart, that *Be a Hero* is not only a word from the mouth of God, but much more from the heart of God. This is a prophetic book—a call to this generation. Yet, for a prophetic book it is intensely practical, in that it not only gives the vision but also provides the tools with which we can carry the vision out. I whole-heartedly commend this book.

Mike Pilavachi
Founder & Team Leader, Soul Survivor England

As "The Call" was to transform a Nation through corporate gatherings of prayer and fasting, *Be a Hero* is a strong trumpet call to mobilize this generation to "do justice and to love mercy."

Che Ahn
Senior Pastor, Harvest Rock Church
CEO and Chairman, The Call

There are very few issues that will demonstrate our alignment with God's heart for the church of the 21st century; one is where we believers stand on Israel, and the other is how we respond to the poor and disaffected of the world. In this book, Wesley Campbell and Stephen Court reveal secrets of the endtime global harvest and demonstrate how every believer in Jesus can impact our earth for the kingdom of God.

Robert Stearns
Executive Director, Eagles' Wings New York

Bless yourself. Position yourself downstream in the River of God's grace. It is flowing to the starving children, the AIDS orphans, and the persecuted refugee. And as you bless yourself, you can potentially bless untold numbers of these dear people for whom the Savior died.

Dutch Sheets
Senior Pastor, Springs Harvest Fellowship & Author

God has been moving His people powerfully toward aggressively transforming society on all levels. *Be a Hero* will show you how to step up to the plate and do your share to help make this happen.

C. Peter Wagner, Chancellor
Wagner Leadership Institute

TABLE OF CONTENTS

TABLE OF FIGURES 15

PREFACE 17

Foreword 21
by Patrick McDonald

SECTION ONE 25

CHAPTER ONE 27
Be A Hero:
Incredible Stories of Heroes and Why We Need Them

CHAPTER TWO 43
Faces and Hearts:
Getting a Lay of the Heroic Landscape

CHAPTER THREE 57
God's Big Idea
The Ingredients of Heroism: Justice,
Righteousness, and Compassion

CHAPTER FOUR 81
The Heroes of the Wars of the Lord:
How Normal People Imbued With the Hero-Maker
Accomplished Superhuman Feats, Serving People

Job—Proto-Revival
Moses—The Egyptian Deliverance
Samuel and David and Solomon—Golden Age of Israel
Asa—The Asa Awakening
Uzziah—When Kings Go To War
Jonah and the King—The Ninevah Headstand
Josiah—The Revival of Religion
John, Jesus, and the Apostles—The Kingdom of God at Hand

SECTION TWO 105

CHAPTER FIVE 107
Victorian England:
    The Best of Times
    The Worst of Times
    Revolution?
    Sanitation
    Outrageously Overworked and Underpaid
    Sex? No Thanks, We're British
    A Drugged Culture?
    The Hero Army Mobilizes

CHAPTER SIX 119
Revolution
    Conceived In Prophecy
    Birthed in Fire
    Heroes All
    The Fruit and the Root
    One-Track Mind
    The Daring, Reckless, Determined Standard
    Mission Crafted System
    An Unleashed Holy Spirit
    Thorough Repentence
    Persecution
    The Conquest of Devil's Island

CHAPTER SEVEN 137
In Darkest England And The Way Out
    The Cab Horse Charter

Lights in Darkest England
Deliverance
The City Colony
The Farm Colony
The Overseas Colony
Promoted to Glory

SECTION THREE 149

CHAPTER EIGHT 151
Who Are They and Where Do They Come From?

CHAPTER NINE 173
Seven Deadly Sins
Dirt Poor
Children in Chains
Orphans of the Street
Sex and the City
AIDS and Plagues
The Exigencies of War
Religious Persecution

CHAPTER TEN 215
This Bud's For You

CHAPTER ELEVEN 221
What Is A Hero?

CHAPTER TWELVE 239
A Paradigm For End-Time Harvest

EPILOGUE 247
A Blueprint For Action

APPENDIX ONE 255
Five Organizations:
Hope For The Nations
The Salvation Army in Bangladesh
HopeHIV

    Viva Network
    Be a Hero

APPENDIX TWO 261
  Organizations Attacking the Seven Deadly Sins

APPENDIX THREE 265
  Child Sponsorships

END NOTES 267

AUTHOR RESOURCES 311

TABLE OF FIGURES

1. God's Heart For Invisible People 62

2. Great Commission Believers: Proportion of World Population . . .156

3. The Spread of Christianity 157

4. The West vs. The Rest 165

5. Women v. Men 166

6. 40% of the World's Population is Children 166

7. The World 169

8. Western World 170

9. Latin America and the Caribbean 170

10. Eastern Europe and Central Asia 170

11. Middle East and North Africa 171

12. East Asia and Pacific 171

13. South Asia 171

14. Sub-Saharan Africa 172

15. The YOU Charts 232

PREFACE

For years we wondered why we could not find a simple one-stop resource that contained a clear, biblical call of the whole gospel of the kingdom of God, including mercy and social justice. Seeing the need, we endeavored to create a resource that placed this call in the context of historical biblical revival as well as modern revival experience. The result is a call to *Be a Hero* by mobilizing mercy and social justice toward fulfilling the worldwide Great Commission.

We are convinced that for the end-time harvest to come in, and for the gospel to be relevant in our time, the proclamation of the good news gospel must be combined with the prophetic action of the good news—mercy and justice. Because substantial proportions of the world's population consist of the very poor and the young, our analysis and solutions give primary attention to them.

We have spoken on these subjects year after year, and the never-ending chorus is, "Don't you have anything in print?" Succumbing to the pressure, we have produced a one-stop resource that addresses the biblical basis for mercy and social justice. Basically, it is an overview of the historical record and examples, the most up-to-date listing of statistics and facts on our present world, and it offers direction for what you, a hero-in-the-making, can do in response.

Be a Hero provides all of these elements in a user-friendly text featuring workable models. The canvas on which we display this beautiful picture is the biblical concept of the Hero Army, the vehicle God has used throughout history to establish His Kingdom on earth.

Be a Hero is composed of three sections. Section One introduces the intent of the book with examples of real-life heroes who are making a difference in the lives of others and, ultimately, are changing the world. A chapter is given to prove that the application of mercy and social justice is not just the responsibility of a few liberal-minded "do-gooders," but rather it is a characteristic of the kingdom of God, and a substantial part of the entire message of the gospel. After establishing the theological basis of God's interaction with people—His plan to redeem "invisible" people through mercy, righteousness, justice, and compassion—we trace the implementation of that plan through heroes of several biblical wars of the Lord, the historical revivals of the Bible.

Gritty detail punctuates the two-page revival reports from the Old Testament, our chapter on "The Heroes of the Wars of the Lord." This is Old Testament history, perspectives, and lessons, to which most Christians have never been introduced.

We suggest that there are four kinds of people:

- **"People people,"** those individuals who are important to us for the relationships we share, people for whom we naturally care;
- **"machine people,"** those people from whose efforts we benefit;
- **"landscape people,"** the extras in the movie of our lives; ...and a peculiarly Judeo/Christian acknowledgment of the
- **"invisible people,"** those whom the Bible describes as marginalized by society—the poor, the widowed, the alien, the orphaned, the needy—who are conveniently out of sight and out of mind of "People people" of every culture. God's big idea is that invisible people can become "People people."

Section Two places the divine plan into an extra-biblical historical context of how God empowers heroes to change the world. One of history's most powerful manifestations of the Hero Army is the primitive Salvation Army. Nestled in the context of the Victorian era, heroes William and Catherine Booth confronted a very godless society. While reading of their many battles in the chapter entitled "In Darkest England and the Way Out," you will rejoice as you understand the great visionary plan that Booth implemented.

Although not a complete success, the plan weds the reality of spiritual revival with the responsibility for social justice in an unprecedented way. In so doing it provides a blueprint for prophetic boldness and action that is intended to mobilize the next generation of the Hero Army.

Section Three time-warps us straight into millennium three. We set our last landscape, that of our world, focusing on our version of the seven deadly sins: extreme poverty, orphans of the street, children in chains, sex and the city, AIDS and plagues, war-affected children, and religious persecution. Sins, in this case, are not things of which the people are guilty, but rather the evils that are perpetrated upon the victims. Our "Seven Deadly Sins" are sins against humanity. In this section, we swamp the reader with current facts and statistics about the world situation. It is senses-assaulting.

However, through generous helpings of story and illustration, we also piece together a biblical response. We present the stories of normal people, drafted and deployed by the Hero God, who are now fighting in the ranks of the Hero Army. We offer practical steps for the convinced reader to make a difference in the world. We introduce the five characteristics of a hero, and suggest ways that you can adopt them in your life.

The appendices include helpful contact information for Christian organizations already on the front lines battling some of the seven deadly sins. The idea is to transform an interested Christian into a hero who mobilizes mercy and justice for end-time harvest.

Be a Hero has the potential to enlist the hearts, the imaginations, the time, the resources, and the lives of millions of Western Christians to fight history's largest war of the Lord! Come with us and join the Hero Army!

FOREWORD

Nothing is more noble, nothing more worthy, nothing more important than to consume oneself with preoccupations of God. And nothing distresses God more than the unprecedented, wholesale destruction of children witnessed across the world today. Children suffer like never before! This is the quiet genocide of our day. This is our modern Auschwitz. This is our generation's shame. This is a full-blown disaster!

More than any other segment of humanity, today's children are suffering from the vileness of mankind and the neglect and abuse of our families and communities. Numbering in the millions they face some of the most inhumane conditions ever experienced by anyone—in the sewers of our cities, in the brothels and bars, locked into baking hot shacks in the slums, forced to work, wasting away from basic curable diseases. And friend, we study it, watch it, report on it, and yet fail to take the necessary action.

When 3,000 middle class citizens died tragically in the twin towers of New York City, we saw the power of the free world mobilized—billions of dollars spent in a war on terror and flotillas of the best trained armies sent to war. But every day almost 30,000 defenseless, vulnerable children die from preventable diseases and hunger and we, the citizens of the world, don't get mad enough to stop it. Please note the word *preventable*.

Be a Hero is mobilizing an army to make the difference. Do you want to join?

You, my friend, are called to follow Christ, to do His stuff. God rescues the weak from those too strong for them and the poor and needy from those who rob them. Pure religion is to look after the fatherless and the widows in their affliction. God hears the desire of the afflicted. He encourages them and He listens to their cry, defending the fatherless and the oppressed.

This is the stuff of God. He's the ultimate Hero God—the prime Child Advocate, the major inspiration behind the guy in the UN lobby bashing away at the ignorant, the apathetic, and those maliciously pursuing their own ends. He is the compassionate God...and He cares. Our God cares. He is there in the brothels late at night when an eight-year-old girl meets her first client. He is there on the rubbish dumps when dinner is served for whole communities of children by the arrival of the latest rubbish van. He is there in the street sewers when kids huddle together for warmth and protection and for some form of warning against rats eating their ears.

He is there on the floor of the mud huts when children grow gaunt, pale, and then quiet. He is our God of love, and we have been called to follow Him, to be like Him, to do His stuff, and to hang out where He would hang out. As it says in Ephesians 5:1: "Be imitators of God, therefore, as dearly loved children."

Winston Churchill described a mandate as akin to your head: *You've got it; whether you choose to use it or not is up to you, but it's yours!*

The Church has a mandate, and her mandate is nothing short of glorious. This is the heady stuff that makes Richard the Lion-hearted or even Aragorn of *The Lord of the Rings* fame pale into insignificance. It is the wondrous offer of godly power to overturn evil, promote justice, reconcile enemies, provide hope, restore sight to the blind, and set the captives free! To bring light, life, and love where death, doom, and darkness reigns! To bring order, peace, and community where chaos, war, and strife rides victorious!

Middle Earth, *Star Wars*, and the *Matrix* are fiction. This is deadly real. In the balance hang the destiny of multitudes, the fate of nations, the legacy of our generation, the future of our children. In the balance hang goodness, honor, and all that is worthy.

Friends, it is a battle—a fierce, furious, all-consuming battle. This is *the* battle, *our* battle, but do *you* want to fight?

Jesus is not only the Alpha and the Omega of history, the beginning and the end. He is not only the Lord of the universe, a historic Nazarene carpenter, or even just the future returning "Lord of hosts." Jesus faces this year with an agenda full of objectives, goals, and tasks, which seek to make His will be "done on earth as in heaven." To accomplish His goals, He needs *you* to get involved. Fully, completely, utterly.

An avalanche begins when rocks start to move. This book seeks to start an avalanche, and it invites *you* to become a rock. Read it, adopt it, practice it, do it, share it. Buy a bunch and hand them out!

Go on, I dare you. *Be a Hero* and join us in changing the world, one precious child at a time.

Patrick McDonald
Founder/President, Viva Network
June 2004

SECTION ONE

CHAPTER ONE

BE A HERO

Incredible Stories of Heroes and Why We Need Them.

> *"Heidi, did you hear? They are blowing up Red Cross trucks in Mozambique!" I was reading TIME magazine's article on the civil war there, and I couldn't believe such evil.*
> *"Oh," she called back. "Let's go there. They need help."*[1]

Heroes, like Heidi and Rolland Baker, rush into crisis when everyone else is retreating.

Something inside each of us shouts "Amen!" to such conviction. Our God, the "mighty" God, the heroic God, instills in us and then extracts from us the urge to be heroic.

History is animated by heroes. We're inspired, stimulated, and challenged by the stories of normal people who did extraordinary feats for noble purposes.

A long time ago, the joy of a provincial people was suppressed by an alien power. Fear was so pervasive that even the harvesters threshed and thrashed in pits so that the oppressors wouldn't raid the crop. One such cow-ard, the youngest child of the least family in the smallest tribe, was a man named Gideon.

In the dreary monotony of persecution, Gideon rose, as from ashes, to lead a remnant to liberation. He overcame enormous odds to defeat an army of superior strength and armor. He was a hero.

How did he do it? How do anonymous farmers become celebrated heroes?

HOLY SPIRIT: HERO-MAKER

Rolland and Heidi Baker are not alone. Gideon, Samson, Samuel, and others rose from humble beginnings to accomplish great things for God. They emerged from the anonymous masses as heroes.

How did it happen? Each encountered the Holy Spirit. The Holy Spirit is the Hero-maker.

> *In the last days, God says, I will pour out My Spirit on all peo-ple. Your sons and daughters will prophesy, your young men will see visions, your old men will dream dreams. Even on My servants, both men and women, I will pour out My Spirit in those days, and they will prophesy. I will show wonders in the heaven above and signs on the earth below, blood and fire and billows of smoke. The sun will be turned to darkness and the moon to blood before the coming of the great and glorious day of the Lord. And everyone who calls on the name of the Lord will be saved (Acts 2:17-21).*

Now, remember, the Holy Spirit is the Hero-maker. Though there are heroes in every culture and every time, the Holy Spirit is the prime Hero-maker. Since He is poured out onto all kinds of people, all kinds of people can become heroes. Heroes don't need miraculous births or blessed upbring-ings. They don't need Masters of Divinity or treasure chests of resources. Every person can be a hero.

Even as the reluctant first king of Israel found out, He can fill you and come upon you and you can be changed into a different person (see 1 Sam. 10:10). He can use a normal person like you or me to do extraordinary things for His glory. Intrigued?

ONE SOLITARY LIFE

Here is the model:

> He was born in an obscure village, the child of a peas-ant woman. He grew up in another obscure village, where He

worked in a carpenter shop until He was thirty. Then for three years He was an itinerant preacher.

He never had a family or owned a home. He never set foot inside a big city. He never traveled two hundred miles from the place He was born. He never wrote a book, or held an office. He did none of the things that usually accompany greatness.

While He was still a young man, the tide of popular opinion turned against Him. His friends deserted Him. He was turned over to His enemies, and went through the mockery of a trial. He was nailed to a cross between two thieves. While He was dying, His executioners gambled for the only piece of property He had—His coat.

When He was dead, He was taken down and laid in a borrowed grave.

Nineteen centuries have come and gone, and today He is the central figure for much of the human race. All the armies that ever marched, and all the navies that ever sailed, and all the parliaments that ever sat, and all the kings that ever reigned, put together, have not affected the life of man upon this earth as powerfully as this "One Solitary Life."[2]

Jesus is the Hero of heroes, the Prototype of all that follow. But even Jesus said that He could do nothing by Himself. What He did, He did by the power of the Holy Spirit (see John 5:19,30).

Heroes aren't all exotic characters from musty old books.

HERO TO THE ORPHANS

Heidi Baker earned a Ph.D. in systematic theology from King's College, University of London—and that may be the least significant fact about her. Called with her husband Rolland to Mozambique, Heidi has been in touch with the Hero-maker. That country is a hurting country. Half of the children die before they turn five. Two-thirds of homes lack even a pit latrine. Five percent have electricity. There is no immunization. Drought, civil war, and AIDS have displaced millions.[3]

Their life story, encapsulated in *There Is Always Enough*, is enthralling.

Heidi met the Holy Spirit in a reinvigorating fashion, and He, the Hero-maker, did His unique work in her life. The Bakers headed to ravaged Mozambique with little more than this Holy Spirit power, and from the beginning the Holy Spirit used them to transform lives, one at a time. Here is an account of one.

In Heidi Baker's words:

> Last week my daughter, Crystalyn, and I were out buying bread, and in the street we came upon a motionless boy dressed in rags and covered in sores. We thought this precious child was dead. I walked over to him and laid my hands on his shoulders. He woke up and looked frightened. I gave him some bread and began to ask him his story. Everista could not talk very well. He had not spoken for a long time. He did not know how old he was. He had never been to school. He knew his parents were dead and he was alone and hungry.... His body bore the marks of years of abuse.... He scurried along the ground more like an animal than a human being. I asked Everista if he wanted to come and live with us.... I took him home and washed his wounds. Crystalyn happily gave him some clothes and things to play with. We hugged him and prayed for him, and let him know he was loved.[4]

Everista is one of many orphans whom Heidi and her Christian community have determined not to pass by. And they add up. Here are the numbers we like to cite about the Bakers:

- 8
- 2,000
- 10,000
- 20
- 5,000
- 5

These are the numbers of orphans they've personally adopted, the number of orphans living with them in their children's home, the number of people they normally feed, the number of dead people who've been raised to life by leaders in their churches, the number of churches they've started, and the number of years during which they've started them all.[5] Did you catch that? They took over the management of a dilapidated children's home—500 kids joined them. A handful of these children actually came under their roof. Authentic Christian community was cultivated and its contagious strain of Christianity has spread through to start 5,000 churches so far. And God has accompanied this explosive growth with signs and wonders!

They've touched multitudes. She has been a hero to each of them.

UBUNTU

Paul Hewson is one of the most famous people on the planet. For 25 years, he and his mates have been writing hit music. A child of a mixed marriage, Catholic and Protestant, he sought some spiritual direction in the early 1980s with a group called *Shalom*. Some time before that he picked up a nickname that grew on him as it grew in accuracy. They called him *Bono Vox*, or "good voice."

Bono is the lead singer of the rock band, *U2*, which has sold well over 100 million albums and won 14 Grammys. U2 has walked an extremely unlikely tightrope, bridging relevance in two generations.

Bono jumped on the advocacy bandwagon early, in the mid 1980s, with *Band Aid* and "Do They Know It's Christmas?" (which sold 50 million singles). Band Aid raised more than $144 million during the seven years of its existence[6], and *Live Aid* (the live concert seen by 1.9 billion people) raised $70 million.[7] Both fought the famine in Ethiopia.

After Live Aid, Bono actually went to Ethiopia, where the famine was killing thousands of people. He spent six weeks on a "hero holiday," working on an orphanage in Wello, Ethiopia.[8] "You'd wake up in the morning, and mist would be lifting," Bono recalls. "You'd walk out of your tent, and you'd count bodies of dead and abandoned children."[9]

One day, an Ethiopian man asked Bono to take his son and raise him. "He is sure to die. But if you take him, he is sure to live," the father told Bono. At that point, Africa no longer was a cause for Bono. It became a calling.[10]

Since then he has led the *Jubilee 2000 Drop The Debt* initiative and created a group called *Debt, AIDS, and Trade in Africa* (DATA) to organize his efforts for Africa. He is effectively using his mass appeal as a platform to make these crises popular issues. Jubilee 2000 was an appeal to Western nations to cancel the debt owed by African countries. About 24 million people signed the petition. Amazingly, this got the attention of G8 countries, which agreed to forgive Heavily Indebted Poor Countries (HIPC) debts[11] totaling $100 billion.[12] DATA tackles the AIDS crisis, the Trade crisis, the Debt crisis, and the Development Assistance crisis.[13] He has been called Africa's Number One Advocate in the West.[14]

Early on, Bono was convicted about the essential role of faith in solving the problem.

> I really do feel, looking at this problem so out of control, that synagogues, temples and chapels are really, in the end, my only hope across Africa. As you look at this, if it isn't

going to happen through the church, it's going to be so very difficult for government.[15]

He hasn't always been thrilled with their reaction. "If you remember the story of the Good Samaritan, well, when it comes to Africa, we're not just crossing the road to avoid the man who needs help, we're catching a bus in the other direction."[16]

In 2002, his criticism of the Church was direct:

> Christ's example is being demeaned by the church if they ignore the new leprosy, which is AIDS. The church is the sleeping giant here. If it wakes up to what's really going on in the rest of the world, it has a real role to play. If it doesn't, it will be irrelevant.[17]

What a difference a year makes! In 2003, Bono admitted, "I really am surprised and even a little disappointed that I can't continue to beat up the church, because they have really responded."[18]

He continued, "The sleeping giant kind of woke up and is really playing a huge role in getting the job done. I'm amazed and moved by it, actually."[19]

Bono emphasized that "I'm not here as a do-gooder. This is not a cause; it's an emergency."[20]

Bono also said:

> Archbishop Tutu introduced me to a word: *ubuntu*. Essentially, what it means is "I am because we are." And it's about the interdependence, how we need each other and we have a stake in each other. One part of the community can't thrive truly while the other part of the community is in the dirt.
>
> In tending to them, we will be better off ourselves. It's that simple. *Ubuntu*.[21]

Years ago, Bono dropped the imagined surname, Vox, leaving him to live up to the name, "Good." And he is. He is a hero to the AIDS victims in Africa.

HERO TO THE HUNGRY

The Breakfast Club of Quebec and larger international NGO, *Breakfast World*, seek to give children an equal opportunity to succeed in life. The founder, Daniel Germain, is a hero.

Years ago Daniel traveled to French-speaking Haiti on a short-term missions trip with his church. Later Daniel reflected back to his pre-trip thoughts and commented, "Passionate but inexperienced, I thought, 'Let's go save the world!' Ironically the day I arrived was the day of the sea disaster where the commercial ship *Neptune* sank off the coast of Haiti."

Daniel found himself conscripted to recover hundreds of bloated dead bodies floating in the ocean and washed up on the beaches. What an introduction to your "hero holiday!"

Not only that, what he saw during these times broke his heart.

> The misery was unbelievable. I saw children whose job was to sort through garbage, and as a salary received a bag of "good" garbage. Their plight touched me deeply, and perhaps it was this experience more than any other that opened my eyes to the conditions of children. I resolved to do something![22]

The next line in the chorus of this beautiful story came from Jackie Pullinger. She'd invested her life in heroin addicts of the Walled City of Hong Kong. After hearing Daniel's concern for the children of the world she questioned him as to how he was contributing to the welfare of children in his country. "Yes it's bad all over the world, but have you done anything in your own hometown?" she probed.

Daniel discovered that 1.5 million Canadian children are living below the poverty line. This need became the basis for the Breakfast Club of Quebec.

The first Breakfast Club was born in November of 1994, at Lionel-Groulx de Longueuil School in Montreal. Today, thanks to the help of more than 1,400 volunteers, the Breakfast Club of Quebec serves a total of 1.5 million breakfasts a year, in 166 schools throughout the province, feeding a total of 12,500 children every school day.

In October 2000, Daniel was recognized as Person of the Year. Daniel is a hero to kids who need breakfast.

A LIFE WORTH $31.00?

Sridhar lives in southern India. When he was 10 years old his family sold his labor to a local *mudalali* (money lender) so they could buy necessities to live. His freedom was sold for 1,500 rupees (approximately $31.00 USD) and for a year, Sridhar spent the day sitting on a dirt floor rolling *beedi* cigarettes. He was required to complete a minimum of 1,000 cigarettes a day, 6 days a week and was paid a meager 10.00 rupees a day (approximately 20 cents), which was far below the legally-required minimum wage. Sridhar reported that he was beaten with a stick by the *mudalali* if his quota was not met. His debt had to be repaid to the *mudalali* in a lump sum, which would be impossible since Sridhar's family desperately needed the money to live and buy food, and the *mudalali* forbade Sridhar from working for anyone but him until the debt was repaid. It is through this system that many children are bonded, grow to adulthood still working to pay off their debt, and eventually pass this same debt onto their children. It is a vicious cycle that is virtually inescapable for impoverished families.

In July 2001, Christian investigators with the International Justice Mission learned of Sridhar's slavery and after determining that he was illegally bonded, helped him fill out an affidavit that was submitted to local government officials. Sridhar was released from his debt and is now in the 7th grade, no longer spending his days rolling *beedis*.[23]

Someone cared—an unidentified person, but a hero in the life of Sridhar and other children in chains.

EATING DIRT

Chrissie Chapman was on her deathbed. Here's a story that will blow your mind.

In her own words she says:

> I was attached to a life support machine and in the intensive care unit for several weeks and became paralyzed down my right side. When I was eventually taken off the life support machine I was in agony, and couldn't move. My lungs were full of fluid and I required a procedure every few hours in order to drain them. All my hair had fallen out. In this state, I asked, "Am I going to die?"
>
> The doctor said, "We've done everything we can, but your lungs are so badly damaged, it is unlikely you will survive more than a few months."
>
> I was transferred to a medical ward to die. Since I had only been a Christian for two years, I didn't really know much about healing—or anything else for that matter! I began to read books on healing but I came to the conclusion that God only healed people who could write books—I'd never met anyone who had been healed.
>
> Then one day I heard the audible voice of God. There was no one in the room; I knew it was the Lord. He said, "It's time to go home, Chrissie, I am going to heal you."
>
> I managed to persuade some friends to ask the doctors to let me go home. After a lot of talk they agreed to let me

out for a weekend—thinking I would return much sooner! I was rolled out of the hospital in a wheelchair, still with my right-sided paralysis, no hair, and my joints in agony. I had a collar around my neck to support my head and I was still having a lot of problems breathing.

Several hours after getting home, I began to feel that maybe I had got it wrong. Maybe what the Lord meant was that he would take me "home" to give me my new body, that it was time to go and be with him. Suddenly 1 Peter 2:24 popped into my mind. I struggled with my good hand to turn and read. As I read, "He Himself bore our sins in His body on the cross, so that we might die to sin and live to righteousness; for by His wounds you were healed" (1 Peter 2:24, NASB). I began to have an encounter with the Holy Spirit. My head began to have this tremendous feeling of pins and needles on it. I reached up with my good arm to feel what was going on—it was like catching hold of a toilet brush—my hair was growing! I crawled across the bedroom floor to try and look to see what was going on; when I got a mirror the first thing I noticed was not my hair, but my face. It was pink and healthy looking—after so long of looking so pale and my lips blue with death!

Over the next 48 hours, I grew a full head of hair, and all the feeling came back into my limbs. The pain left my joints, and my breathing became normal—for the first time in years. I took off the collar and danced before the Lord. I was 29 years old and felt like I was 16 (since that day 23 years ago I have never had another asthmatic attack).

The young doctor who had looked after me for so many months came by to see me in the ward. Shocked, he reached out to touch my hair, and then fell on his knees and began to speak in tongues. I told him he couldn't do that—that he needed to get saved first—they say ignorance is bliss! That young doctor became a Christian and ended up serving the Lord in India. Over the next few weeks 17 of the hospital staff gave their lives to Jesus as a result of my miraculous healing.[24]

Chrissie had an encounter with God that left her with new lungs and a complete healing, including the asthma! A single lady, miraculously healed of fatal diseases, Chrissie has not only received her own healing but now disseminates it to others in need.

Not surprisingly, she intended to invest her redeemed life in redeeming others. So, after some biblical training, she headed to Burundi on a short-term missions trip, and promptly fell in love with the country. Chrissie returned to Burundi for good in 1990 to establish a maternity clinic and dispensary. Burundi has about 5 million people, of whom 22,000 are war orphans and a staggering 600,000 are AIDS orphans. Chrissie left a busy London hospital full of doctors and equipment to go to a lonely little clinic on a mountaintop with no running water or electricity, to which only the most complicated cases came. That's where she learned to pray.

Children were among the first casualties of the war that soon started. One baby was shot in Chrissie's arms! Chrissie, who had been forced to evacuate the whole clinic from the mountain, began serving among the displaced people. She remembers, "I came across so many babies and young children who had been abandoned after their families had been killed. They were left on rubbish dumps and at the side of the road to die. I simply did what my hands found to do and started collecting them and bringing them home."

The genocide in neighboring Rwanda swamped her with orphans. This wasn't the only time she saw "children *eating dirt* to try and take away the hunger, so they [could] sleep." One night Chrissie took in 17 of these traumatized treasures, all under the age of one. She jokes that, with dozens of babies living in her home, she didn't get a good night's sleep for the next two years!

God has recruited people from all over the world to help Chrissie, who now has five houses full of vibrant kids who love Jesus and who know that God has rescued them because He has a plan for their lives. She emphasizes, "They are not poor orphans, they don't act like poor orphans. They are children of the King and that's how they act!" Almost all of the children in her schools give their lives to Jesus.

The government has given Chrissie their orphanage, to go along with the street children feeding program, the two schools, and the AIDS center she has started. And she's not finished:

> I will continue to look for ways to reach out to the children in this land. I do not believe that God ever intended to have babies sleeping in the streets, hundreds of children who have never had the experience of feeling a mother's arms wrapped round them, never been told by anyone that they are loved…. I am a mama. I will continue to reach out my

arms to embrace these children, to love and feed them and most importantly, to introduce them to their Heavenly Father. That's what I am, just a mama, that's what I do, love children.[25]

That's not completely true. Once terribly afflicted herself, Chrissie now represents healing to the afflicted. This single woman now has an enormous family, to whom she is "Mama." Those plagued by AIDS and other pestilences in Burundi are the recipients of her heroism. Not only a mama, Chrissie is a hero to the orphan and the afflicted.

PEDOPHILE PARADISE

Shuvaloy Majumdar is Deployment Leader of *The Future Group*, a Calgary-based non-profit organization fighting the sex trade. He works in the Cambodian capital, Phnom Penh.

While The Future Group features a bold and informative web site called youwillbecaught.com, Majumdar and his partners on the ground are the advance troops in this war against child prostitution.[26] Probably 80 percent of Phnom Penh's street children have been sexually abused.[27] In *Maclean's* magazine reporter Susan McClelland's words:

He leans out his window and lies, telling [a] boy he wants a girl much younger than those on the street. Majumdar has brought me to Svay Pak to show the scale of the child-sex trade, and he knows that children as young as four are available but kept hidden by their pimps in an attempt to avoid police raids. After a brief conversation in Vietnamese with a rough-looking brothel manager, the boy leads Majumdar and three others down a narrow pathway to a small cabin.

Inside, Majumdar takes a seat in a creaky metal chair beside a stained mattress. Within seconds, two girls, who claim they're 6 and 8, join him. Just awakened, they're wearing cotton pajamas and rubbing the sleep out of their eyes. At first, the girls stand silently and rigidly together. The pimp slaps one on the back of the head and the girls begin to awkwardly and unenthusiastically flirt with Majumdar. Shaking, the 6-year-old mumbles, "no boom-boom, just *ngam-ngam*" (Vietnamese slang for oral sex). But when a photographer who has accompanied Majumdar begins to take some pictures, the pimp and his bodyguards draw guns, thinking Majumdar and the photographer are undercover informants. Thinking fast, the visitors defuse the situation by telling the angry pimp the pictures are for their business—organizing sex tours out of Thailand. The ruse works and the danger passes.[28]

Majumdar and his partners will rescue tens of thousands of children like these two. He and The Future Group are an impressive bunch. Birthed in 2000 by some young people who found "something worth dying for, and live for that," the average age of this international organization's members is 23.[29] Majumdar is a hero in Pedophile Paradise.

HERO TO THE HOMELESS

In the '90s there were at least 3.5 million Afghan refugees in Pakistan. This was before the infamous September 11, 2001. It was a result of the 1979-1989 Russian-Afghan War. They were displaced by war.

Man Enough?

When nightfall comes I can make the cold hard earth
Disappear
I can dream my special dream that makes everything
Alright again.
My heart is filled with laughter
Again
As I play with my friends
Scrambling up and down the hillside,
Pinching fruit and pulling my sisters' pigtails.
We were so happy
My brothers and sisters and I
Until the war
And father went away
And mother, "Bibi" cried a lot,
And ten the soldiers came
With big guns and toy-bombs.
There were eight of us
Now there are three
I am scared to go near "Bibi" now
So old and scarred she cries no longer
Just stares and stares.
I long to be away from here

> *To be a mujahid*
> *Like my brother*
> *To fight beside him*
> *For my country*
> *My Afghanistan.*
> *I am twelve*
> *Man enough to be a soldier*
> *If only I could walk.*[30]

There are 80,000 such stories, maybe not all as eloquent, from Afghan people uprooted and stuck in a camp, across the border in Pakistan, run by The Salvation Army in Pakistan. In the name of Jesus, Colonel Joyce Ellery and a band of heroes housed, fed, trained, served, and medically cared for each author of each story.

THE ONE-ARMED BARBIE

David Waines is a friend. He is also Community Health Ambassador with EQUIP Canada serving in post-war Liberia. He daily delves into the heroic while serving the displaced people of Liberia. The day before heading into the center of a war zone, David asked us to pray:

> Please pray for my trip behind the frontlines into Ganta tomorrow [October 13, 2003]. There is fighting in nearby Duo and no law or order in Nimba. The UN Military Helicopter has agreed to carry me, and our "cold boxes" of vaccines, in to support our EQUIP CHA emergency health teams restart vaccination coverage. 350,000 people in Nimba are cut off from Monrovia and all other humanitarian assistance. Hundreds of children are dying in Nimba because medicines, vaccines and food cannot get through. As the fighting continues in Nimba virtually the entire population of the county are becoming internally displaced and in desperate need for health care and food.
>
> I am in awe of the dedication of our four EQUIP Liberia CHA Frontline Emergency Health Teams who with overcoming faith are doing the seemingly impossible. They are risking their lives on flimsy rafts bringing medicines across the raging St. John River from Guinea. [They] endure threats and abuse at checkpoints as they buy locally available high protein biscuits and Corn Soya Blend plus fish, peanuts,

beans, [and] sesame seeds to feed approximately 100 moderately to severely malnourished children every day in four areas. [31]

The next day proved why prayer was needed!

October 13, 2003, vaccine success! We had precious vaccines to get to the children of Nimba County. However, our Russian MI-8 helicopter didn't start at 8:45a.m. as planned. Perhaps I'd been in Liberia a little too long, because I recommended that we all push and jump-start it. None of the UN soldiers or officers laughed. The technicians spent three hours and lots of fuel trying to get the starters working right. By 1:00p.m. we were on our way to Gbangar. At Gbatala LURD fighters with AK-47's (likely stoned) start shooting at our helicopter. The pilot swerved and dove to the right. Cracking of machine gun fire. We were not hit as far as I know. We landed in Gbangar, then the general, all of us, and the UN military convoy drove 35 km towards Ganta up to the Balia Bridge over the St. John River where Nimba County starts. This was supposed to be the front lines but there has been active fighting today and yesterday LURD has attacked more villages in Nimba. LURD boy soldiers with their huge BZD gun mounted in the back of a pick-up want to make a quick retreat when our convoy of UN soldiers arrive at the bridge; comically they have to push start five times before the old Ford pick-up fires to life. There is lots of shooting in the air. The UN Force Commander is getting nervous. We hear the gunfire and explosions of active fighting not far from the bridge. On the way back to Gbangar he tells me there is not enough time, not enough fuel, not enough security in the area to go to Ganta and drop the vaccines as planned. I plead "General O'Pande, I will name my next child after you, *please* at least get the vaccines to the children." He motions that I should say not another word about it; he has made up his mind we are not going. I pray hard for the next twenty minutes. Just as the chopper is about to lift off it is announced we will go to Ganta. I cheer—arms in the air.

We drop the vaccines quickly but neither Ruth nor Joseph is there. Where are they? The command is to leave the engines going, blades beating, drop the boxes, and get right back up in the air. I have cash for Ruth to care for needy children. Cash for Joseph to run the health work. No one to give it to. A jeep arrives, then a pick-up. No Ruth. No Joseph. The UN point soldier rushes over and grabs my arm, "The commander says if you are not in the chopper now we are lifting off without you!" "I will be there…in one minute!" Then I see Ruth rushing towards me. I give her a huge hug, pass the money and other gifts, run back and jump on the helicopter. We lift off before I get to my seat. Mission accomplished. The General first said no but God changed it to YES. [32]

Help Wanted!

"We have over 350,000 people to try to care for this month—HELP WANTED."

September 19, 2003: The mortar detonated as soon as it came in contact with the roof of the house next door to ours [Waines house] on Mamba Point. Every one in the family of six was home and were all wounded by the red hot metal bomb fragments. Alpha, the husband, lifts up his t-shirt to show me where a chunk of metal is still embedded in his shoulder. Musu, their six-year-old daughter, with a delightfully shy smile, had her right arm ripped up. It had to be amputated below the elbow. She greets me many times a day as I come and go down the footpath away from our house. "Hello, white man," she says softly, waving her hand-less right arm out of habit then remembering it's not the same anymore and waving with her left hand instead. Musu has an old Barbie doll she hugs very tight. Her Barbie is also missing her right arm.[33]

David Waines and his coworkers are heroes to the displaced people of war-ravaged Liberia.

CASE CLOSED

Radha was held in forced prostitution behind the padlocked door of a Bombay brothel. She was originally from Calcutta, but was sold into prostitution. She was forced to provide sex to the brothel's customers, or face beating. Bombay has one of the highest rates of AIDS infection in the world.[34]

The *International Justice Mission* was not about to allow Radha to continue suffering.

> "Jim" infiltrated the brothel and found Radha being held in forced prostitution. Using surveillance equipment, "Jim" was able to document her plight and refer the information to a trusted police contact. "Jim" assisted the police in raiding the brothel and secured Radha's release. Although Radha was unable to return home, "Jim" was able to find her a safe government home, free from daily abuse.[35]

"Jim" cared as Jesus cares. He went out of his way. He even put himself in harm's way. And he did it to rescue a young, trapped girl. He is a hero to the prostitutes, fighting for biblical justice in unbiblical haunts.

HERO TO THE PERSECUTED

Pastor Richard Wurmbrand was "Prisoner #1" in Romania. Outside of the prison and the country he was known as the "Voice of the Underground Church" and the "Iron Curtain St. Paul." After more than a dozen years of beatings, he was released. He started a group called *Voice of the Martyrs* (VOM) to fight for the subjects of religious persecution.

In restricted nations, many times when pastors or evangelists (usually the main income earner in a family) are imprisoned for their activities, their families are left with little means of financial support. When a minister like Pakistani Pastor Emanuel Ditta is murdered for his faith in Jesus, often his children must drop out of school because they can no longer pay their school fees. A martyr's family also incurs heavy debts with funeral and medical expenses. Wurmbrand's VOM supports the Ditta family.[36] He is a hero to the persecuted.

HOW ABOUT YOU?

These aren't musty old stories. And most of the people I described aren't superstars. They are normal people with names like Gideon and David and Daniel and Chrissie and Heidi and Joyce and Jim and Richard. They are normal people inspired by the Holy Spirit, the Hero-maker. And they are heroes. They've mixed mercy and justice to change conditions and circumstances, to introduce love and peace, to launch redemption in the lives of marginalized people around the world. You can add your name to the list. You, a hero? Intrigued? Read on.

CHAPTER TWO

FACES AND HEARTS

Getting a Lay of the Heroic Lanscape.

The face of the earth will be changed as we see the hearts of its people transformed. Our heavenly Father wants no one to perish (see 2 Pet. 3:9). And His means of accomplishing His will today is as shaky as when He trusted 11 *doubtfuls* the first time—this time it is *us*.

Our heroes don't wear their boxers on the outside. They don't show up on Saturday morning television. Most don't leap over tall buildings in a single bound.[1] The Bible sometimes calls them champions, or warriors, or valiant men, "the mighties," or mighty men.[2] Though the Hebrew word *gibbowr* can be translated "hero," it is more often translated "mighty," "strong," or "valiant."[3] This word appears 159 times in the Old Testament.[4] And these heroes changed the shape of their spiritual and social landscapes.

People are heroes, and even God is a hero! He is described as the *Gibbowr*—"Mighty" or "Hero" God (Isa. 10:21). The messianic hope of Israel was, "For to us a child is born, to us a son is given, and the government will be on His shoulders. And He will be called Wonderful Counselor, Mighty God [*Eel Gibowr*—the Hero God]" (Isa. 9:6). And through the power of the Holy Spirit, the Hero God raises up heroes.

Vine's Dictionary explains this hero phenomenon:

> In the context of warfare, these *heroes* were literally "mighty men of valor" (e.g. Joshua 1:14). David, a proven victor on the battlefield, attracted heroes while being pursued by Saul (2 Samuel 23). When he became king, he epitomized the power of his kingdom. As commander of the Israelite forces, he was expected to be a hero. The king is described as a "*hero*" (Psalm 45:3, emphasis added).

There was even a *House of the Heroes* (see Neh. 3:16).

So it's the Hero God and His Hero Son, with the Holy Spirit, the Hero-maker, who craft heroes out of the stuff of humanity so that they, like God Himself, reach out to change the life of another.

In this vein, "The Christian religion presupposes an intense interest in transformation, both of self and of society. 'Your Kingdom come, Your will be done on earth as it is in heaven,' is a prayer that is not yet answered."[5] The Hero-maker, the Holy Spirit, was promised to disciples, and He is to convict the world of its guilt with regard to sin, righteousness, and judgment through those disciples.[6] So there is a great burden of responsibility on fellow workers, partners, co-laborers with God, His heroes—us—to faithfully obey and see to it that His will is done on earth as it is in heaven.

It is inconceivable that anyone can dispute the preeminence of Christianity as a force for good in humanity. Here is a short primer of positive change that came through the heroes of this faith:

- Hospitals
- Universities
- Literacy and education for the masses
- Free enterprise
- Civil liberties
- Abolition of slavery
- Modern science
- Elevation of women
- Benevolence and charity
- Higher standards of justice
- Condemnation of sexual perversion
- Sanctity of life

- Codifying many of the world's languages
- Inspiration and development of art and music
- Salvation[7]

Protestantism proved to be a vehicle with much horsepower for effecting change worldwide. "Max Weber, one of the founders of modern sociology, called it the 'lead' society of our age. The reason is that all other societies, willingly or unwillingly, have followed its style and adopted its values."[8] Will such adoption prove an essential precursor to the adoption of our faith? Belonging, will they believe? Is Catalytic Christianity the answer?

At the dawn of this new millennium, the Protestant-lead culture has expanded in hemispheric directions that have left the rest of the world without Weber's "Protestant Ethic" and its concomitant economic blessing.[9]

THE ALTRUISTIC HANGOVER

Despite the cynicism of postmodern Western intellectuals, the Wall Street Journal still thinks that spiritual morals generate social value.[10] We agree. Christianity generates a compassionate love that compels action. So it is both a lifestyle standard and a mission means. Faith generates works. As James wrote, "Faith without works is dead" (James 2:26). We assert that Christianity without compassion lies in a grave beside faith without obedience.

Although Western society is now considered post-Christian, the hangover of Protestantism's "altruistic activism" lingers in the form of such efforts as the September 11 "Heroes" Telethon, which raised $150 million two weeks after the 9-11[11]; the "We Are Family" Benefit[12]; Live Aid; Jerry Lewis telethons; and the like.[13] The irony is that this hangover has left unbelievers without a sense of the driving force behind their charity. One advertisement for the hotline of an organization that included the word "Samaritan" in the name explicitly requested that only non-religious people were welcome to apply. They didn't realize that the Good Samaritan was one of Jesus' great ideas![14] How did we ever get to this place? It has not been without pain.

THE GREAT DIVORCE

As the Protestant culture expanded, a serious cancer was poisoning the body of the movement itself. In the wake of the European Enlightenment, everything was put under the scrutiny of the scientific method, including the very force that birthed the enlightenment—the Bible itself. God was demoted to non-personal force status that could be experienced only through human reason or in nature. The newly enthroned Rationalism looked with disdain at biblical accounts of creation, resurrection, and miracles. The cancer attacked the rule of God and the authority of Scripture, usurping both and gifting them to "reasonable" people.

Truth was one of the first casualties, eradicated by reason and feeling. Sin was slaughtered soon after, as humans were now seen merely as "incomplete and needing perfecting." In essence, a new religion was created out of the old. As H. Richard Niebuhr wrote, criticizing the nineteenth century liberal "gospel": "A God without wrath brought men without sin into a kingdom without judgment through the ministrations of a Christ without a cross."[15]

In this environment, the discipline of biblical criticism breeded, causing, and then filling the void left when biblical authority was exterminated. The "*sola scriptura*" battle cry of the reformers who had birthed Protestantism was replaced with a selfish whining, "Bible as it means to me." It was a time when many of the great Protestant universities rejected their roots, and Protestantism began to implode.

The fallout was huge. Those who bought into this humanistic reformation had nothing left but to pour themselves into the non-supernatural elements of a social gospel—that is, faith in the betterment of mankind and a helping hand to those in need. Repentance, conversion, discipleship, and mission were all avoided like the plague.

On the other hand, the conservative element grew alarmed and congealed into an even more conservative brand of right-wing fundamentalism in reaction to the modernist controversy. If the modernists rejected the authority of the Bible, the fundamentalists would major on it. If the liberals rejected miracles and holiness, then the new offshoot called "Pentecostalism" would make it a singular focus. If the liberals replaced mission with mercy, then the conservatives rejected mercy and focused almost exclusively on mission. Whatever the liberals did, the conservatives wouldn't.

As in every divorce, the ones who suffered most were the children. The liberal churches eventually began to die out more and more, and their social programs died out with them. The call to morality and social justice was present but the internal power and virtue for maintaining it disintegrated. Conversely, before the great divorce, it never occurred to the Church that proclamation was ever supposed to be separated from compassion and action. Indeed, it was the great evangelicals like Wesley, Whitefield, and Wilberforce who did so much through the presentation of the whole gospel—words with deeds—so as to even establish the title, "evangelicals." But now Western Christianity morphed into a strange state where, for the first time since the days of Rome, it devolved into a fringe group on the edge of society. The very programs that the Protestant revivals had birthed were now taken over by the state and/or government, and even the preachers abdicated responsibility for them. This terrible split within Protestant Christianity lasted close to a hundred years. Only recently have many evangelical/charismatic Christians actually acknowledged their accountability to both save the heart as well as minister to the body so that the face of the world will be changed.

EXTREME MAKEOVER

That acknowledged, within the larger scope of history, both the face and heart have been shaped by the Church. An exhaustive search through the historical documents of antiquity has left no trace of any organized charitable effort before Christ![16] Astounding! And then Jesus came.

> The Christian community stressed the support of its widows, orphans, sick, and disabled, and of those who because of their faith were thrown out of employment or were imprisoned. It ransomed men who were put to servile labor for their faith. It entertained travelers. One church would send aid to another church whose members were suffering from famine or persecution. In theory and to no small degree in practice, the Christian community was a brotherhood, bound together in love, in which reciprocal material help was the rule.[17]

OUR HERITAGE!

This is not just a good idea—it works. Listen to this avowal: "The Christians were strongly opposed to child exposure, actively rescuing foundlings, and deplored abortions which they did not think defensible except with arguments that equally justified infanticide."[18] This assertion is not describing the American Moral Majority or Republican Right Wing; it is talking about the early Christian community in the Roman Empire. And there's more!

Whereas today we often treat theology as luxury or irrelevant, the first century Christians found in the realities of mission the "mother of theology."[19] In the middle of the third century, one Roman church is recorded as caring for 1,500 widows. A church in Syrian Antioch in the late fourth century is remembered for feeding 3,000 hungry people.[20] How did Christianity become the religion of choice in a completely pagan Roman Empire? They won the moral and compassionate higher ground.

Mercy

Even a casual look into Church history reveals how intricately revival is tied to showing mercy. The examples of this are numerous. Early Christians were known for rescuing abandoned Roman babies and then raising them as their own. Orphans and the poor could always find help from the Church (see James 1:26). For centuries the monks and nuns gathered together in communities called monasteries. These monasteries became centers for learning, hospice or medical work, care for the poor, and evangelization. Entire religious orders were organized throughout the Middle Ages with a specific focus on preaching the gospel and helping the poor. Some of the most famous would be the Order of the Franciscans founded by the radical St. Francis of Assisi, and the Poor Clares, a female order started by "Gentle" Clare, also of Assisi.

Besides the more strict religious orders of monks and nuns, there were voluntary lay movements made up of Christians totally devoted to preaching the gospel and serving the poor. A mass women's movement called the *Beguines* impacted "Christian" Europe for hundreds of years. At times the numbers of these volunteer women reached as high as 10 percent of a city's population, as they banded in semi-communal structures to work for the good of others.[21]

A modern-day equivalent of 10 percent of a city's population living together in communal context would be, for example, a *Youth With A Mission* base, or some other para-church organization, in order to serve the poor. The great Catherine of Siena was a member of one of these lay movements that practiced selfless sacrifice to the poor, the sick, and the dying.

Revival and Mercy

Examples from the "Awakenings" over the last 250 years identify a similar pattern. In a sweeping historical overview of revival and social reforms, Earle Cairns maintains that, "Revival goes hand and hand with the application of Christian principles to government and with antislavery, antiwar, and temperance activities."[22] Revival historian J. Edwin Orr found the same. All of the great revivals—from John Wesley on—resulted in huge thrusts of ongoing evangelization and social action.[23]

In England, it was first the Quakers and then Wesley and the Methodists who began to oppose black slavery. Wesley and his converts ministered in the prisons, hospitals, and workhouses, and they tried to abolish slavery. At age 88, six days before he died, Wesley wrote his last letter, which was to William Wilberforce, an evangelical member of parliament. With faltering hand

Wesley exhorted him to keep on fighting that "execrable sum of all villainies—slavery" until it shall utterly vanish away.

Wilberforce did keep up the fight, and with the help of the rest of the Clapham Sect—evangelical leaders in business and politics—brought bill after bill to bear in the House of Commons. For 40 years they fought the system, with Wilberforce losing most of his money and health. In the last year of his life he saw the reward of his suffering, as the "Emancipation Act of 1833" freed 781,000 slaves throughout the British colonies.[24]

The list of charitable works, organizations, and accomplishments done by those revived Christians who obeyed Jesus' command to "show mercy" in a literal way are so numerous as to boggle the mind.

John Howard, founder of the *John Howard Society*, was encouraged by John Wesley to reform England's prisons.

Elizabeth Fry, mother of 11 children, became a Quaker preacher, as well as a prison reformer.

The YMCA (Young Men's Christian Association) was founded to provide religious services and culture in a "home away from home."

Florence Nightingale believed that God had called her with an audible voice to help the sick. She impacted an evangelical named Henri Dunant who went on to found the Red Cross.

Even the *Royal Society for the Prevention of Cruelty to Animals* (R.S.P.C.A.) was founded by an Anglican cleric, Arthur Bloome, with the aid of Wilberforce and friends.[25]

Mercy to children has always been a focus of the Church. Lord Shaftesbury became a member of Parliament in 1826 and wrote in his diary that he would found his "policy on the Bible," and practice "active benevolence in public life" in order to advance religion and "increase human happiness."[26]

Shaftesbury spent most of his time fighting the evils of child exploitation in the factories, mines, brickyards, and chimney sweeps. It was rightly called "the white slave trade." Children as young as 4 were racking up to 12 and 14 hours a day in pitch-dark mines. Little orphans picked up off the street were forced up chimneys to clean in the choking claustrophobic dark. Shaftesbury introduced the "Ten-Hour Act" that prohibited factories from working children their common 13 to 16 hours a day. He passed legislation prohibiting using children as chimney sweeps and children under 10 in the mines. Shaftesbury engaged government on behalf of the oppressed.

George Mueller got revived and turned his attention to caring for orphans and eventually was caring for up to 2,050 children at one time.

Thomas J. Barnardo was the product of the revival in 1859. Lord Shaftesbury influenced Barnardo to become a missionary to the slums of London. Barnardo began to open homes for children who were homeless because of drinking parents. Before Barnardo died he had cared for 60,000 children.[27]

RIVALING THE ENTIRE U.S. FEDERAL BUDGET!

In America the "Second Awakening," commencing under the ministry of Francis Asbury and the circuit riders, as well as the camp meetings, and continuing right into the ministry of Charles Finney, created a virtual *tsunami* of mercy ministries. Slavery, vice, world peace, women's rights, Sabbath observance, prison reform, and profanity—the 19th century's version of our "seven deadly sins"[28]—were targeted and attacked by this network of societies, whose total annual income in 1834 rivaled the entire U.S. federal government budget.[29] The *Benevolent Empire* was composed of the "Great Eight" institutions: the American Bible Society, the American Board of Commissioners for Foreign Missions, the American Sunday School Union, the American Tract Society, and the American Missionary Society.[30] Each was championed by a hero.

These and other groups comprised a vast network of volunteer societies all united under one great banner called the *Benevolent Empire*.

By 1834 the total annual income of the Benevolent Empire was about today's equivalent of one hundred thirty million [American] dollars, which rivaled the entire budget of the federal government in those days![31]

They succeeded in bringing Christian values into the mainstream of American society.

It is said that,

This Awakening had a greater impact on secular society than any other in American history through its vast social concern... Christian laypeople organized thousands of societies that touched every phase of American life.[32]

Examine the fruits of Protestantism in the New World. Although followed in fits and starts, within 40 years of landing the Puritans turned to the task of educating a "learned clergy and a lettered people."[33] "The missionary zeal of this 'lead class'...brought the Gospel to countless numbers of people around the world. The compassion of members of the bourgeoisie has led to a global medical program that has cut the death rate of infants, and extended the life expectancy of adults."[34]

Consider this: of the first 119 colleges birthed in young America, 104 were spawned by Christians with the expressed purpose to acquaint Christians with the knowledge of God.[35] Out of a graduating class of 40,000 in 1855, 10,000 became ministers—over 25 percent![36]

In the post-modern societies of the West, there has been an obvious declension following the abandonment of Christian foundations. The president of Johns Hopkins University, Steve Muller, described the current state of education in the West: "The failure to rally around a set of values means that universities are turning out potentially highly skilled barbarians."[37]

HEROES HAVE CHESTS

C.S. Lewis anticipated this in his seminal article, "Men Without Chests," in which he foresaw the effects of rejection of Christian values.

> This process of reinforcing virtue with emotion produced "sentiments" in people, supplying them with "chests" that safeguarded them from savagery. By debunking all sentiments as merely subjective, however, modern critics have generated "men without chests," human beings who are unable to resist their basest appetites because they have been deprived of the very means of resistance. The situation made civilization unsustainable according to Lewis. "We make men without chests and expect of them virtue and enterprise," he observed. "We castrate and bid the geldings be fruitful.[38]

Without the undergirdings of Christian virtue, we produce men and women lacking the conviction and the courage to be the heroes that the world requires. Heroes must have chests.

In the 20th century, Frank Laubach, a missionary to the Maranao people of the Philippines, developed reading programs based on "key words," the "story method," and "picture-word-syllable" charts to teach people how to read in "scores of countries and hundreds of languages."[39] This is the spiritual leader known for his *Game With Minutes*, in which he recounts his efforts to maintain conscious communion with Jesus every minute of the day. Fully 21 years before he died, *LIFE* magazine credited him with teaching 60 million people how to read.[40]

And it continues today. In one Indian state alone (Tamil Nadu) there are already 1,500 childcare projects run by Christians.[41] The bottom line is that whether the area is schools, hospitals, or politics, revived Christians always let their religion flow out to the streets in mercy.

You might be surprised, though, as Viva Network founder Patrick McDonald was, to find that the Church is doing more for children at risk than any other single group on the planet. The Christian Church is making most of this stuff happen right up to this present day. For example, The Salvation Army, which is just one tiny sliver of the worldwide Church, is itself the world's second largest social service provider (behind the United Nations).

PROLONGING THE AGONY?

Don't get this wrong. We're not advocating merely helping the poor, noble as that exercise is. Salvation does not come by sponsoring children; nor do children become saved just by being sponsored. Assisting people to get a step up may only prolong the agony. The ultimate problem remains one of sin. Unless the hearts of the people are transformed, the face of the earth won't be changed. A true advocate asks "why?" Why do we have the poor, and how did they get there? As an ancient Chinese parable suggests, "Of all the 36 ways to get out of trouble, the best way is—leave.[42] And as we seek to serve the needy in Jesus' name, more and more will listen and *leave* their trouble, and repent of their sin.[43]

The *face of the earth* will be changed as the *hearts of its people* are transformed. We need to preach the Good News in its entirety if we want to see our Father pleased that no one perishes. This gospel includes repentance of sin and faith in our Lord Jesus Christ. It will take complete surrender of our will and complete mobilization of the Hero Army of God. Though the gospel includes compassion, holiness is the solution to every problem.

There are tangible consequences for our failure on this front. President Dwight D. Eisenhower asserted, "Every gun that is made, every warship launched, every rocket fired, signifies in the final sense a theft from those who hunger and are not fed, those who are cold and are not clothed."[44]

The clashes of religions have sparked terrorism that has changed our post 9-11 world. From just two wars involving Afghanistan and Iraq, the United States Congressional Budget Office's estimate for the cost of the war, on December 16, 2003, was $90 billion.[45] That overshadows the $12 billion price tag for the initial Afghanistan effort.[46] A further $87 billion was approved by the U.S. Congress for the Iraq and Afghanistan conflict and reconstruction.[47] Britain has spent or earmarked another $1.4 billion in Afghanistan[48] and $9.6 billion in Iraq.[49] That is a round total of $200 billion!

President Eisenhower's statement, applied to these wars, means that this money could provide 60 million children with a year's worth of health care,

2 million affordable housing unitsl[50], or 37,700 missionaries for 100 years at $50,000 USD per year! If the missionaries armed with mercy had been deployed a few generations ago, then maybe the guns would have been irrelevant today. As Bono argues:

> We put it in the most crass terms possible; we argue it as a financial and security issue for America.... There are potentially another 10 Afghanistans in Africa, and it is cheaper by a factor of 100 to prevent the fires from happening than to put them out.[51]

It is our conviction that revival revolutionizes society, that the *face of the earth* will be changed as we see the *hearts of its people* transformed. The temptation is unrelenting to segregate the "spiritual" from the "social" in Christianity. "The Biblical pattern is both working together: ministries of compassion in the context of passion for the Person and presence of Christ."[52]

Indeed, even *Newsweek*, in recognizing the escalating popularity of Christianity in the East, notes, "For most Asians...what makes Jesus attractive is His identification with the poor and suffering."[53] Philip Jenkins has shown that the gospel that is exploding in the South is a gospel that includes the poor.[54] Identification wed to the power of the Hero-maker, the Holy Spirit, becomes a catalyst for metamorphosis. And the *face* changes as the *hearts* are transformed.

BIG PICTURE

Now, the West isn't everything. You may look around and question some of the assertions presented already. But most of the Christians alive today don't actually live in the West. And so, although the lead Protestant culture has left an admirable legacy of ethics and education and sanctity of life, the inheritors of that legacy have discarded many of the treasures. We're not suggesting that everything Western governments have done is right. As difficult as it is while relaxing in air-conditioned halls of worship, we must face the reality that, "More people take part in Christian Sunday worship in China than do people in the entirety of Western Europe. The same is true of Nigeria, and probably true of India, Brazil, and even the world's largest Muslim country, Indonesia."[55]

WARNING: THIS BOOK CONTAINS OVERWHELMING INFORMATION

One danger is that you will bury your head in your hands in despair after reading parts of this book. But be encouraged. Keep the perspective of

Mother Teresa, who, when commended by a senator on Capitol Hill for her marvelous work, corrected, "It's God's work."[56]

Yes, it is true that the current situation stinks and, from a human perspective, is only getting worse: "The 48 least-developed countries, comprising some 55 millions persons with per capita income of less than $500 per head, will have widely divergent fates in the Information Age. Most will become even more marginalized and desperate."[57]

Yet, World Bank president James Wolfensohn indicates that the proportion of world budgets devoted to development assistance has never been lower than it is now.[58] Missiologist Patrick Johnstone has traced the problem to a lack of theological framework for mission.[59] A 1986 British Council of Churches survey concluded that missiology "is either virtually unknown in theological institutions or relegated to the position of an unimportant subsection of pastoral theology."[60]

But the Hero Army is crafting a comeback in the fourth quarter—transforming hearts and changing the face of the earth, as revival revolutionizes society.[61] The acceleration of victories toward the end of the 20th century is staggering. Today the two-legged gospel of repentance and faith on the right and faith in action through mercy and justice on the left is being walked out again. The Great Commission to "make disciples of all nations" will be accomplished by a healthy Hero Army marching with both legs of a full gospel.

Defining Terms

We want to convince you that this is more than an emotional plea or a pretty good idea. The Hero Army, mobilized by God and deployed on the front lines of the agony of this world, was hatched in the mind of God. The whole concept is anything but trendy. This Army is Heroic. It arises from and returns to the roots, the source. It does not rely on the latest fad or the flavor of the month. It intends to perform thorough, extreme, fundamental, and revolutionary change.

The noun that is radical is "Army"—God's armed and trained fighting force. The Hero Army prevailed and experienced revival that revolutionized societies throughout Scripture. But it is not just in the annals of biblical history that the Hero Army triumphed.

We'll show you in the pages that follow, not only biblical precedent, but also history's most powerful manifestation of the Hero Army, the primitive Salvation Army that transformed the face of parts of the earth as it saw Jesus transform the hearts of the people. Then we'll get our hands gritty by showing you the status of the war today. We'll wrench your heart by overwhelming you with the grim reality in a world scourged by what we coin "seven deadly sins": extreme poverty, orphans of the street, slavery and child labor, sex and the city, AIDS and plagues, war-affected children, and religious persecution.

But we won't leave you in despair. We will propose for you a paradigm for end-time harvest, a framework for seeing our Father's will done, that no one perishes, and that everyone comes to repentance. Just as the historical landscape is punctuated by benevolent exertion initiated by courageous individuals, so you, or you and your small group can apply the biblical mandate to make a difference in your world. "Everyone wants to be a hero and God knows that—it is one of the noblest impulses He placed in people."[62]

As Thomas Long noted in his article, "Beavis and Butt-Head Get Saved":

> The word heroic makes us blush. The word seems too big, too romantic, too triumphal. But our embarrassment cannot conceal the truth that to strive to be a hero—to have one's life rise above the mediocre, to really count for something extraordinary, to outshine death, to be capable of the highest generosity and self-sacrifice—is what we most deeply want and need.[63]

You are called to this life. All kinds of people can be heroes. You don't have to be famous or skilled or eloquent or charming. You have to be committed. We intend to deposit within your spirit inspiration wed with praxis to mobilize you to **be a hero** in the end-time Hero Army!

CHAPTER THREE

GOD'S BIG IDEA

*The Ingredients of Heroism: Justice,
Righteousness, and Compassion*

According to the Ambedkar Centre for Justice and Peace, "In August 1995, a five-year-old untouchable girl was blinded in one eye as the result of a beating from her teacher. The teacher was incensed that the girl had used a drinking cup normally reserved for upper caste students."[1]

Chief Justice P.N. Bhagavati wrote of the Untouchables:

> They are a non-being, exiles of civilization, living a life worse than that of animals, for animals are at least free to roam about as they like and they can plunder or grab food whenever they are hungry, but these OUTCASTS of the society are held in bondage, robbed of their freedom, and they are consigned to an existence where they have to live either in hovels or under the open sky and be satisfied with whatever little unwholesome food they can manage to get,

inadequate though it be to fill their stomachs. Not having any choice, they are driven by poverty and hunger into a life of bondage, a dark bottomless pit from which, in a cruel exploitative society, they cannot hope to be rescued.[2]

Today, the Untouchables, "victims of harassment, rape and violence,"[3] are called *Dalits*, which means "broken people." But for all intents and purposes, the Chief Justice may be closer to the truth when he labels them "non-being, exiles of civilization." Today they represent one of the largest people groups in the history of the world—250 million people—and comprise a group that is prepared to convert *en masse* to a different religion. What are they looking for? With what do they want to replace Hinduism? The answer is quite pragmatic and not so outlandish—anything that works! For them, that which *does* no good, *is* no good. *Love us, treat us like humans, and get our kids an education!*

What a quarter of a billion people are saying is that religion that doesn't work is not good. Conversely, if a belief system actually has the answers to life and it works in our daily lives, then it's worth considering. The Dalits of India are looking for heroes like Gideon and Samson and the rest who will hear their cries and deliver them. They are looking for heroes. This is the religion of YaHWeH. This is the history of Christianity—supplying heroes.

This is how it has been for millennia, everywhere, not just in India. People have been subjugated, have been pressed down, have been oppressed when "might is right." Millions of untouchables, of "non-being, exiles in civilization," have been so mistreated. If you can overpower them, you can abuse them. Rape, pillage, bludgeoning, cruelty, and violence are all acceptable if people are not people. God's big idea disposes of this sin on the ash heap of ethical history.

Do not oppress the widow or the fatherless, the alien or the poor.

In your hearts do not think evil of each other (Zechariah 7:10).

God is acutely concerned with the marginalized, the oppressed, and the "non-being, exiles of civilization." In establishing this free-will form of sovereignty, God has emphasized His commitment to the crucial imperative of protection for this engorged group of people around the world. Heroes are His strategy. Holy Spirit, the Hero-maker, transforms normal people like you and me into heroes.

What are the manifestations of the Hero-maker's filling?

*Now to each one the **manifestation of the Spirit** is given for the common good. To one there is given through the Spirit the message of wisdom, to another the message of knowledge by means of the*

same Spirit, to another faith by the same Spirit, to another gifts of
healing by that one Spirit, to another miraculous powers, to
another prophecy, to another distinguishing between spirits, to
another speaking in different kinds of tongues, and to still another
the interpretation of tongues. All these are the work of one and the
same Spirit, and He gives them to each one, just as He determines
(1 Corinthians 12:7-11).

"SPIRIT-FILLED" AND THE "PRESENCE OF GOD"

In the Old Testament a primary understanding relating to the filling is the example of the Holy Spirit *coming upon* individuals.[4] Gradually the teaching begins to unfold that a new day is coming when the Lord will place His "Spirit" *in* us (see Num. 11:29).[5] It will not be just a *"special few"* but *"all"* who possess the Spirit. By the end of Jesus' ministry, the great anticipated event is not far away. Immediately after the crucifixion and resurrection, Jesus appeared for the first time to His disciples and "breathed on them and said, 'Receive the Holy Spirit' " (John 20:22).

This "promise of the Father" would be like being "endued with, or clothed with power from on high" (Luke 24:29). The power Jesus spoke of would follow the "Holy Spirit coming upon them" and would thereby enable the disciples to be His witnesses.[6] Pentecost brought this long-awaited "Spirit baptism," and the same promise was extended to all who are afar off who will believe (see Acts 2:38-39). Today the promised "Comforter" dwells *in* all of God's people (see John 14:14-17). The Holy Spirit is the Hero-maker.

As the prototype of all we will be, Jesus was the Spirit-filled man *par excellence*—the ultimate Hero. Certainly Jesus was endued with that which He promised us. He said that we would be filled with the Spirit, and He was "filled with the Spirit without limit" (John 3:34). Luke records: "One day as He was teaching, Pharisees and teachers of the law…were sitting there. And *the power of the Lord was present* for Him to heal the sick" (Luke 5:17). "And again, the people all tried to touch Him, because power was coming from Him and healing them all" (Luke 6:19). Jesus cast out demons "by the finger of God" (Luke 11:20).

All this Spirit activity sounds a whole lot alike, whether it is found in the Old or New Testament. In the Old Testament, "The hand of the Lord came upon Elisha and he said, 'This is what the Lord says' " (2 Kings 3:15).[7] The way Elisha was filled and worked under the Spirit's control in the Old Testament sounds the same as the way Jesus cast out demons in the inauguration of the "kingdom of God" (Luke 11:20).[8] People have often puzzled over the curious story concerning Elisha's bones:

> Elisha died and was buried. Now Moabite raiders used to enter the country every spring. Once while some Israelites were burying a man, suddenly they saw a band of raiders; so they threw the man's body into Elisha's tomb. When the body touched Elisha's bones, the man came to life and stood up on his feet (2 Kings 13:20-21).

How could this happen? The presence of the Spirit was so mightily upon Elisha, that long after he was dead and gone the Holy Spirit still lingered over his bones—the presence of God resting on a tangible inanimate thing. Then when this dead man's body touched the bones of Elisha, where the glory of God rested, the man was raised to life.

The way Jesus operated with power coming out of Him and around Him is similar to the description of Peter's anointing, as "people brought the sick into the streets and laid them on beds and mats so that at least Peter's shadow might fall on some of them as he passed by" (Acts 5:15). The way healing was transferred through Elisha's inanimate bones is similar to the way healing was transferred through Paul's handkerchiefs and aprons (see Acts 19:12). Why? Because the Holy Spirit is not bound by our bodies. The Hero-maker is both *in* us and comes *upon* us. He moves through us and He moves upon others independent of us.

Warning

Defeat the temptation to bypass this theological basis of our discussion. Everyone needs to read this stuff! The Bible is chock full of it. We're not repeating ourselves here—these are all new verses. We're talking about God's heart on the issue. This is what He thinks about it. So, buckle in and hunker down, with an open Bible and an open heart.

"MACHINE," "LANDSCAPE," AND "INVISIBLE" PEOPLE

Jesus did say that we'd always have the poor with us (see Mark 14:7). That apparent slip of the tongue has been misinterpreted and misused by Christians throughout history. We've misused it to reject participation in the great reclamation operation that started when Jesus parachuted into enemy territory—earth. We figure, "What can I do for the starving kids in Africa? Jesus said we'd always have them." And we've misinterpreted it sometimes, twisting it to make poverty somehow noble, when it really just plain sucks.

Whereas Eastern Christianity and the monastic tradition have recognized the spiritual benefits of freedom from "things," certain streams of

Western Christianity have somehow hallowed poverty, partly because it runs so counter to the prevailing ethic of consumerism. But what is so blessed about being poor? We don't understand it, so we categorize it with celibacy, martyrdom, and some of those other gifts that we respect but really don't want ourselves! But the blessing isn't in the form of a gift. The poor are not blessed intrinsically as poor people. They are blessed when they are poor because their poverty graphically shouts out to them the need for something more.

> Jesus did not say, "Blessed are the poor in spirit *because* they are poor in spirit." He did not think, "What a fine thing it is to be destitute of every spiritual attainment or quality. It makes people worthy of the kingdom."... Those poor in spirit are called "blessed" by Jesus, not because they are in a meritorious condition, but because, *precisely in spite of and in the midst of their ever so deplorable condition,* the rule of the heavens has moved redemptively upon and through them, by the grace of Christ.[9]

Yes, apparently we'll always have the poor among us, but this is more a clarion call to warfare against evil than an excuse for comfortable carnality.

God's big idea is that the marginalized are people too. Ralph Neighbour, Jr., offers three categorizations of people in *The Arrival Kit*: People people, machine people, and landscape people.[10] People people are those we know and care about as people; machine people are those whose efforts we appreciate for how they help us; and landscape people are just extras in the movie of our lives. The Western Church needs to add another category, because we've been successful at hiding a massive collection of people from our view, and the result has been, "out of sight, out of mind." How about calling them "untouchables"? Oh wait, that's been used. Maybe we'll call them the "invisibles."

God's big idea is that the invisible people—the fragile, marginalized, hurting, dispossessed, and oppressed individuals who are more damned than born into this world—are People people. For example, consider that unnamed woman (an invisible person) who'd been bleeding for 18 years whom Jesus healed and renamed a daughter of Israel (a People person). God actually provides a way for invisible people to become People people. That's good news!

He makes invisible people into People people with three essential actions: justice, righteousness, and compassion and mercy.

The meaning of the Hebrew words for justice, righteousness, and compassion flesh out our understanding of these religious words that have starved for lack of meaty use. They are like God's senses. They seem to be how God engages the world. Without plunging into an exhaustive survey, we'll engage these terms with hopes of provoking a new awareness and appreciation of the intensity of God's care and the comprehensive nature of His expectations for us. A fresh experience of God's heart on these issues will enable us to savor His goodness to us.

GOD'S HEART FOR INVISIBLE PEOPLE

The following chart, Figure 1, gives a word frequency count that is enlightening.

FIGURE 1

GOD'S HEART FOR INVISIBLE PEOPLE
Number of appearances of this word in Scripture in the NASB and the NLT

SELECTED WORD IN SCRIPTURE	NEW AMERICAN STANDARD BIBLE (NASB)	NEW LIVING TRANSLATION (NLT)
Poor	138	195
Orphan(s)	36	38
Widow(s)	86	96
Foreigner(s) Alien	114	139
Hungry	46	67
Dying	9	30
Oppressed	36	43
Needy	51	36
Compassion	92	30
Pity	27	32
Righteous ('ness)	296	128
Merciful	10	46
Mercy	91	155
Justice	135	145

Justice: God's Sight

Salaam was a refugee from Eritrea, a small, war-ravaged country on the Horn of Africa, whose political involvement left her the choice of exile or death. She's been detained, interrogated, threatened, and raped. Four times the Australian government rejected her pleas for asylum. Then Ange, who is not a lawyer, decided to care. She appealed directly to the

Minister of Immigration and generated a letter campaign to see Salaam experience justice.[11]

Ange secured biblical justice. She was a hero to Salaam.

The Hebrew word for "justice" is *mishpat*, meaning a verdict.[12] This extremely important concept appears more than 400 times in the Old Testament.[13] If justice, righteousness, and compassion are God's senses, then justice is His sight. Justice is typically symbolized as being blind to partiality, with statues on courthouses even blindfolded. But even more than being blind to partiality, God unwraps the blindfold to perceive and see the plight of the marginalized. Through justice, God sees. Unlike the American tripartite—legislative, executive, and judicial—branches of government, the meaning of this word comprises all the functions of government, as well as the full range of meaning of the English word "justice."[14]

> *But let justice roll on like a river, righteousness like a never-failing stream!* (Amos 5:24)

Justice embraces the related ideas of laws (Exod. 21:1)[15], rules (Num. 9:3), regulations, the same laws for natives and aliens (Lev. 24:22), case and complaint (Num. 27:5)[16], a claim on what is properly due (Deut. 18:3), what is deserving (Deut. 19:6), what is just (Deut. 32:4), the cause of disputes (Judg. 4:5), and judgment (Ps. 1:5). It is to be the same law for the poor as for the rich, the same justice for the weak as for the strong.

God even allows us to hold Him accountable on this issue. When contemplating the destruction of Sodom and Gomorrah, Abraham challenged God on the point of justice, asking, "Will not the Judge of all the earth do right?" (Gen. 18:25) And from this concept of justice being what is right emerges the notion of rights.[17] And yet He will not tolerate our tilting of His priorities to make Him out to be unjust in light of the rights of people: "You have wearied the Lord with your words. 'How have we wearied Him?' you ask. By saying, 'All who do evil are good in the eyes of the Lord, and He is pleased with them' or 'Where is the God of justice?' " (Mal. 2:17)

It is the lack of justice that angers God. Where "truth is nowhere to be found, and whoever shuns evil becomes a prey…. The Lord looked and was displeased that there was no justice" (Isa. 59:15).[18] He specifically looks for instances where justice is denied (see Lam. 3:36).

Justice is closely connected with the second of God's three means of making invisible people into People people—righteousness. Justice appears in conjunction with righteousness frequently in God's entreaties. A father "will direct…his household in the way of the Lord by doing what is right and just" (Gen. 18:19). The Proverbs are written to instruct a person toward a "disciplined and prudent life, doing what is right and just and fair" (Prov. 1:3). After all, "The Lord is righteous, He loves justice; upright men will see His face" (Ps. 11:7). Like two pedals moving in tandem, "I walk in the way of righteousness, along the paths of justice" (Prov. 8:20). And both concepts are active in salvation: "Zion will be redeemed with justice, her penitent ones with righteousness" (Prov.1:27).

Justice is integral to our understanding of Western civilization. It is essential that we understand the concept in order to appreciate God's feelings toward the invisible people.

Righteousness: God's Taste

When my wife, Danielle, was seven years old she had two classmates who were twins. They were from the wrong side of the tracks. They were a little slow, they dressed less fashionably than the other kids, and they sometimes smelled bad. Their family situation was poor. This was obvious to all. To the amusement of the other students, one day the teacher spanked them both in the front of the class. Danielle told her father. The next morning this man of God showed up at the principal's office, demanding that the twins and their teacher also appear. He insisted that their teacher apologize to them in front of the class. When told by the principal that it wasn't any of his business, he replied, "I've made them my business!"

My father-in-law brought righteousness to that school. He was a hero to the twins.

The Hebrew word for righteousness is *tsedaqah*, which means to be morally right.[19] If these are God's senses, righteousness is His taste. The salt, the enriching moral goodness that He deposits in the world through His followers, improves that taste. Just in its feminine form, the word righteousness appears in the Old Testament 157 times.[20] It is essentially a legal term defining the fair and honest responsibilities of parties in a relationship.[21]

Throughout Scripture, love is recognized in obedience.[22] Scripture also defines faith in terms of obedience (see John 3:36).[23] This perception of faith, love, and obedience is grounded in Abraham's response to God, when "Abram believed the Lord, and He credited it to him as righteousness" (Gen. 15:16). Further, "If we are careful to obey all this law before the Lord our God, as He has commanded us, that will be our righteousness" (Deut. 6:25).

The term is used to characterize David's kingship: "David reigned over all Israel, doing what was just and right for all his people" (1 Chron. 18:14). Job's defense captures it from a different perspective: "I will maintain my righteousness and never let go of it; my conscience will not reproach me as long as I live" (Job 27:6).

The holy character of God is defined and proven by this term: "The holy God will show Himself holy by His righteousness" (Isa. 5:16).

Thus, "The effect of righteousness will be quietness and confidence forever" (Isa. 32:17).

Compassion: God's Touch

> We don't argue compassion.
>
> —Bono, U2

The simplest act of compassion is to not look away.[24]

A traditional Zulu greeting is "I see you." The proper response is "I am here." It is the recognition that makes us truly human.[25] It is the simple act of not looking away from deformity, from ugliness, from repulsiveness, that is the simplest act of compassion.

At a gathering of a school for the disabled, a distraught father stood up and cried:

> "Where is the perfection in my son, Shay? Everything God does is done with perfection. But my child cannot understand things as other children do. My child cannot remember facts and figures as other children do. Where is God's perfection?"
>
> The audience was shocked by the question, pained by the father's anguish and stilled by the piercing query. "I believe," the father answered, "that when God brings a child like this into the world, the perfection that he seeks is in the way people react to this child.[26]

Shay's father was a hero. But let us look at Shay. Let's remove his invisibility.

The Hebrew word for compassion is *racham*.[27] If justice, righteousness, and compassion are God's senses, then compassion is His sense of touch. Yes, He dwells in a high and holy place, but He also dwells *with* the contrite and lowly of spirit (see Isa. 57:15).

Two closely related words mean "to fondle," and "bowels" or "womb." And when you touch, you feel. With compassion—which in Latin means to *suffer with*—the bowels are stirred up or the womb cherishes the fetus. There is strong connotation of tender, loving intimacy and guts-yearning emotion.

More than a mere feeling, however, it is an active word, possessing the sense of "love with its sleeves rolled up."

The King James Version of the Bible inclines toward translating compassion in these colorful ways:

- *And Joseph made haste; for his bowels did yearn upon his brother: and he sought where to weep; and he entered into his chamber, and wept there* (Genesis 43:30 KJV).
- *The Lord is good to all: and His tender mercies are over all His works* (Psalm 145:9 KJV).

And again, these key words of activating personhood for invisible people are inter-related:

- *This is what the Lord Almighty says: "Administer true justice; show mercy and compassion to one another"* (Zechariah 7:9).

Remember, God's big idea is that "invisible people" are "People people." And God invests a significant amount of space in the Bible to establish this truth toward various flavors of invisible people that He redeems. Watch as God takes the poor, the needy, the alien, the widow, and the orphan and instills within them rights, justice, a sense of belonging and dignity, through the unstinting deployment of justice, righteousness, and compassion.

INVISIBLE PEOPLE: THE POOR

I live in Vancouver's Downtown Eastside. Let me tell you about some of my neighbors on East Hastings Street:

A boy's dreams are easily ground to dust here in El Guantillo, Honduras.

Dreams like earning enough to build your family a house to replace the one Hurricane Mitch tore apart two years ago.

Dreams like new jeans and a stylish shirt.

Dreams like eating until your belly is full.

In El Guantillo and half a dozen nearby villages sprinkled across the dusty red-dirt countryside of Francisco Morazan state, the farmers try to grow coffee, but the only sure crop is poverty.

El Guantillo is a hard four-hour drive on blacktop, gravel and dirt. The last leg of what is a road in name only fords two streams and winds its way up a sparsely forested mountain, snaking between fast-moving fires. It's the dry season, and work-weary subsistence farmers are burning off the previous season's crops.

There is no other way to live in these villages—Cedros, Agua Caliente, Porvenir, Quebrada, El Pedernal. A few years ago, village leaders say, some boys left the area and returned months later with new clothes and gold chains around their necks. It seemed like a miracle.

So now the villages are sending their future to East Hastings Street. Boys desperate for something more are leaving in droves.... This is their Never-Never Land, a squalid strip where child prostitutes strut and sirens scream.... The children are selling a mountain of crack cocaine, one $10 rock at a time, on Vancouver's most crime-ridden street.... Here on East Hastings Street, the lost boys of Honduras chase visions of a better life.[28]

Each of these young people is in need of a hero.

The Poor

This word is sometimes translated "needy." It connotes destitution. The New Testament word comes from a word meaning "to crouch," as a beggar cringes.[29] How insipid! The Untouchables. The Invisible. We slap a name on this aggregation of three billion people and sit at attention to flick the channel should World Vision or the Christian Children's Fund be so brazen as to interrupt Sunday afternoon football with 30 seconds depicting their graphic desolation, their unequivocal destitution.

Justice for the Poor

- *I know that the Lord secures justice for the poor and upholds the cause of the needy* (Psalm 140:2).

God sees and defends them.

- *He will defend the afflicted among the people…He will crush the oppressor* (Psalm 72:4).
- *With my mouth I will greatly extol the Lord; in the great throng I will praise Him. For He stands at the right hand of the needy one, to save his life from those who condemn him* (Psalm 109:30-31).
- *Sing to the Lord! Give praise to the Lord! He rescues the life of the needy from the hands of the wicked* (Jeremiah 20:13).

As you can see, this is the cause of much rejoicing and praise! Not only does God do it, but He directs *us* to do it as well.

- *Do not deny justice to your poor people in their lawsuits* (Jeremiah 23:6).
- *Do not take advantage of a hired man who is poor and needy, whether he is a brother Israelite or an alien living in one of your towns* (Deuteronomy 24:14).
- *Speak up and judge fairly; defend the rights of the poor and needy* (Proverbs 31:9).

And when God doesn't seem to be moving according to our own timetable, He encourages us to join with Him by "reminding" Him.

- *But the needy will not always be forgotten, nor the hope of the afflicted ever perish. Arise, O Lord, let not man triumph; let the nations be judged in Your presence* (Psalm 9:18-19).
- *Rescue the weak and needy; deliver them from the hand of the wicked* (Psalm 82:4).

Either way, the end result is that "The poor have hope, and injustice shuts its mouth" (Job 5:15-16).

Righteousness for the Poor

He defended the cause of the poor and needy, and so all went well.

Is that not what it means to know Me? (Jeremiah 22:16)

Righteousness toward the poor is equated with revering God! "He who oppresses the poor shows contempt for their Maker, but whoever is kind to the needy honors God" (Prov. 14:31).

Righteousness, God's taste, is manifest in the sweetening of social relationships. God laid down rules that poor slaves would be freed after seven years of service (see Deut. 15:9). Associated with the cancellation of debts and with slavery, Moses instructed that "There should be no poor among you, for...He will richly bless you, if only you fully obey the Lord your God and are careful to follow all these commands I am giving you today" (Deut. 15:5). God instructed the people, "During the seventh year let the land lie unplowed and unused. Then the poor among your people may get food from it, and the wild animals may eat what they leave. Do the same with your vineyard and your olive grove" (Exod. 23:11).

The unrighteous are identified by their treatment of the poor. "The scoundrel's methods are wicked, he makes up evil schemes to destroy the poor with lies, even when the plea of the needy is just" (Isa. 32:7). And Jeremiah criticizes the fat and sleek: "Their evil deeds have no limit; they do not plead the case of the fatherless to win it, they do not defend the rights of the poor" (Jer. 5:28). God applies this measure on nations: "This is what the Lord says:

'For three sins of Israel, even for four, I will not turn back [My wrath]. They sell the righteous for silver, and the needy for a pair of sandals' " (Amos 2:6); and most scandalously, cities: "Now this was the sin of your sister Sodom: She and her daughters were arrogant, overfed and unconcerned; they did not help the poor and needy" (Ezek. 16:49).

Imagine! God considers apathy toward the poor to be as evil, and worthy of punishment, as sodomizing sexual sin! This may offend some Christians out there. It may even convict some!

Amos, the shepherd of Tekoa, berates and lambastes the people of Israel for their unrighteousness on this issue:

- *Hear this word, you cows of Bashan on Mount Samaria, you women who oppress the poor and crush the needy and say to your husbands, "Bring us some drinks"* (Amos 4:1)!
- *For I know how many are your offenses and how great your sins. You oppress the righteous and take bribes and you deprive the poor of justice in the courts* (Amos 5:12).
- *Hear this, you who trample the needy and do away with the poor of the land…* (Amos 8:4).
- *Buying the poor with silver and the needy for a pair of sandals, selling even the sweepings with the wheat* (Amos 8:6).

What a way to win friends and influence people! Whew! No wonder Amos asserted that he was neither a prophet nor the son of a prophet. But he did see evil and unrighteousness through God's eyes and was inflamed over it.

Like the Old Testament prophets, Jesus measured righteousness by treatment of the poor: "Jesus answered, 'If you want to be perfect, go, sell your possessions and give to the poor, and you will have treasure in heaven. Then come, follow Me' " (Matt. 19:21). The apostles made it a fundamental condition of right relationship in the Hero Army of God of A.D. 33: "All they asked was that we should continue to remember the poor, the very thing I was eager to do" (Gal. 2:10). And in remembering the invisible people labeled "the poor," by acting righteously toward them, we transform them into People people.

Compassion for the Poor

- *I was a father to the needy; I took up the case of the stranger* (Job 29:16).

Whereas righteousness could be enacted by not doing something harmful, compassion must be exercised in reaching out to the disenfranchised. And when you touch, you feel.

First of all, God instructs us to show compassion to the poor:

- *If there is a poor man among your brothers in any of the towns of the land that the Lord your God is giving you, do not be hardhearted or tightfisted toward your poor brother. Rather be openhanded and freely lend him whatever he needs* (Deuteronomy 15:7-8).
- *You have been a refuge for the poor, a refuge for the needy in his distress, a shelter from the storm and a shade from the heat. For the breath of the ruthless is like a storm driving against a wall* (Isaiah 25:4).

Second, He models it.

- *He has scattered abroad His gifts to the poor, His righteousness endures forever; His horn will be lifted high in honor* (Psalm 112:9).
- *But He lifted the needy out of their affliction and increased their families like flocks* (Psalm 107:41).
- *He raises the poor from the dust and lifts the needy from the ash heap* (Psalm 113:7).

Third, He promises compassion.

- *He will take pity on the weak and the needy and save the needy from death* (Psalm 72:13).
- *The poorest of the poor will find pasture, and the needy will lie down in safety. But your root I will destroy by famine; it will slay your survivors* (Isaiah 14:30).
- The poor and needy search for water, but there is none; their tongues are parched with thirst. But I the Lord will answer them; I, the God of Israel, will not forsake them (Isaiah 41:17).

Mordecai formalizes the exercise of compassion to the poor during the festival he established (see Esther 9:20-22).

God is entreated to show compassion to the poor (see Psalm 74:21).[30]

And in a compelling manner, Jesus Christ defines His mission in terms of compassion to the poor:

- *The Spirit of the Lord is on Me, because He has anointed Me to preach good news to the poor. He has sent Me to proclaim freedom for the prisoners and recovery of sight for the blind, to release the oppressed* (Luke 4:18).

And He defends His identity as the Messiah by the measure of compassion He has exercised toward the poor:

The blind receive sight, the lame walk, those who have leprosy are cured, the deaf hear, the dead are raised, and the good news is preached to the poor (Matthew 11:5).

INVISIBLE PEOPLE: THE NEEDY

Poor and needy are synonyms. And yet God distinguishes between the two experiences and speaks to the needy[31] specifically, in terms of protection, righteousness, and mercy. These are people like Annie, who lives down the street from us and sometimes "acquires" neat used outfits for our infant son. She has some mental challenges. She has a husky singing voice and a funky taste in clothes. Annie has a rare room with a shower in our neighborhood. But she doesn't work. She does drugs regularly. And she is needy. God speaks to Annie in terms of protection, righteousness, and mercy. Any individuals who attract that kind of divine attention are indubitably People people.

Justice for the Needy

- *"Because of the oppression of the weak and the groaning of the needy, I will now arise," says the Lord. "I will protect them from those who malign them"* (Psalm 12:5).
- *My whole being will exclaim, "Who is like You, O Lord? You rescue the poor from those too strong for them, the poor and needy from those who rob them"* (Psalm 35:10).
- *I know that the Lord secures justice…and upholds the cause of the needy* (Psalm 140:12).
- *Do not crush the needy in court* (Proverbs 22:22).

Righteousness for the Needy

- *If you lend money to one of My people among you who is needy, do not be like a moneylender; charge him no interest* (Exodus 22:25).
- *If the man is poor, do not go to sleep with his pledge in your possession* (Deuteronomy 24:12).

Compassion to the Needy

- *There will always be poor people in the land. Therefore I command you to be openhanded toward your brothers and toward the poor and needy in your land* (Deuteronomy 15:11).
- *But those who suffer He delivers in their suffering; He speaks to them in their affliction* (Job 36:15).

INVISIBLE PEOPLE:
THE ALIEN, REFUGEE, AND FOREIGNER

Yolande Mukagasana is an alien. A Rwandan author and human rights campaigner, she fled her country:

> I had no husband left, no children, no friends, no roof over my head, no past in short. I never imagined that when I left Rwanda, I would feel abruptly and profoundly torn apart.

> Especially as the bodies of my husband and children lay in common graves, in this country which never wanted us. As far as I was concerned, I had nothing left to do on that soil, which swallowed up my family in an ocean of torture, humiliation, suffering unmatched—perpetrated by our brothers the Rwandans. I thought myself disgusted with my own country.

> Europe…was the continent that would accept me perhaps, where I would have the right to live simply like a human being. A human being at the very bottom of the ladder: a refugee.

> No, I thought, I cannot be a refugee. I will be a tourist who will sleep soundly, without fear of a machete descending on my neck. Without seeing every morning the criminal people who I love, who have just betrayed me. I will be back in two months.

> Farewell to family.

> This decision gave me goosebumps! Three children. Abandoning my family, my past, this life of 100 years in 100 days as if I were abandoning myself. I got up and went to see my children. Or rather their common grave, there down below behind Gaspard's house, the man who led them to be killed. Sitting on the grave, I started talking to them.

> Sifting through the bones of my children. "My dear children, forgive me for abandoning you. Forgive me for not being able to lead you to adulthood. Forgive me for letting you die so young. Forgive me for not having the courage to fend off with another machete the machetes that killed you.

> "Forgive me for having been an unfit mother. I abandon you. I am going off to live in a country which knows virtually nothing of your ordeal. I am off to smile to people who may be partly responsible for your death.

"I am off to look for the protection of those who were unable or unwilling to protect you. I am a cowardly mother, even more cowardly than your assassins."[32]

I know this reads a little like the umpteenth sequel to a classic sci-fi horror flick but it's really a rebuke to all of us who are patriots at heart. In very real ways our flag-waving nationalism epitomizes our succumbing to the enemy. The devil has used national anthems to draw lines that restrict our concern for justice, for righteousness, and for compassion.[33] But God will not allow us to persist in this sin.

God is about to show us that the aliens like Yolande Mukagasana are People people too.

Justice for the Alien, Refugee, Foreigner

The principle means of accomplishing this goal is to establish one set of rules for everybody.

- *The community is to have the same rules for you and for the alien living among you; this is a lasting ordinance for the generations to come. You and the alien shall be the same before the Lord: The same laws and regulations will apply both to you and to the alien living among you* (Numbers 15:15-16).

This goes both ways—not just blessing but also punishment:

- *One and the same law applies to everyone who sins unintentionally, whether he is a native-born Israelite or an alien. But anyone who sins defiantly, whether native-born or alien, blasphemes the Lord, and that person must be cut off from his people* (Numbers 15:29-30).
- *And I charged your judges at that time: Hear the disputes between your brothers and judge fairly, whether the case is between brother Israelites or between one of them and an alien* (Deuteronomy 1:16).

It is considered unjust to deprive the alien (see Deut. 24:17), and a curse is on anyone who deprives an alien of justice (Deut. 27:19).

Righteousness for the
Alien, Refugee, and Foreigner

God's emphatic tactic on righteousness is that the Israelites don't have to put themselves in the alien's shoes—they have their own pair! If God's righteousness is not taste, maybe, in this instance, it is smell! And so God merely reminds them, "Do not mistreat an alien or oppress him, for you were aliens in Egypt" (Exod. 22:21); and, "Do not oppress an alien; you yourselves know how it feels to be aliens, because you were aliens in Egypt" (Exod. 23:9).

Most people do not leave their home and land unless there is a problem. Aliens are aliens because of persecution or war or hardship or famine. This "one law" policy of righteousness even extends to the issue of precious land: "'In whatever tribe the alien settles, there you are to give him his inheritance,' declares the Sovereign Lord" (Ezek. 47:23).

Then God shows the Israelites that it is right to leave a little behind. "When you are harvesting in your field and you overlook a sheaf, do not go back to get it. Leave it for the alien, the fatherless and the widow, so that the Lord your God may bless you in all the work of your hands" (Deut. 24:19).

An interesting application of this principle pertains to the tithe. God teaches that, "When you have finished setting aside a tenth of all your produce in the third year, the year of the tithe, you shall give it to the Levite, the alien, the fatherless and the widow, so that they may eat in your towns and be satisfied" (Deut. 26:12). So the alien is to directly benefit from our tithing! This is a good verse to yank out at church budget meetings.

God defines righteousness in relation to our treatment of the alien:

> This is what the Lord says: Do what is just and right. Rescue from the hand of his oppressor the one who has been robbed. Do no wrong or violence to the alien, the fatherless or the widow, and do not shed innocent blood in this place (Jeremiah 22:3)[34]

And Ezekiel points out the same thing to the people of God, that their denial of justice to the alien is unrighteous: "The people of the land practice extortion and commit robbery; they oppress the poor and needy and mistreat the alien, denying them justice" (Ezek. 22:29).

> Do not go over your vineyard a second time or pick up the grapes that have fallen. Leave them for the poor and the alien. I am the Lord your God (Leviticus 19:10).
>
> When you reap the harvest of your land, do not reap to the very edges of your field or gather the gleanings of your harvest. Leave them for the poor and the alien. I am the Lord your God (Leviticus 23:22).

Compassion for the Alien, Refugee, and Foreigner

Showing justice and righteousness is one thing, but asking us to show compassion to the alien is really pushing it. You want us to touch them? To feel for them? Jesus did that in the story of the Good Samaritan. And God calls on Israel to do it as well.

Don't just be nice; love the alien. Like a guy at The Salvation Army asked, "I don't mind most people, but you want me to love them?" Love someone who acts and looks and smells and eats and speaks and recreates and labors and believes differently than us?

- *For the Lord your God is God of gods and Lord of lords, the great God, mighty and awesome, who shows no partiality and accepts no bribes. He defends the cause of the fatherless and the widow, and loves the alien, giving him food and clothing. And you are to love those who are aliens, for you yourselves were aliens in Egypt* (Deuteronomy 10:17-19).

- *When an alien lives with you in your land, do not mistreat him. The alien living with you must be treated as one of your native-born. Love him as yourself, for you were aliens in Egypt. I am the Lord your God* (Leviticus 19:33-34).

INVISIBLE PEOPLE: THE WIDOW

Susan grew up in the beautiful historic city of Kabul, Afghanistan. She remembers the freedom of being able to go out with her friends and shop without being watched or followed. Clean water once ran through the Kabul River. Once the beautiful architecture and greenery of the Kings Palace was a center of attraction, but it now lies in shambles. Half of the city was destroyed by factional fighting. Women are scared to go out. "The beautiful city of Kabul is only memories," Susan shared.

"We suffered very much. We lost our home and two brothers. Twice my husband, five children and I fled to Pakistan. We returned six years ago thinking the situation in Kabul was back to normal. To our dismay, it was not. We suffered much more. My husband could not find a job and without the help of friends we would not have made it. We could not depend on our friends for long as they were suffering too."

Susan continued, "To take care of the family, my husband joined one of the local warlords who promised to pay well in order to fight for power. I did not see him for six months and did not receive any money. When I could not take it any longer, I sent a message to the warlord through a neighbor to see the welfare of my husband. 'I am sorry, your husband was killed three months ago,' was the reply from my neighbor.

"I looked at my children and did not know what to do. I cried for days. The children were crying from hunger and at times I wanted to kill myself. After searching for help I found a job in making quilts. I was promised 50 cents a quilt and hurried home to try to finish as many as possible. Not knowing how to sew, I hurt my fingers badly. Even with pain, I was only able to do one in three days. Within two weeks I was able to complete two per day. With little money I was able to keep my children fed."

More widows in the quilt project came to me and began to share and show their scarred hands. I prayed for wisdom. I felt the Lord saying, "Feed them."[35]

Even in our society, widows are often forgotten. In the ancient times they were destitute. The Bible offers stunning glimpses of counter-culture and counter-history as widows play starring roles in significant events. Two widows, Tamar and Ruth, are immortalized in Matthew's genealogy of Jesus (see Matt. 1). Abigail, the widow of Nabal, was married to David before he was King David (see 1 Sam. 27:3).

It was a widow who sustained and ministered to the renowned prophet Elijah during the notorious drought, when he was a wanted man (see 1 Kings 17). It was a widow who was commemorated by Jesus for giving more to God than all the wealthy people (see Mark 12:42-43). It was Anna, a widow, who was blessed to recognize the Messiah at His dedication in the Temple (see Luke 2:36-38). It was a widow who wrenched compassion from Jesus' innards such that He raised her son to life (see Luke 7:12-16). And Jesus makes it a widow who compels an apathetic judge to give her justice (see Luke 18:2-8).

Now, several of God's injunctions concerning widows appear with the alien and the fatherless, but there are others in which she is singled out.

Justice for the Widow

The Lord sustains the widow (see Ps. 146:9). He teaches us to defend widows and plead their case (see Isa. 1:17).

Righteousness for the Widow

We're instructed not to "take advantage of a widow or an orphan" (Exod. 22:22).

Compassion for the Widow

Job, in the defense of his integrity, assured that "from my birth I guided the widow" (Job 31:18).

INVISIBLE PEOPLE: THE ORPHAN

Some 12 million children in Africa have been orphaned by AIDS—and that number is rising, according to the Save the Children Fund (SCF).

Teddy lives in a village in southern Uganda. Her parents died of AIDs-related illnesses when she was 11. She now lives with her three brothers and sisters and helps to look after three other boys whose parents also died of AIDS-related illnesses.

"My mother and father died in 1996. My father died in the hospital.

"But I saw my mother die here. Because I was a bit older than the others, I looked after her.

"I used to cook food for her, wash her clothes, and boil herbs for her.

"She told me she was suffering from AIDS, but she didn't tell me how she got it or how to avoid it.

"I wish she'd told me more about it. I'd like to know how it's transmitted.

"When my mother died we suffered so much. There was no food, and there was no one to look after us.

"We didn't even have money to buy soap and salt.

"We wanted to run away to our other grandparents, but we didn't have transport to go there.

"I tried to be positive, but it was difficult.

"I missed my mother because I loved her so much.

"When my mum was here we didn't suffer. We had food and money for buying things.

"Some neighbors say bad things about us: 'Those children are so poor; they don't even have relatives. They don't belong. They don't have a clan.'

"Some people also call us 'AIDS orphans,' and they say that maybe our parents infected us.

"We don't say anything. At least no one oppresses us.

"We're also free to play when we want, and there's nobody telling us to do this or that.

"A while ago some neighbors came here and asked us to sell them our trees.

"We agreed and we sold them.

"But they haven't given us the money.

"We've tried getting the money from them, but they won't give it.

"Sometimes people come and steal food from our garden. My grandfather's brother comes and takes the coffee.

"He just steals it when the beans are still on the trees.

"I don't go to school. I'd like to go, but my grandparents and neighbours told me to stay at home and look after the others.

"If I were educated I'd like to be a nurse.

"I want to treat other people and heal them from whatever they're suffering from.

"I want to do this because when my mother was sick, there was nobody to look after her because we had no money."

She is one of 12 million African children orphaned by AIDS.[36]

As Teddy's story suggests, the plight of too many orphans is deplorable, and their voice is muted. And, although God's directives to substantiate justice, righteousness, and compassion to the orphan have frequently emerged as we've attended to the other invisible people, He does tackle their plight specifically, and in so doing, designs these invisible people into People people.

JUSTICE FOR THE ORPHAN

We've all heard the expression, "It's like taking candy from a baby!" Why, what does that mean? It means a baby doesn't know what it has, that her candy is treasure. A baby is easily duped. A baby couldn't resist if she wanted to. God doesn't like that. He sees and defends the orphan (see Ps. 10:17-18). He instructs us to do the same (see Ps. 82:3). Those who oppress the orphan are in for "quick" judgment (see Mal. 3:5).

Righteousness for the Orphan

Again, God instructs us to leave off evil toward the orphan: "Do not move an ancient boundary stone or encroach on the fields of the fatherless" (Prov. 23:10). Don't leave a bad taste in their mouths.

Compassion for the Orphan

God is "the helper of the fatherless" (Ps. 10:14), and "A father to the fatherless, a defender of widows, is God in His holy dwelling" (Ps. 68:5). He touches them, and feels. And the prophet declares, "In You the fatherless find compassion" (Hos. 14:3).

NEW TESTAMENT RECORD

There are three kinds of laws in the Old Testament: moral law, civil law, and ceremonial law. The moral law continued into the New Testament era largely intact; the civil law became the basis of much of our Western legal codes; and the ceremonial law was fulfilled in Christ.

Jesus stamped His endorsement on the law in Luke 10:28. There are 613 commands in the Torah.[37]

How does the New Testament record compare with the Old? To a man, the main characters in the new era endorse the Jewish moral and the basics of the civil law.

Jesus, as we'll see in more detail later, is all about the marginalized. His standard for Kingdom choice seemed, in Matthew 25, to be all about feeding hungry people, clothing naked people, visiting sick people, befriending lonely people, attending imprisoned people. Ouch!

John the Baptist was just as clear-cut. If you have two jackets, give one to the guy who only has one. If you have some food, share with the person who doesn't have any. Don't rip people off. Don't slander or manipulate people. Be content (see Luke 3:10-14).[38]

James, the brother of Jesus, followed his big Brother's example. He asserted, "This is pure and undefiled religion in the sight of our God and Father, to visit orphans and widows in their distress, and to keep oneself unstained by the world" (James 1:26). Does that sound familiar?

And Paul confirms both his heart and modus operandi, and the prevailing ethic of the original apostles, when he repeats his meeting with Peter, James, and John, noting that they wanted him to "remember the poor—the very thing I was eager to do" (Gal. 2:10). Let this eager spirit pour out justice, righteousness, and compassion to the marginalized in our world.

God doesn't pretend. He can't feign with the monkey, "See no evil, hear no evil, speak no evil." God is fully alive. He sees all oppression and brings justice. He can taste all of the wickedness and fights for righteousness. And He feels all of the agony through divine compassion. All of His senses are in operation. God exercises all of His senses through justice, righteousness, compassion, and mercy to redeem and restore the invisible people of this world.

The invisible people can become People people. It happens as heroes, under the Holy Spirit's power, apply God's senses and exercise justice, righteousness, mercy, and compassion toward them in Jesus' name. This application makes us fully alive, as we finally fully sense the world as God does. When Yolande and Susan and Teddy and Annie and the Lost Boys experience God's heart through us, something supernatural has begun. And so it remains true that the face of the earth will be changed as the hearts of its people are transformed. It is time for us to "get" God's big idea.

CHAPTER FOUR

THE HEROES OF THE WARS OF THE LORD

How Normal People Imbued With the Hero-Maker
Accomplished Superhuman Feats, Serving People.

He is there, and He is not silent.

—Francis Schaeffer

Throughout history, cutely rendered "His Story," God is at work. He is often seen behind major battles, revolutions, and international crises.

The wars of the Lord are fought with the weapons of justice, compassion, and righteousness to establish mercy, justice, compassion, and righteousness on the earth. From this perspective, revival is simply a war of the Lord. The wars of the Lord pave the battlefields of heroes. And real revival impacts society. The face of the earth changes as the hearts of its people are transformed.

"HOLY HEROES"

Throughout history God has deployed heroes to this end. A quick "Google" search finds you a multitude of hero sites. Our generation comes by it honestly. The 19th century featured literature like evangelist D.L. Moody's *Paul: The Christian Hero,* and Charlie Coulson's *A Christian Hero of the American War.* William Carey and Hudson Taylor left marks that changed the world. Previous to that, in 1701, Sir Richard Steele penned *The Christian Hero.* Count von Zinzendorf, leader of the Moravians, began one of the most phenomenal missionary movements in history, with nearly 1 in every 12 members sent out to mission fields. They actually started more missions in 10 years than the whole of Protestantism did in the previous 200.[1]

Dante refined the concept of a Christian hero in the 14th century. Francis Xavier was living it, baptizing 750,000 Asians in 10 years.[2] In the 8th century his ilk were called *"sacer heros miles Christi,"* literally, "the holy heroes of Christ." The holy hero "wishes to fight against his passions, flees the world, takes refuge in solitude, undertaking the severest fasts and sometimes eccentricities."[3]

It was during this general era that the heroic Celtic monks evangelized much of Britain and West and Central Europe. Saint Patrick is the most famous of a group of notable heroes such as Ninian, Columba, Columbanus, Aidan, and Boniface.[4]

Nestorius and followers took the gospel through Syria, to Iran, Yemen, Central Asia, Mongolia, Tibet, China, India, Thailand, and Burma, growing to 12 million between A.D. 430-1000.[5]

With the gradual organization of monasticism, these heroes expressed their conviction in charity directed toward the common good, mobilizing the "zeal of the fervent for the social benefit of Christian civilization: the exercise of various crafts, agriculture, building and rebuilding, the care of the deserted children and the poor and the sick, the redemption of captives and relief of prisoners."[6] In the 6th century Walfroy spent the winter on a pillar.[7] And from the 4th century's St. George and the fifth's St. Simeon Stylites,[8] from St. Catherine through to the 20th century's St. Maximilian Kolbe (who willingly died in the place of another prisoner who had familial connections), Catholics have called their heroes… saints.[9] Despite varying perspectives and experiences, these heroes find their inspiration in the Bible.

Let's take a first trip again to some of the biblical battlegrounds of the wars of the Lord.

JOB—PROTO-REVIVAL
(JOB 29-31)

A hush swam over the gathered crowd. Each head turned to catch a glimpse. Like the long chase of the setting sun, appreciative smiles crossed every face. Young people were blown away by the light of a smile aimed in their direction. It was not the rarity of the event but its magnitude that attracted every eye. Waves of people parted in deference. Individual benedictions rolled to individual minds and lips, how this great and good man had rescued that family when the crop failed, how he had taken this one in after his parents died of the plague, how he undertook for that one after her husband died in battle, how he cared for those over there who made a meager living by begging, how he established a home to nurse several who were handicapped and ill, how he smashed the fangs of the wicked slimeball intent on robbing this one of his land and snatched the victims from his teeth.... Clothed in righteousness, bedecked by justice, the Chief arrived at the Gate. Job was as a king amongst his troops.[10]

No one is quite sure when Chief Job lived and ruled in Uz. But this man of integrity left a legacy that continues to shine. Long before God granted us the law on stone, Job manifested the law written on his heart, and in delineating it, he left for us an embryonic code for social justice, a nascent charter for the Hero Army.

At the inception of God's plan for world blessing, possibly during the lifetime of Abraham, an obscure, benevolent man named Job fashioned the charter of the Hero Army. It is the enactment of the revived life. From him we have the essence for a transformed society.

Most of us know the popular tale of Job. We've heard about the patience of Job. We might know about the suffering of Job.

After disaster strikes Job and his family, he responds: "The Lord giveth and the Lord taketh away; blessed be the name of the Lord" (Job 1:21). His wife is a little less magnanimous. Her advice is, "Curse God and die" (Job 2:9)! His friends aren't much better, and for dozens of chapters we follow their conversation with Job.

Finally Job defends his lifestyle, the enactment of a revived life, and the essence of a transformed society. It is worth reading at length:

If I have denied the desires of the poor or let the eyes of the widow grow weary, if I have kept my bread to myself, not sharing it with the fatherless—but from my youth I reared him as would a father, and from my birth I guided the widow—if I have seen anyone perishing for lack of clothing, or a needy man without a garment, and his heart did not bless me for warming him with the fleece from my sheep, if I have raised my hand against the fatherless, knowing that I had influence in court, then let my arm fall from the shoulder, let it be broken off at the joint.

For I dreaded destruction from God, and for fear of His splendor I could not do such things. If I have put my trust in gold or said to pure gold, "You are my security," if I have rejoiced over my great wealth, the fortune my hands had gained, if I have regarded the sun in its radiance or the moon moving in splendor, so that my heart was secretly enticed and my hand offered them a kiss of homage, then these also would be sins to be judged, for I would have been unfaithful to God on high. If I have rejoiced at my enemy's misfortune or gloated over the trouble that came to him—I have not allowed my mouth to sin by invoking a curse against his life—if the men of my household have never said, "Who has not had his fill of Job's meat?"—But no stranger had to spend the night in the street, for my door was always open to the traveler—if I have concealed my sin as men do, by hiding my guilt in my heart because I so feared the crowd and so dreaded the contempt of the clans that I kept silent and would not go outside ("Oh, that I had someone to hear me! I sign now my defense—let the Almighty answer me; let my accuser put his indictment in writing. Surely I would wear it on my shoulder, I would put it on like a crown. I would give him an account of my every step; like a prince I would approach him.)—If my land cries out against me and all its furrows are wet with tears, if I have devoured its yield without payment or broken the spirit of its tenants, then let briers come up instead of wheat and weeds instead of barley. The words of Job are ended (Job 31:16-40).

This was the lifestyle of a "blameless and upright" man, who "feared God and shunned evil" (Job 1:1). For Job, revival was not defined by how loud he sang, how often he went to a spiritual gathering, or whether he danced to the Lord with all his might. Spirituality was accompanied by tangible humanitarian action. This was a great man, a king and a chief, whose conduct and behavior was scrupulous and whose armor was without chink. He was so good a man that God removed all protection from him, making him vulnerable to frontal assaults by satan. He became heaven's righteous showpiece, the target of all of hell's fury. But his good works were ingrained within his character. While not boasting, he pointed confidently to the way that he made People people out of invisible people. He factually recounted that he did not deny the desires of the poor, that he did not let the widow's eyes grow weary, that he reared the fatherless, that he took up the case of the stranger, that he fed the hungry, and that he clothed the naked. This activity emerged from within. He explained that he dared not turn to materialism or idolatry, that he would not exercise pride or envy.

Blessing accompanied his righteousness and social justice. After his ordeal, Job lived 140 years and watched this budding code of social conduct extend to bless his descendants to the fourth generation (see Job 42:16). It laid the groundwork for our understanding of the consequences of revival in terms of social justice. Job made invisible people into People people. He proved our aphorism that the face of the earth changes as the hearts of its people are transformed. Every revival since then reflects back to the truths God spoke to the heart of the hero Chief of Uz.

MOSES—THE EGYPTIAN DELIVERANCE (EXODUS 4:29-31)

Egypt, the primary exporter of false religion, was at a crossroads. The Egyptian Pharaoh Amenophis IV devoted himself to the sun god, Aten, whom he proclaimed the only god.[11] You'll note that the Egyptian first-borns were killed at midnight, and that Moses and the people of God left Egypt at night, when Aten must have been sleeping (see Exod. 12:29,31).[12] Of course, such monotheistic devotion really cut into the Egyptian idol trade, not to mention the priest and priestess professions. And so, sooner than you can say "King Tut," the Egyptians returned to their extensive pantheon represented by animals such as the bull, cow, vulture, hawk, crocodile, ape, falcon, frog, serpent, and cat.[13] And, eventually, the Pharaohs were deified as the incarnation of the god, Ra.

It is probably Ramses II, Yul Brynner's half brother of Charlton Heston's Moses,[14] who reigned as Ra-in-the-flesh during the great Egyptian Deliverance. Talk about sibling rivalry! Of course, the revival involved the People of Yahweh, not the Egyptians, and as Hebrew hearts were transformed, you can be sure that the face of the earth (that empire certainly) was changed. Revival revolutionizes society.

About this Pharaoh—who is deemed (and whose god is deemed) so insignificant in Scripture as to remain unnamed—his name, extracted from archeology, is a combination of his god Ra and Moses, thus *Ramses*. In Hebrew these two words meant "evil" and "to bring forth," so, to the people of Yahweh, Pharaoh was, "he who brings forth evil."[15] He was the parallel universe evil counterpart to Moses. Just in case the modern reader overlooks the subtle nuances and dynamics of the interaction, let me spell it out for you: This is God's deliverer, Moses, against Ra Moses (Ramses).

And Ramses' god was no match for Moses' God, the Hero-maker. No wonder *The Ten Commandments* and *The Prince of Egypt* were such enormous theatrical smashes! This segment of Israelite history contains all the intrigue and drama of a "whodunnit" soap opera, combined with the supernatural mystery of horror and sci-fi genres, laced with the archetypical good versus evil storyline. Moses, the wilderness-shepherd leader of the slave revolt, takes on his arch nemesis Ramses, ruler of the evil empire.[16] *Mano a mano*. Yah versus Ra. God versus god. A subtext for the heroic.

Moses, the Egyptianized Hebrew exile, who had settled for an anonymous existence as a shepherd in the desert, returned to his hometown ready to conquer the world. Moses had a spiritual experience. He'd encountered the God-of-the-Burning-Bush. But rather than stay on the mountain and worship forever, this God with the burning heart commissioned Moses to go save those whom His heart burned for.

The apostle Paul exhorts us to "never be lacking in zeal" (Rom. 12:11). Zeal comes from a word meaning, "boiling liquid, glowing solids."[17] Though both David and Jehu were renowned for their zeal (see Ps. 69:9; and Jehu said, "Come see my zeal for the Lord" in 2 Kings 10:16), the original Zealot, the One who set them on fire, was God.

The Hebrew word *qana'* has a strongly competitive sense. In its most positive sense the word means "to be filled with righteous zeal or jealousy." It is used in the context of husbands suspecting their wives of adultery (see Num. 5:30). Jealousy cannot tolerate rivalry in a marriage relationship.[18] "Jealous Zealot" is one of nine Old Testament names of God.[19] He will not tolerate rivalry within the relationship He enjoys with you.[20]

Majestically, the Jealous Zealot, this Burning God dismissed all of Moses' excuses against the mission for which he was being commissioned. This God was a potent God, who could burn in your heart and not consume you.[21] This is a God who didn't blink at the power of other gods and who was willing to make Moses as a god to Pharaoh, to demonstrate His glory through Moses. What a confidence builder!

As Moses is on the way to his destiny, God reveals Himself to Moses as He revealed Himself to Abraham earlier, as the God of Covenant. It took the quick thinking Zipporah, Moses' wife, and an even quicker flint knife to circumcise her son and touch the blood to Moses' uncircumcised "feet" (see Exod. 4:25) to bring the family into covenant relationship with Yahweh and spare her husband's life.

Such experiences can produce perspective for an ambassador of God! His heart was transformed, and he went directly for the hearts of his people.

> *Moses and Aaron brought together all the elders of the Israelites, and Aaron told them everything the Lord had said to Moses. He also performed the signs before the people, and they believed. And when they heard that the Lord was concerned about them and had seen their misery, they bowed down and worshipped* (Exodus 4:29-31).

Not to get too technical, but the whole episode breaks down cleanly into components of revival:

1. Moses encountered a God who saw the misery, heard the cries, and was concerned with the sufferings of His people (see Exod. 3:7). This is a theme for God through to millennium three.
2. This burning bush encounter burned through Moses' heart. A personal, life-altering experience with God removes the necessity of leaning only on the faith of our fathers.
3. Moses became acquainted with God's power. The God we read about in the Bible comes alive for us today.
4. He was commissioned. There was no questioning, in the words of an old Southern preacher man: "Was you sent, or did you just went?" God's anointing attends God's commission.
5. And he entered covenant. God's modus operandi seems to include committed relationship.
6. Obediently, Moses took this revelation to the people, and proclamation was accompanied with demonstration. God wants to sell us the entire package.
7. The result is genuflection. People bend the knee and worship God.
8. The Egyptian Deliverance revolutionized society. Slaves were freed. Idols were toppled. Evil systems were dismantled. Economic imbalances were corrected (see Exod. 12:35-36). Frogs were piled. History was altered. God was glorified.

Moses Took Dictation

Numbers 8 deserves some elaboration. God not only turned over the Egyptian slave system and freed His people, but also, very shortly thereafter He blessed them with the written code, the Ten Commandments and the Law. Catch this—*out of thin air, God dictated this bedrock of civil life to Moses.* This is enormous.

God promised Moses, "There, above the cover between the cherubim that are over the ark of the Testimony, I will meet with you and give you all My commandments" (Exod. 25:22). Moses responded obediently; then "The Lord called to Moses and spoke to him from the Tent of Meeting. He said...." The rest is known as the Book of Leviticus (see Lev. 1:1)!

That is why Thomas Cahill entitles his popular book, *God's Gift of the Jews: How a Tribe of Desert Nomads Changed the Way Everyone Thinks and Feels.* We're talking about a meandering tribe, fresh out of the shackles of bondage, gifting the world with the basis for civil government!

Ten Commandments

The Ten Commandments are inextricably linked to monotheism. This war of the Lord enabled the people of Israel to follow Yahweh, who is both Lord and Law-giver.[22] These attributes authorize Him to step into history with rules. After their victory over the Egyptian Pharaoh, the people came out to the desert to worship and God told them how to approach Him.

In fact, He set up rules for how to approach and worship Him. The first one is very well known: "Love the Lord your God with all your heart, with all your soul, and with all your strength" (Deut. 6:6). That He instructed them to love their neighbors is sufficiently demonstrated in Chapter 3, "God's Big Idea." The third part of His rules is now known as the Ten Commandments.

Then, further Jewish law operationalizes, or gives expression to, these *meta* commands. These are the laws that become the foundation of right and wrong for Western civilization.

These rules are so significant for social life. Show spiritual loyalty. Don't go flirting with other gods. Don't speak poorly of God. Follow God's commands. Honor your parents. Don't murder people—you're killing God in effigy.[23] Don't cheat on your spouse. Don't lie about your neighbor. Don't go lusting after your neighbor's spouse.

Among criminals, if everyone steals, the one who doesn't will be trusted. Among adulterers, if everyone fornicates, the one who doesn't will be trusted. Among liars, if everyone lies, the one who doesn't will become trusted. Among murderers, if everyone murders, the one who doesn't will become trusted. The people who observe these command-ments rise to become the dominant culture! And every revival is a return to the application of the law.

Think about this for a moment. Humans figured that you could work your servant seven days a week. God said "six." In fact, "the reason given in Deuteronomy (5:15) for remembering the Sabbath is that our ancestors in Egypt went 400 years without a vacation."[24] Humans figured that you could hate your enemies. God said, "Love your enemies and pray for those who per-secute you" (Matt. 5:44). Humans always look to increase their personal pan-theon of idols. God said, "Have no other gods before Me" (Deut. 5:7). Invisible slaves became People people.

Enthused by God, this puny little people group established the basis for Western civilization! Is it too much to see the partial fulfillment of God's promise to Abraham to bless the nations through him? Is it too much to perceive the Egyptian deliverance as the prototype of revival? To see in it the plumb line for measuring every revival since? To see it as the root, the archetype, of what God will do throughout the rest of history? If it is the root, the radical basis of revival, then it becomes a model for understanding societal upheaval in response to the moves of God. This granddaddy of them all becomes a standard for the Hero Army because, as the Egyptian deliverance attests, the face of the earth is changed as the hearts of its people are transformed.

SAMUEL AND DAVID AND SOLOMON— GOLDEN AGE OF ISRAEL (1 SAMUEL 7)
From Ichabod to Ebenezer

It was a revered place with a storied history. After the initial conquest of Canaan, Shiloh became the first permanent home of the tabernacle of God (see Josh. 18:1). The commander Joshua set up the first government there (see Josh. 21:1-2). In so doing, it evolved into the hub of the nascent nation of Israel (see Josh. 22:9,12) and became the seat of the last judge, Eli the priest (see 1 Sam. 1:3).[25]

Presumption of grace is the only sin that satan wouldn't dare commit.[26] But the Israelites weren't as squeamish. Following their leader Eli and his sons, the priests Hophni and Phineas, they presumed upon God's grace.

After a defeat that cost the lives of 4,000 soldiers at the hands of the Philistines, the Hebrews presumed upon God's grace. While licking their wounds and mourning their dead, they figured, "Let us bring the ark of the Lord's covenant from Shiloh, so that He may go with us and save us from the hand of our enemies" (1 Sam. 4:3). The consequences of this presumption were enormous.

"The Israelites were defeated and every man fled to his tent. The slaughter was very great; Israel lost 30,000 foot soldiers. The ark was captured" (1 Sam. 4:10-11). And the shrine at Shiloh was destroyed.[27] And worst of all, "The glory...departed from Israel" (1 Sam. 4:22).

While the Israelites languished for seven months outside the protection of God, God was demonstrating His sovereignty in neighboring Philistia, where His Ark was taken after it was stolen. After a comedic series of mishaps during which God punished the Philistine god Dagan, and visited the people with tumors of the groin (see 1 Sam. 5:9)[28] and an infestation of rats (see 1 Sam. 5:6)[29], the Ark of the Covenant was returned to Israel by their conqueror Philistia. But more presumption, and the judgment that accompanies it, was still to follow.

Some of the men who found the Ark presumed to look into it. The consequence of this sin was the death of many more men (see 1 Sam. 6:19).[30] And the mourning of Israel continued for 20 years (see 1 Sam. 7:2).

Then...

> Samuel said to the whole house of Israel, "If you are returning to the Lord with all your hearts, then rid yourselves of foreign gods and the Ashtoreths and commit yourselves to the Lord and serve Him only, and He will deliver you out of the hand of the Philistines" (1 Samuel 7:3).

In obedient repentance the Israelites smashed their household idols, the local gods, the statues, their high places, and all the pagan paraphernalia they had accumulated, and began to serve Yahweh only.

"All Israel" assembled at Mizpah. Probably thousands of representatives of the people of God made the trip to this town. They traveled light, planning no meals due to the fast they would endure. This solemn assembly featured ritualistic repentance and cleansing. The Israelites poured out water to baptize themselves from their idols,[31] and to pour out their hearts in repentance before the Lord.[32] All day long, through the heat and the dust, the Hebrews cried out to the Lord.

"And the Lord answered" (1 Sam. 9). Israel enjoyed godly leadership from Samuel, a preferred peace with the Philistines and the Ammonites, and the presence of God. Safe borders, secure administration, and true religion, or, in the terms of Canadian pioneers, "peace, order, and good government," were the social effects of this revival. The people of Israel were prophetically named "Ichabod," which means, "the glory has departed." But by the end of their repentance, they were able to exclaim, "Ebenezer!" or, "thus far has the Lord helped us!"

God Splurged!

In fact, the acknowledgment of "Ebenezer!" inaugurated the Golden Age of Israel. Samuel established the Golden Age. However, like another one calling out in the wilderness, he prepared the way, not for the Son of David, but for David himself. David, the flawed romantic, the man after God's heart, reigned over the halcyon days of the Golden Age. David was less your prim Sunday School teacher than William Wallace's Braveheart.

This uneducated man, David, grew up in the fields as a herder, surrounded by sheep as companions. From his teenage years, he was skilled with a slingshot. After killing Goliath, he was a warrior. He spent the next 14 years fighting on the run. As he worshiped God from the field to the tabernacle, his heart was to bring the Ark to Jerusalem. Why? Because he wanted God in his own backyard. He wanted to sing in the presence of God. A revival takes place and the Golden Age is born. The humanities flourish in the presence of God. God's presence backwashes these people who have become truly human, and lofty arts and humanities result.

Imagine the background of this uneducated shepherd-warrior, dirty, scavenging, trying to stay alive. Within 20 years David gives the world the Psalter. How did such brilliance come about? This brave man—composer, singer, worshiper, warrior—dragged his people into revival, from barbarism to incredible heights. This elevated era produced the gut-wrenching elegance of the Psalms, the passionate intimacy of the Song of Songs, the ancient wisdom of the Proverbs, the cultured organization of new instruments and new sounds and new ensembles. Starting with Psalm 1, David lives a life that epitomizes the virtues of justice, righteousness, and compassion.

During David's era and its aftermath, Israel enjoyed unequaled prestige and prosperity. Moses introduced the law. But not since Moses had someone animated the Law of Moses so heartily as David. In so doing, David created a new template for biblical revival, a new definition of what it means to be radical, a new measure *for* the Hero Army, and a new enactment *of* the Hero Army.

The Golden Age of Israel denoted not only the abolition of evil but also the fruition of excellence. And although this excellence included such important facets of society as trade, politics, war, architecture, and the arts, these manifestations were mere splashes from the river of God's grace that was flowing through Israelite society during this period.

Although Samuel set the time and key, David set the tone. Samuel crafted a harmony for David's melody—one we're singing to this day.[33]

From the wilderness intimacies of youthful shepherd days through the wilderness reliances of exile, David knew God like few before or after him. Yahweh and David enjoyed a friendship, even a camaraderie, that smacks of scandal. David, the dancing man, was the one who not only returned the Ark of the Covenant, the epitome of God's presence, to Israel, but also set up leagues of professional worshipers to dance and genuflect and sing and pray to the God resident there *within the veil*. In fact, there was no veil! That is, there was no separation. Individual scandal of intimacy is macro-sized as legions of "unordained" saints express their adoration and affection directly to God, not once a year through a priest and an ornate series of rituals, but both systematically and spontaneously right in the face of God! Invisible people danced in God's presence. Just as David's tabernacle became the prophetic model for worship today (see Acts 15:15-17),[34] so his reign has become the prophetic model for revival today.

But there's more. The tabernacle prepared the way for the temple. David handed off the baton to his son Solomon, who learned, in graphic terms, that where God lands, God expands (see 2 Chron. 7). Where we, in humble obedience, prepare a landing pad for the Holy Spirit, He not only settles down but also spreads around. Where the Godhead congregates, the glory disseminates.

The 24-hour House of Prayer and worship were the underpinnings of the Golden Age. They buttressed the eternal aphorisms of economic and social justice, righteousness, and compassion that pervade the Book of Proverbs. In fact, like the wisdom of Benjamin Franklin, the Proverbs serve as social commentary on the age in which they originated. The Proverbs establish a radical root for Franklin's adages. Strains of Solomon's proverbs are still heard in sayings such as "Waste not want not," "A stitch in time saves nine," "Early to bed, early to rise, makes a man healthy, wealthy, and wise," and "The early bird gets the worm."

The transition from Ichabod to Ebenezer, and the accompanying Golden Age, served to rip up tent pegs and reorder boundaries as Israel blossomed from an insignificant tribe to an influential country. In more than one way, the Golden Age enacted further fulfillment of God's promise to Abraham to bless all the nations through him. In a sense, the Mizpah Outpouring and its enormous repercussions put Yahweh on the map as it solidified Israel as a light to the world. And without doubt, the face of the earth is changed as the hearts of its people are transformed.

Asa—The Asa Awakening
(2 Chronicles 15)

From the Compromise of Comfort
to the Commitment of Covenant

Two-to-one odds are pretty daunting—maybe not in tiddlywinks, but certainly in war. Judah's third king, Asa, faced just these odds as his 480,000 soldiers—half of whom were armed with large shields and spears, the others equipped with small shields and bows—faced the million-strong army of Cush, which was led, in person, by General Zerah (see 2 Chron. 14:8-9), and they had chariots.

How's this for strategy? Asa prayed:

> Lord, there is no one like You to help the powerless against the mighty. Help us, O Lord our God, for we rely on You, and in Your name we have come against this vast army. O Lord, You are our God; do not let man prevail against You (2 Chronicles 14:11).

The army of Cush was crushed beyond recovery (see 2 Chron. 15:13), and every village around Gerar was sacked and pillaged by the Lord and His forces.

What a blessing! Israel had enjoyed a decade of peace and righteous leadership under Asa, and now the army had lambasted Cush. The people of God were also living in a period when God manifestly spoke through His prophets. Michael Brown suggests that times of social stability can provide "fertile ground for revolution, and it is out of such soil that revolutionary movements (both good and bad) often grow."[35] Social stability nourished spiritual compromise. And so, though King Asa practiced righteousness, many of his people dabbled in idolatry.

It was into this context that Asa marched his army in triumph.

We know nothing about Oded, except that he had a prophetic son named Azariah. Azariah went out from his tent on the morning after the victory. What he encountered was a celebratory parade atmosphere. Cheers and shouts accompanied the songs that the weary but joyful soldiers sang as they skipped and danced and strutted and sauntered in loose formation to the wild appreciation of the surrounding crowds. The happy pandemonium consisted of a smorgasbord of dusty colors wrapped around gaudy treasures, children playing among Cushite donkeys and sheep, victorious shofar blasts, and the rumbling rhythm of thousands upon thousands of stomping Hebrews, delirious with conquest.

He found the king and prophesied this qualified commendation and cautionary encouragement:

> *Listen to me, Asa and all Judah and Benjamin. The Lord is with*
> *you when you are with Him. If you seek Him, He will be found*
> *by you, but if you forsake Him, He will forsake you. For a long*
> *time Israel was without the true God, without a priest to teach and*
> *without the law. But in their distress they turned to the Lord, the*
> *God of Israel, and sought Him, and He was found by them. In*
> *those days it was not safe to travel about, for all the inhabitants of*
> *the lands were in great turmoil. One nation was being crushed by*
> *another and one city by another, because God was troubling them*
> *with every kind of distress. But as for you, be strong and do not*
> *give up, for your work will be rewarded* (2 Chronicles 15:2-7).

How we respond to the word of the Lord not only says a lot about who
we are but also determines who we will become. In the din of his success Asa
could easily have shrugged off the warning aspect of this prophecy. He could
have complacently basked in the glow of the promise. He could have let it
get to his head. He did none of these things.

Instead, Asa took courage. He was spurred on by the word of the Lord
to even greater works. He completed his repentance on behalf of Judah,
removing all of the detestable idols from the whole of the lands under his
control. And then he re-established the spiritual priorities of the nation by
repairing the altar of the Lord. In doing so, Asa made it possible for the daily
sacrifices and offerings to be made, and for the people of God to serve God in
obedience.

But Asa did not stop there. He deposed his wicked grandmother,
Maacah, from her position as queen mother because she was an idol worshiper. He chopped down her repulsive Asherah pole, smashed it up, and had
it burned. Here he was purifying himself and his household and ridding himself of pagan, contaminating influences.

Asa brought to the temple all the gold and treasure that he and his
father had dedicated to the Lord, belatedly honoring his promises to God.
Then King Asa assembled the people of Judah in Jerusalem. In a melee of
neighing and "baah-ing" and spraying blood and glistening swords, they sacrificed thousands of animals to the Lord in repentance and acknowledgment
of His sovereignty. And all of the people swore an oath to enter a covenant
with God that they would seek Him with all their heart and soul! They also
determined to put to death all who would not seek Him with all their heart
and soul.

The results were dramatic. Imagine a country wholeheartedly dedicated to
serving God! We're talking about social and spiritual revolution—a generation

of shalom! The religious hypocritical parody was displaced by the voluntary imposition of the Law on what emerged into covenantal community. The Torah not only steers daily life, it pervades it. Once again, the dietary laws, relationships, attire, leisure activities, family time, work schedules, reading habits, life ambitions, worldviews, business practices, disposable income, and hobbies were all transformed at the individual and family level (see Nah. 3:19).

The landscape changed as horizons dotted with idolatrous high places were abandoned and dismantled. Even the breezes of the towns wafted with a different aroma, as the exotic incenses of idolatry were superceded by a mingling of the earthy odors of raw, sacrificed meat with the unique scents of Levitical perfume sacrifice. The widows were honored and cared for. The poor were blessed—in fact, their socioeconomic class was almost eliminated. The orphans were defended. The aliens were integrated into community. Invisible people became People people. Everyone committed, heart and soul, to the Lord.

We're describing paradise on earth. This godly utopia is the goal of everyone seeking revival. And so the Asa Awakening is a model for the Hero Army today. The face of the earth is changed as the hearts of its people are transformed.

UZZIAH—WHEN KINGS GO TO WAR (2 CHRONICLES 26:1-15)

The country was in shambles. The political posturing and religious opportunism of the leader had bitten him back. His military victories were ruined by bowing down to the gods he'd just defeated. Besides exercising utter stupidity in such idol worship (see 2 Chron. 25:14), King Amaziah showed contempt for his people and their God. His selfishly ambitious challenge to Israel, pouring salt in the wounds of division, was rewarded with death. It was not an honorable death.

Amaziah left the nation in disarray, without a moral compass, and shackled with a 16-year-old heir, his son Uzziah. It was in this compromising situation, this spiritual malaise, that Uzziah assumed the throne.

Directed and discipled by the visionary prophet Zechariah, Uzziah sought the Lord. And as long as he sought the Lord, God prospered him (see 2 Chron. 26:5).

Uzziah is an Old Testament type of the New Testament apostle. Helped by God, Uzziah warred with and defeated the Philistines, the Arabians, the Meunites, and the Ammonites. He tore down their walls and established cities in their midst (see 2 Chron. 26:6-8).

It was obvious that the people of God benefited from Uzziah's largesse. He properly invested the perks of success in his people. Uzziah built towers in Jerusalem and buttressed its gates (see 2 Chron. 26:9). He invested in the infrastructure of the capital and the protection of the people.

He prophetically built towers in the wilderness (see 2 Chron. 26:10). Uzziah determined to do a new thing, to raise up civilization where there was only desolation—streams in the desert, if you will.

He dug a system of reservoirs and wells (see 2 Chron. 26:10). He managed agricultural lands, overseeing different kinds of crops and raising livestock (see 2 Chron. 26:10). Having invested in the infrastructure of the capital, Uzziah also invested in the infrastructure of the countryside. He developed an irrigation system and a series of crop and livestock-based farms, creating employment and provision for his people.

He developed and maintained a standing general army plus an elite army, for which he prepared armor and weapons and invented war machines (see 2 Chron. 26:11-15). Uzziah was proactive in his military stance. He invented new weapons of war! This not only created industry to supply the needs he created, but also protected Judah's military position.

This is the textbook for what happens when kings go to war. Revived by God, kings multiply the blessing by generating sources of income, employment, provision, and safety through vision, entrepreneurship, and ingenuity. Construction projects, catalytic inventing, systems of irrigation and agriculture and trade, and vision initiatives all blessed the people of God during this time of revival.

Not only was Uzziah marvelously helped, but he grew marvelously famous (see 2 Chron. 26:15).[36]

Uzziah is a model for Christians today who are blessed with wealth. Unlike some of his predecessors, he didn't break the bank on extravagantly memorializing himself and searching for materialistic bliss. He was intent on war, defending and keeping what God had given him, as well as extending his authority as far as God would allow. And so today's kings, whether they be crowned in small businesses or stock market or corporate leadership or some other area, must choose their lifestyles. If they are seeking God and blessed by Him, they will go to war, and the fruit of their success will be invested in blessing the people. Invisible people will become People people as kings undertake great projects, as they act as catalysts for creativity and mobilization, as they establish systems to serve the poor, as they build cities in the desert, and as they enable, through entrepreneurship and ingenuity, the poor to grow self-sufficient.

God, bring individual revival to the hearts of today's kingly leaders and marketplace apostles so as to motivate them to go to "war" as Uzziah.

Then, the face of the earth will be changed as the hearts of its people are transformed.

JONAH AND THE KING—THE NINEVEH HEADSTAND (BOOK OF JONAH)

The plunge was exhilarating at first. After days of struggling to keep balance and hold down breakfast it was liberating to go with the flow. Thunder and splattering drops on wood were quickly drowned out by gurgling, washing stereo sounds. The scare of seasickness was quickly overcome by a sinking feeling. The emotional anguish of days of disobedience had sucked the fight out of weary arms and sea legs, and after a short round of flailing, the battle was conceded. Both the vision and mind faded inexorably to black.

Jonah is famous for reasons for which he should be notorious. He is popular because he took on a big fish from the inside out. He spent a long weekend in the stomach of a fish. Of course, this was the immediate result of Jonah's disobedience toward God. Characteristically, God uses the consequences of Jonah's disobedience for His glory.

God commanded Jonah to preach a message of coming judgment to the prosperous citizens of Nineveh, the capital of Assyria. This was a wicked city, absorbed with evil ways and violence (see Jon. 1:2; 3:8). This was not a pleasant assignment for a Jew. It could have been similar to an Israeli today being sent to Nineveh today (northern Iraq) to preach judgment. Today, although it might be a satisfying message, one might hesitate to obey for fear of his personal safety. Although that may have been a factor for Jonah, he had a baser motivation for disobedience. He disobeyed because he believed that he'd be successful!

You might not blame him. The Ninevites of Assyria had a terrible reputation (see Nah. 3:19). Assyrian sculptures of chained slaves with their eyes being pecked out by birds still exist. They proudly recorded their exploits, mutilating, skinning, and burning people alive. Shalmaneser III made a pyramid of heads. Among many other things, Ashurbanipal put a dog chain through a captured king's jaw and made him live in a dog kennel.[37] King Ashurnasirpal II (883-859 b.c.) wrote:

> I slaughtered them; with their blood I dyed the mountain red like wool.... The heads of their warriors I cut off, and

I formed them into a pillar over against their city; their young men and their maidens I burned in the fire.... I destroyed, I demolished, I burned. I took their warriors prisoner and impaled them on stakes before their cities...flayed the nobles, as many as had rebelled, and spread their skins out on the piles (of dead corpses)...many of the captives I burned in a fire. Many I took alive; from some I cut off their hands, from others I cut off their noses, ears and fingers; I put out the eyes of many of the soldiers.[38]

In any case, three days of soaking up the inner fluids of a big fish made Jonah a ghostly apparition that likely struck horror in the hearts of the Ninevites. Not only did word of his miraculous survival for three days in the belly of the fish flabbergast them, but his appearance left them dumbfounded. In this context his message that they were history in 40 days put the fear of God into their hearts.

You see, God is establishing His standards to the pagan king. Torturing your enemies after you've caught them? That's a "No no." Mutilating them, cutting off their noses? Hmmm? No. If you want God's mercy, then feed them. Have compassion on them. Give them something to drink. God is not saying, here, that you can't make them slaves, but flaying, skinning, and blood sport are out. If they didn't repent, God would destroy them.

The Ninevite response was right out of the textbook. "The people of Nineveh believed in God and they called a fast and put on sackcloth from the greatest to the least of them" (Jon. 3:5). Not just the poor people on the wrong side of the tracks, but also the trendy cappuccino drinkers, the power-suited business leaders, and the pagan devotees strapped on the coarsest of attire to remind themselves of their sins and refrained from eating food.

When word reached the king, he traded in his royal robe for sackcloth and his throne for ashes. He issued a decree that no living thing in the city should eat or drink, that every living thing be covered in sackcloth, that each person call out earnestly to God, and that each person turn from personal wickedness and violence (Jon. 3:7-8). The king's hope was that God might withdraw His burning anger and so spare their lives.

When God saw their deeds, that they turned from their wicked
way, then God relented (Jonah 3:10).

On that day, 600,000 were spared. Each of them had repented and believed in God. They had seen and heard of His power. Their lives were forever changed. The city was transformed and enjoyed the blessing of this revival for a century and more.[39]

Can you imagine a wholesale repentance of a city the size of London, England, today? Both Nineveh and London are known as great cities, and their relative populations might be similar.[40] Can you grasp the picture of 600,000 citizens, soccer moms and soccer players, bus riders and bus drivers, plumbers and pluggers, employees and employers, manufacturers and consumers, writers and readers, the high and the low all fasting—no McDonalds, no Krispy Kreme, no anything—discarding the fashions and luxuries of the day—palm pilots and cell phones, internet and cable—to cry out to God in repentance? Hordes of animals on imposed fasts bleating and barking, ribbeting and roaring. We're talking about the most sensational revival in history!

This was no mere evangelical response to a passionate sermon. This is not just asking Jesus into your heart. This is transformation from pagan evil and violence to a God-fearing lifestyle. How does that look?

The sway of the wicked king was comprehensive. While he lived an iniquitous lifestyle, his people reveled in it. When he traded depravity for ascetic humility, his people followed suit.

Jonah and the king were two of history's oddest heroes. As individuals, they each turned from their sin and wailed to the Lord for mercy. They both encountered His love, and it turned their lives upside down. They stopped doing evil. They abandoned their violence.

A city liberated from violence is blessed in multiples as money is saved in medical bills and repair, as "good-for-nothings" begin to contribute to the economy, and as a population, freed from fear, optimizes life and work. I can conjure up images of rusting chains, flattened stakes, and redeemed gravesites. History leaves us blanks where details of the expunging of paganism and the overthrow of evil would be welcome. For some reason there are no records extant of wholesale transition to Yahweh worship. These records, if they survived, would likely tell the wholesome tale of the adoption of practices foreign to the Assyrians: protection of the widow and orphan, defense of the poor and needy, adoption of the alien, and uplifting of the poor, as invisible people became People people.

Truly, the face of the earth was changed as the hearts of its people were transformed.

JOSIAH—THE REVIVAL OF RELIGION (2 CHRONICLES 34–35)

Josiah was the grandson of the "Abomination of Judah," the "Doctor of Divination," the "Ultimate Evil," the original "Master of Disaster," the perpetrator of the "Massacre of Manasseh." His grandfather filled all of Jerusalem with innocent blood (see 2 Kings 21:16). After Manasseh's death, Josiah's father Amon took over and "multiplied guilt" (2 Chron. 33:23) for two years, until his own servants killed him.

For 57 years, with a brief repentant blip, Judah had abased herself in all kinds of wickedness. Chaotic cries vied for ascendancy with the crackling sizzle escaping Molech's gaping mouth upon ingesting sacrificed babies. But even this debauchery was exceeded, by the setting up of an idol in the temple to worship and to which to sacrifice (see 2 Chron. 33:). At the risk of sounding like a broken record, this was a time fraught with baby killing, homosexual temple prostitutes, genocide, and despicable evil. It was one of the lowest points in Jewish history.

In the aftermath of Amon's death, the eight-year-old boy named Josiah was crowned king of Judah.

What an overwhelming situation! One might accurately describe it as hopeless.

Josiah's is a blessed account of how one person can make an enormous difference for God. After his 16th birthday Josiah began to seek the Lord. By his 20th birthday he was going whole hog after God.[41] The Chronicler of Scripture needed chapters to outline the aspects of his repentance that set the stage for revival and built on that platform.

Suffice it to say, Josiah was ruthless in dealing with wickedness. He pulverized idols. He trashed abominations. He chopped down incense altars. He even got personal with the outlawing of child sacrifice (killing), and homosexuality in worship. Josiah basically expunged sin from the country. But he exercised even more enthusiasm, if that were possible, in chasing God. When he re-discovered the lost book of the Law, he repented and humbled himself before God. Then he covenanted with God to be obedient. He was instrumental in re-establishing the Jewish religion. He celebrated the best Passover since the days of Samuel. No king could match him.

Because Josiah stepped into the gap, God refrained, during Josiah's lifetime, from bringing judgment on His people. Terrifying curses were postponed for nearly two decades. The people of God experienced mercy and peace for 19 years because of their repentance.

God ultimately, within three months of Josiah's death, brought about judgment on the Jews. The geo-political, social, and spiritual aspects of this judgment literally changed the face of the earth. But Yahweh acknowledged their repentance and the covenant made by their leader. And the face of the earth was changed as the hearts of its people were transformed.

JOHN, JESUS, AND THE APOSTLES—
THE KINGDOM OF GOD AT HAND
(MATTHEW 3; MARK 1; LUKE 3; JOHN 1,3)

It was a blindly arrogant religion that had infected Israel. Although having the less than praiseworthy distinction of being conquered by some of the greatest empires of history—Egypt, Babylon, and Rome—its proponents could still insist they'd never been enslaved by anybody, and they believed it! Lacking the corporate will to submit to the Torah, Israelites settled for the outward trappings of the inward truth. They were sacramentalists of the very worst kind, and their religious traditions accommodated a sinful society.

It was ripe for revival.

This popular revival was prophetic on various levels. The son of Zechariah, who experienced a miraculous birth, led it. His father was made mute following an angelic encounter during vocational service to the Lord. That angel foretold his birth. During the pregnancy he was filled with the Holy Spirit. From birth he was set apart to a Nazarite lifestyle. His name was also the answer to prophecy. His parents called him John.

John the Baptist was cut from the Old Testament mold. He lived in the wilderness in a decidedly counter-cultural style. He seemed a modern-day Elijah. His diet consisted of honey and locusts, and even that was prophetic. He received the sweet things of the Lord, from His word and communion with Him. And he devoured the devourer.[42]

The revival itself was prophesied by Isaiah.

John preached uncompromising repentance for the kingdom of God was at hand. And he boldly insisted that the chosen people be baptized for repentance, maintaining that their Jewish birth did nothing for their spiritual state. He curried to no one and thought nothing of publicly rebuking the leaders whose lives also needed mending.

By the power of God and the example of an abandoned life, he succeeded in seeing "all the people of Jerusalem" (Mark 1:5), and "all Judea, and all the district around the Jordan" (Matt. 3:5) actually repent of their sin and publicly acknowledge their need of forgiveness. This, in and of itself, was revolutionary.

It had the power to change relationships as food and clothing re-distribution systems of the heart replaced a self-interested climate (see Luke 3:10-11).

It had the power to change social structure, as the militia was told to refrain from force, abuse, and revolt (see Luke 3:14).

It had the power to transform the financial structures, as tax-collecting arrangements would begin to reflect reality, rather than coercion and manipulation (see Luke 3:12-13).

It had the power to change the religion of the day, as efficacy was wrestled from the professional religious class and returned to the penitent religious convert (see Luke 3).

The revival really was, as Isaiah prophesied and as John the Baptist himself asserted, a preparation for the Lord's arrival.

Once the nation repented, they were softened up for Jesus' ministry to them. And, as we well know, this was eternity change. Who can imagine a world today without the influence of Jesus Christ?

Jesus ushered in the kingdom of God—the Super Bowl of revivals.

Jesus brought the kingdom of God into the banalities of religious parody. What a shock!

Worlds were changed. Eternity was rearranged. And the invisible people received special attention, as Jesus came expressly for the sick. His coming out party was based on Luke 4:18-19:

> The Spirit of the Lord is on Me, because He has anointed Me
> to preach good news to the poor. He has sent Me to proclaim
> freedom to the prisoners and recovery of sight for the blind, to
> release the oppressed, to proclaim the year of the Lord's favor.

All this happened to a measure that few could predict. Jesus accomplished all these purposes. Near the end of His mission, Jesus outlined the standard for future judgment. It consisted of our revived responses to the invisible people. High marks were given for feeding the hungry and thirsty, for showing hospitality to the alien, for clothing the naked, for visiting the sick, and for being with the imprisoned (see Matt. 25:35-36). In other words, any "so-called" revival that doesn't turn invisible people into People people, that doesn't turn the tables of social injustice nor dispense mercy, isn't real and doesn't fit within the stream of historical biblical revival. In magnificent and magnanimous ways, the face of the earth changes as the hearts of its people are transformed.

SUMMARY

The revolution birthed by Jesus accelerated through the heroics of Peter, Paul, and "the many." The gospel spread, social divisions were overturned, religious exclusivities were blown wide open, economic inequities were rectified, and injustice was overcome.

What it all comes down to is that revival is more than good meetings and a spiritual tickle. Biblical revival is the manifestation of the holistic gospel, comprised of a truth to embrace and a lifestyle to animate. The current separation of church and state has relegated God to a spiritual experience. We've proven that this is not the case. Faith manifests itself through works. The two legs of the gospel must work in tandem.

We can prove from the Bible that revival always transforms society. From Job, through Moses and David, all the way through to the New Testament, the Bible testifies that the face of the earth changes as the hearts of its people are transformed. And heroes are the strategy.

If our religion isn't transformative, is our religion real?

The accounts of the wars of the Lord do not end in the Book of Revelation. They continue on through history as the Hero Army fights with compassion, righteousness, and justice to establish compassion and righteousness on behalf of the poor, the widows, the orphans, and the alien.

One of the classic historic examples of this occurred in Victorian England.

SECTION TWO

CHAPTER FIVE

VICTORIAN ENGLAND

THE BEST OF TIMES

Sauntering up the downtown West End of London under these new-fangled electric streetlights, you'd have to agree with me that these are the best of times. This sprawling metropolis epitomizes all that is great about the Empire. Imagine, me, in a city of well over 3 million people, being able to find a hotel that is hooked up to both the brand spanking-new telephone (invented by Alexander Graham Bell in 1876) exchange and the just-completed city sewage system! I can phone and flush! Not only that, but I can buy Australian frozen meat at the market, and read Mark Twain's new best-seller, **Tom Sawyer,** *in paperback! And next year, I hear that they're going to a parcel postal system!*

The year 1879 looked very good at the center of the British Empire. On the fringes, with the Suez Canal recently sold off, the newly added gems in Queen Victoria's crown—Egypt, along with Ethiopia, Fiji, South Africa, and India—might beg to differ.

George Eliot, W.B. Yeats, Emily and Charlotte Brontë, Elizabeth Barrett Browning, Robert Browning, Lewis Carroll, Rudyard Kipling, Henry James, George Bernard Shaw, H.G. Wells, Oscar Wilde, Alfred Lord Tennyson, Sigmund Freud, and Sir Arthur Conan Doyle were among those writing their legacy into the history of this unforgettable era. Preachers Charles Spurgeon and D.L. Moody; Amy Carmichael, who left her native England at age 22 for India; David Livingstone, an explorer, cartographer (map maker), and abolitionist who served in Africa; George Mueller, a German missionary who devoted his evangelistic ministry to English orphans; and Hudson Taylor, who became the legendary missionary to inland China, all left their stamp on the world.

Romantic notions of Victorian England not only abound, they pervade our 21st century consciousness. Collective sentimental reminiscences of a moral period of history and nostalgic heart-yearnings for a better day hearken back to 19th century Britain. But for many that day never really existed.

THE WORST OF TIMES

Charles Dickens was not making it up.[1] Florence Nightingale was famous for a reason. (She introduced modern nursing to the world rife with atrocious conditions.) It was a time in which, thanks to the Contagious Diseases Act of 1864, prostitutes could be humiliated, stopped by plainclothes police, and required to submit to physical examination for venereal disease.[2] So bad was the poverty that nearly a million Irish emigrated to America in the previous decade, followed by nearly half a million English after them.[3] Fully 30 percent of all full-time workers in York, England, earned below poverty wages.[4] Jack the Ripper was running amok (1888).

Not that it was much better across the water. Slavery ignited the American Civil War. When the Civil War ended, the Ku Klux Klan was born (1865).

Even the improvements implicitly point to the sad state of affairs. It was not until 1869 that British Debtor's Prisons were abolished. (Before then, if you failed on a debt you often went to prison until someone on the outside paid up.) The Industrial Revolution was being taught in history class by the time a British Act of Parliament legalized labor unions (1871). It was 1872 before voting by secret ballot became law in Britain.[5]

REVOLUTION?

Our friend sauntering up the street in the West End of London undoubtedly shared the common disdain for those who lived in "Outcast London," and joined in the general fear of social revolution on the part of the poor of the East End.[6] The expectation was that the poor would "burst their barriers at last, and declare open and violent war against law and order and property."[7]

Social observers considered the East End a place where the "vilest practices are looked upon with the most matter-of-fact indifference...[and where] the filthy and abominable from all parts of the country seem to flow."[8]

In the Whitechapel district of the East End of London, 39.25 percent of its citizens lived on or below the poverty line. There were 63 brothels in Whitechapel. There was also a huge number of "casual prostitutes."[9] The Society for the Suppression of Vice estimated that there were 80,000 prostitutes in all of London. According to historian Judith Walkowitz, we're talking about 1 prostitute per 12 adult males.[10]

SANITATION

The state of affairs was tough for everyone, not just the down and out. Anthony Wohl describes the problem from a uniquely affluent perspective:

> Despite its wealth and social prominence the family found that it was unable to isolate itself from the stinks, pollution, and health hazards of the day. As newly-weds they had wanted the latest sanitary appliances, but the inexperience of the workmen putting in the water closet resulted in the waste overflowing into the rainpipe and down the dressing-room window. The cesspools beneath their Thames-side residence were notoriously foul, even by the standards of the day and when, at last, they had a new drainage system installed, the stench from the old cesspools remained and made parts of the dwelling almost uninhabitable. Some twenty years later the sewers blocked up after heavy rains and became "most offensive and putrid." Although living by the Thames was certainly most scenic, whenever the river rose their lawns were saturated with the raw sewage, which

habitually floated on the surface of the water. Resigned to this inevitability, they simply had the lawns raked and the filth shoveled back into the river. In dry weather, on the other hand, the Thames' muck was left high and dry along the banks and gave off an appalling odor.[11]

Affluence and resources couldn't coax a better lifestyle. This family, ripped to shreds by the loss of a father, a daughter, and a grand-daughter[12] from bad sewers and filth diseases[13] (and very nearly a son), forced to live amidst stink, and water and air pollution, was the Royal Family.[14]

The concept of sewage had to be converted from "inconvenient runoff" to "dangerous pollution" in the Victorian mind before it could be drained from the cities via "underground waste removal pipes" instead of "open streams" in the Victorian gutter.[15]

Chadwick's Report on Sanitary Conditions determined that the annual loss of life from filth and bad ventilation was greater than the loss from death or wounds in any wars in which the country had been engaged up to that time period. Chadwick elaborated:

> That of the 43,000 cases of widowhood, and 112,000 cases of destitute orphanage relieved from the poor rates in England and Wales alone [poor rates were householders tax that was the sole help for the poor], it appears that the greatest proportion of deaths of the heads of families occurred from the above specified and other removable causes; that their ages were under 45 years; that is to say, 13 years below the natural probabilities of life as shown by the experience of the whole population of Sweden.[16]

Clearly, in, "Outcast London," the celebrated Victorian era left something to be desired.

> Two millions of people, or thereabout, live in the East End of London. That seems a good-sized population for an utterly unknown town. They have no institutions of their own to speak of, no public buildings of any importance, no municipality, no gentry, no carriages…they have nothing. It is the fashion to believe that they are all paupers, which is a foolish and mischievous belief…. Probably there is no spectacle in the whole world as that of this immense, neglected, forgotten great city of East London. It is even neglected by its own citizens, who have never yet perceived

their abandoned condition.[17]

SEX? NO THANKS, WE'RE BRITISH

Prim and proper Victorian England offered some strange juxtapositions on this issue. Although women were expected to be so naïve about sexual awareness that no British law against lesbianism was written,[18] they were recognized to be knowledgeable enough that prostitution was acknowledged to be "the great social evil."[19]

Quick on the heels of increasing prostitution was a rise in the prevalence of gonorrhea and syphilis. Venereal asylums and lock hospitals served to punish and separate these "social lepers of the 19th century" from the general populace.[20] The capacity of asylums and lock hospitals was challenged by the British Army, where soldiers, not to be outdone by civilian cads, were infected to the tune of one out of three.[21]

A DRUGGED CULTURE?

One of the major causes of infant mortality was the widespread practice of giving children narcotics, especially opium, to quiet them. A common dose of opium equaled the price of a pint of beer, and, until late in the century, sale was unregulated. Laudanum, opium in alcohol, was the drug of both the rich and the poor.[22]

In Manchester, according to one account, five out of six working-class families used laudanum habitually. In Nottingham, one member of the Town Council, a druggist, sold 400 gallons of laudanum annually. At mid-century there were at least 10 proprietary brands, with Godfrey's Cordial, Steedman's Powder, and the grandly named Atkinson's Royal Infants Preservative among the most popular.

In East Anglia, opium in pills and penny sticks was widely sold and opium-taking was described as a way of life there. Doctors reported how the infants were wasted from it. "Shrank up into little old men" and "wizened like little monkeys" is the way they were described.[23] Of this era, Richard Davenport-Hines concludes, "Absolute sobriety is not a natural or primary human state."[24]

OUTRAGEOUSLY OVERWORKED AND UNDERPAID

"Nothing is more characteristic of working-class life, and harder for us to imagine today, than this virtually total absence of social security."[25] The Poor House was the only recourse of the indebted, the unemployed, and the invalid. My great, great, great grandmother, Susannah Court, was a resident there for a time. The power of the mighty empire teetered precariously on the feeble backs of outrageously overworked and underpaid servants and workers. While innovation is celebrated as the heart of the industrial revolution, the unskilled 16-hour workday was the blood coursing through society's veins, keeping it alive. MP William Cobbett characterized the situation like this:

> A new discovery had been made in the House that night, which would doubtless excite great astonishment in many parts; at all events it would in Lancashire. It had formerly been said that the Navy was the great support of England; at another time that our maritime commerce was the great bulwark of the country; at another time that our colonies; and it had even been whispered that the Bank was; but now it was admitted, that our great stay and bulwark was to be found in three hundred thousand little girls, or rather in one eighth of that number. Yes; for it was asserted, that if these little girls worked two hours less per day, our manufacturing superiority would depart from us.[26]

An 1832 parliamentary investigation of conditions in the textile factories featured numerous accounts of beatings, child labor, and 14-16 hour days.[27] Many left their habitations for long days of work. Others stayed home. Throughout the 19th century domestic service constituted the largest single employment for English women, and the second-largest employment for all English people, male and female. "Eighty hours of actual work a week, against fifty-six for the factory worker, may well be a fair estimate for the late nineteenth century, and must have been exceeded in many single-handed households."[28] The incidence of poor, single-handed households was exacerbated by the Poor Law:

> One of the harshest elements of the 1834 Poor Law Amendment Act was the practice of splitting up families as a deliberate policy. Keeping husbands and wives apart prevented them from "breeding"—a term used by the middle classes who thought that the poor produced more and more children in order to claim greater amounts of money from the poor rates. Keeping children separated from their parents was supposed to turn the children into useful human beings—which, it was thought, their parents were not: otherwise they would not have entered the workhouse in the first place… People in the same family might see each other during meals or in the chapel but they were not allowed to speak to each other.[29]

Child labor, one of our seven deadly sins in the third section of this book, was a scourge of industrial Britain. In 1860, half of the children between 5 and 15 were in some sort of school, if only a Sunday school; the others were working. There were over 120,000 domestic servants in London alone at mid-century, who worked 80-hour weeks for one half pence per hour.[30] Some worked in the mines. Sarah Gooder, age 8, was one such child:

> I'm a trapper in the Gawber pit. It does not tire me, but I have to trap without a light and I'm scared. I go at four and sometimes half past three in the morning, and come out at five and half past. I never go to sleep. Sometimes I sing when I've light, but not in the dark; I dare not sing then. I don't like being in the pit. I am very sleepy when I go sometimes in the morning. I go to Sunday school and study "Reading made Easy." (Comments by mine investigator: "She knows her letters, and can read little words. She can repeat the Lord's Prayer, not perfectly.") "God bless me and make me a good servant. Amen." I have heard tell of Jesus many a time. I don't know why he came on earth, and I don't know why he died. I would like to be at school far better than in the pit.[31]

One report to Parliament in 1840 presented veritable horror stories: "Women and children chained and belted, harnessed like dogs in a go-cart, black, wet, half-naked crawling on their hands and feet, and dragging their heavy loads behind them."[32] Underground rape was an even darker sin than the coal.

Ultimately, such brutal conditions claimed the attention of legislators, who dallied for decades before protecting children. Described one such law-maker, in an argument about the relative ease of factory work:

> [There] is the old, the often-repeated, and as often-refuted, argument that the work is light. Light! Why, no doubt, much of it is light, if measured by the endurance of some three or four minutes. But what say you, my Lords, to a continuity of toil, in a standing posture, in a poisonous atmosphere, during 13 hours, with 15 minutes of rest? Why, the stoutest man in England, were he made, in such a condition of things, to do nothing during the whole of that time but be erect on his feet and stick pins in a pincushion, would sink under the burden. What say you, then, of children— children of the tenderest years? Why, they become stunted,

crippled, deformed, useless. I speak what I know—I state what I have seen. When I visited Bradford, in Yorkshire, in 1838, being desirous to see the condition of the children—for I knew that they were employed at very early ages in the worsted business...I asked for a collection of cripples and deformities. In a short time more than 80 were gathered in a large courtyard. They were mere samples of the entire mass. I assert without exaggeration that no power of language could describe the varieties, and I may say, the cruelties, in all these degradations of the human form. They stood or squatted before me in all the shapes of the letters of the alphabet. This was the effect of prolonged toil on the tender frames of children at early ages.[33]

Many children worked 16-hour days under atrocious conditions. It was considered commendable that scarcely anyone over the age of four was idle.[34] Beatings were as regular as sunrise. Mr. Matthew Crabtree is just one example of many workers interviewed in Michael Sadler's 1832 parliamentary investigation of conditions in the textile factories.[35] The following is part of that interview:

When trade was brisk what were your hours?

—*From 5 in the morning to 9 in the evening.*

Sixteen hours?

—*Yes.*

With what intervals at dinner?

—*An hour.*

How far did you live from the mill?

—*About two miles.*

Was there any time allowed for you to get your breakfast in the mill?

—*No.*

Did you take it before you left your home?

—*Generally.*

During those long hours of labor could you be punctual; how did you awake?

—*I seldom did awake spontaneously; I was most generally awoke or lifted out of bed, sometimes asleep, by my parents.*

Were you always in time?

—*No.*

What was the consequence if you had been too late?

—*I was most commonly beaten.*

Severely?

—*Very severely, I thought.*

In those mills is chastisement towards the latter part of the day going on perpetually?

—*Perpetually.*

So that you can hardly be in a mill without hearing constant crying?

—*Never an hour, I believe.*

Do you think that if the overlooker were naturally a humane person it would still be found necessary for him to beat the children, in order to keep up their attention and vigilance at the termination of those extraordinary days of labor?

—*Yes; the machine turns off a regular quantity of cardings, and of course, they must keep as regularly to their work the whole of the day; they must keep with the machine, and therefore however humane the slubber may be, as he must keep up with the machine or be found fault with, he spurs the children to keep up also by various means but that which he commonly resorts to is to strap them when they become drowsy.*

At the time when you were beaten for not keeping up with your work, were you anxious to have done it if you possibly could?

—*Yes; the dread of being beaten if we could not keep up with our work was a sufficient impulse to keep us to it if we could.*[36]

Even after "short time" laws, the textile industry, gas works, shipyards, construction, match factories, nail factories, the business of chimney sweeping and other occupations employed children at the age of 5.[37]

THE HERO ARMY MOBILIZES

Into this self-contradictory environment emerged one of history's most powerful manifestations of a Hero Army. Victorian critic and dramatist George Bernard Shaw, who wrote the play *Major Barbara* about The Salvation Army's tension with idealism and realism, clearly saw the necessary conditions of a British revolution:

It has been said that the French Revolution was the work of Voltaire, Rousseau and the Encyclopedists. It seems to me to have been the work of men who had observed that virtuous indignation, caustic criticism, conclusive argument and instructive pamphleteering, even when done by the most earnest and witty literary geniuses, were as useless as praying, things going steadily from bad to worse whilst the Social Contract and the pamphlets of Voltaire were at the height of their vogue.[38]

Shaw argued that, though necessary, the social outcry was insufficient to generate revolution. His unexpected confession admitted the futility of talking up a revolution:

> The problem being to make heroes out of cowards, we paper apostles and artist-magicians have succeeded only in giving cowards all the sensations of heroes whilst they tolerate every abomination, accept every plunder, and submit to every oppression.[39]

Paper apostles can only conjure up paper "heroes" out of cowards with talk. Real apostles transform cowards into heroes by action. Where talking fails, action succeeds. Action is the sufficient condition to the revolution, and it comes from an unlikely, apostolic source.

> Yet in the poorest corner of this soul-destroying Christendom vitality suddenly begins to germinate again. Joyousness, a sacred gift long dethroned by the hellish laughter of derision and obscenity, rises like a flood miraculously out of the fetid dust and mud of the slums; rousing marches and impetuous dithyrambs rise to the heavens from people among whom the depressing noise called "sacred music" is a standing joke; a flag with Blood and Fire[40] on it is unfurled, not in murderous rancor, but because fire is beautiful and blood a vital and splendid red; Fear, which we flatter by calling Self, vanishes; and transfigured men and women carry their gospel through a transfigured world, calling their leader General, themselves captains and brigadiers, and their whole body an Army: praying, but praying only for refreshment, for strength to fight, and for needful MONEY... preaching, but not preaching submission; daring ill-usage and abuse, but not putting up with more of it than is inevitable; and practicing what the world will let them practice, including soap and water, color and music. There is danger in such activity; and where there is danger there is hope. Our present security is nothing, and can be nothing, but evil made irresistible.[41]

So it was that the pagan playwright George Bernard Shaw heralded the spiritual revolution led by the 19th century Hero Army, also known as The Salvation Army. The cynic Shaw's classic play, *Major Barbara*, profiles what he considers a Dionysia[42] alternative to the established religions (Dionysus represented the rebellion against rational culture by appealing to the basic sensory pleasures of his followers, who were oppressed by society[43])—an "army of joy, of love, of courage…[that] picks the waster out of the public house and makes a man of him: it finds a worm wriggling in a back kitchen, and lo! a woman!"[44]

And so this religious alternative, this mythical hybrid, this Hero Army, arose from the steaming, streaming excrement of the Victorian East End gutters to usher in a spiritual revival of biblical proportions.

CHAPTER SIX

REVOLUTION

Christianity is heroism.

—Catherine Booth Jr.

We are revolutionists.
—George Scott Railton (Booth's first Commissioner)

They regard us as dangerous, which we are.

—Herbert Booth

Let us begin with a bold avowal of our flag, for we are not the children of darkness, but of light.... Those who do not feel the urgent need of radical changes in themselves and in mankind, or those who cannot reconcile themselves to the desperate measures required by so desperate a case, have nothing in common with us. The world is lost, and Jesus has come to save it; and it must be saved, at any cost, and whatever that may require, because whoever is not saved will be damned forever.[1]

History is punctuated by other generals raised up to lead the great wars of the Lord. Joining the biblical heroes are such greathearts as Patrick, Francis, Hus, Knox, Wesley, and Mother Teresa. Two of the most outstanding of these leaders were Catherine and William Booth, the founders of The Salvation Army. From the masses of England, Generals William and Catherine Booth mobilized an army of dangerous revolutionists that swept the world in the latter 1800s. Primitive Salvationism epitomized one of the purest, most powerful manifestations of the Hero Army of God in history. To understand its popular social action, we must understand its spiritual motivation, for The Salvation Army experienced the truth that the face of the earth changes when the hearts of its people are transformed.

In God's wonderful sense of humor, He raised an answer to the social disaster of Victorian England from its own ashes. The invisible people became the foot soldiers of His heroic response to the problems of Victorian England. The prostitute became the rescuer of the prostitutes. The poverty-stricken woman became the virtuous slum sister. The orphan became the den mother to orphans. The rebellious drunkard became the courageous officer. The victims became the aggressors. The survivors became heroes.

The primitive Salvation Army burned with revival fire, driven by a sense of calling. General Catherine Booth prophesied:

> The decree has gone forth that the kingdoms of this world shall become the kingdoms of our Lord and of His Christ, and that He shall reign whose right it is, from the rivers to the ends of the earth. I believe that this Movement is to inaugurate the great final conquest of the Lord Jesus Christ.[2]

CONCEIVED IN PROPHECY

Although The Salvation Army was born in the fire, it was conceived in prophecy.

> Fully four years before the Christian Mission morphed out of what was initially called the East London Special Services Committee, on January 23, 1861, a member... named Baptist Noel truly prophesied to some 200 Christians: "If this work is done, we shall see some unknown Luthers and

Whitefields excavated out of this dark mine, to spread the Gospel farther and wider than we have any idea.... I believe we are on the eve of a greater work than England ever saw, and the East End of London is the right place to begin."[3]

This was an accurate prophecy. Along with pioneer heroes like John Lawley, chimney sweep Elijah Cadman, and James Dowdle, God raised up world-traveling George Scott Railton, Samuel Logan Brengle (D.D.), and Frederick Tucker (imperial magistrate), heroes all, who, between them, began to spread the gospel farther and wider than any of the 200 in attendance could have imagined.

The Hebrew word *naba*, translated "prophecy" in the Old Testament, means to bubble up. Prophecy bubbles up and then gushes forth. The next bubbling gurgle came in late 1863, in an incident while staying at the home of a host:

"Excuse me Mr. Booth...what is it that engages your thoughts so frequently and protracted as you pace the garden?" Mr. Booth, with face all ashine, answered, "My friend, I am thinking out a plan, which, when it is implemented, will mean blessing to the wide, wide world."[4]

Who can deny that this bubbling, that this movement, subsequently blessed the wide, wide world?

BIRTHED IN FIRE

If we go on as we are we shall have the whole country saved by Christmas!

—George Scott Railton to William Booth mid 1880s

The Salvation Army is all about heroes and heroics. That's why God thought us up. The vast majority of His Church was being ignored by three-quarters of the populace. The remaining quarter, it was boring to tears. It was boring Him.... So He came up with us and, like all God's ideas, it worked magnificently, spreading like wildfire around the globe—no apologies, no compromises, no identity confusion.[5]

In 1879, just one year after becoming The Salvation Army, 4,000 soldiers in the heat of revival fires attended the first Council of War. General Catherine Booth implored them:

> The time has come for fire. All other agents have been tried: intellect, learning, fine buildings, wealth, respectability, numbers. The great men and the mighty men and the learned men have all tried to cast out these devils before you, and have failed. TRY THE FIRE. There are legions of the enemies of our great King. Fire on them. There are legions of strong drink, damning millions; of uncleanness, damning millions more; of debauchery, blasphemy, theft, millions more! Charge on them, pour the red-hot shot of the artillery of heaven on them, and they will fall by thousands![6]

Primitive Salvation Army revival spread like prairie fire. In December 1882, five Salvationists invaded New South Wales, Australia. Two years later, The Salvation Army boasted 20,000 soldiers and adherents in 46 Corps! (The Corps was a mission station where the gospel was preached and the saints were trained.) The invasion of Victoria, Australia, grew similarly from nothing to 20,000 in two years.

In New Zealand, 5,000 conversions were recorded in the first nine months!

In Buffalo, New York (USA), 250 soldiers were made in the first 13 weeks. And they impacted the town. Police reported a three-week period where there was no one to arrest! The spiritual overflow was such that one local church gained 100 members!

The Salisbury (South Africa) newspaper, after a few months of The Salvation Army's invasions, proclaimed that, "The Salvation Army has 'occupied' Salisbury, the Devil having retired into the 'fly' country without having offered a single blow."[7]

The flamboyant teenager, "Happy" Eliza (Lieutenant Eliza Haynes) raised a crowd of 3,000 in Marylebone, England, in no time. She became famous throughout that country in the early 1880s. Songs were sung about her in the music halls, and dolls, toys, and candy were named after her![8]

Invaded simultaneously in Toronto and London, Ontario, in 1882, within two years Canada was home of 73 Corps and 35 outposts under 142 officers.[9]

In 1884, three teenaged girls opened the Army in Owen Sound, Ontario (Canada). In bold faith they rented a hall seating 1,500 people. It was packed on the first Sunday! Across the country, 73 Corps were started in that year.

An indoor riding school seating 5,000 was leased in Sweden. Less than two weeks passed before the crowds outgrew the school. A timber yard was leased and thousands stood in the ice and snow to hear the gospel!

Globally, the primitive Army experienced amazing, "great awakening" growth between 1881 and 1886. During this period there were more than 250,000 conversions. That's more than 1,000 each week! During this period five mission stations were opened per week![10] The number of officers increased from 533 to 3,600. The next year was even better! In 1887, The Salvation Army exploded by 50 percent, from 1,552 to 2,328 Corps. That is 15 new mission stations each week![11]

The Hero Army attacked with Holy Spirit fire, and the various demons Catherine Booth described began to fall as society was transformed. Between 1876 and 1886, annual sales of alcohol in England fell 46,980,000 pounds! In one of Major Jack Stoker's appointments, 13 pubs went bankrupt in the first three months after his arrival! By 1901, there were 30,000 converted drunks in the ranks of the Army in the UK! Labor and prostitution laws, criminal codes, employment standards, unemployment relief, and social welfare service were all stamped by this radical Army birthed in fire. Truly, the face of the earth changed as the hearts of its people were transformed.

HEROES ALL

Salvationist historian Geoff Ryan explains:

> We didn't just talk about evangelism and read books on it. We kitted up and headed for the front and never stopped to inquire politely of people "would you like to join us?" We lived our heroic lives amid the everyday and people flocked to our colors. The only question we asked was "can you keep up?" We were heroes, to saints and sinners alike.[12]

THE FRUIT AND THE ROOT

Now, most today have no clue as to the spiritual DNA of The Salvation Army. Even though William Booth was recently voted one of the 100 Greatest British Heroes,[13] most would be at a loss to offer any meaningful details of his life. Although The Salvation Army shield is one of the most recognized logos in the world, and the "Salvos" are the most-loved charity in the Western world[14], the majority of people are a little vague as to what they really do. The Salvation Army's stereotypical image is an older person ringing a bell beside a "kettle" outside a liquor store at Christmas time, a friendly lady giving out toys to the underprivileged, or, for those with very good memories, a donut girl on the front lines of a world war.

As the solution to Victorian England's problems, and some of today's as well, The Salvation Army has been applauded for decades. But although the

world acknowledges the magnificent social and humanitarian accomplishments of the Army, most don't recognize its spiritual motivation. Many phil-
anthropists want nothing to do with enthusiastic religion or frothy
spirituality but they love the results of drunks sobered, addicts cleaned up,
abused women rescued, broken marriages restored, prostitutes redeemed,
orphans adopted, and so on. As one Canadian Prime Minister asserted, "The
Salvation Army is a vital spiritual force with an acute social conscience."[15]

People might prefer to conveniently overlook the revivalist basis of the
Army. But one cannot have the fruit without the root. Society likes the fruit.
And yet the tree is the tree. A different tree would produce different fruit. Jesus
said that. People may want to divorce the fruit from the root but it cannot be
done. Without understanding and embracing the dynamic principles and vital
experiences that generated their success, mere superficial imitation is doomed
to failure. So we must let those who birthed this powerful movement speak for
themselves. What did they say about Salvationism?

ONE-TRACK MIND

Overcome, conquer, subdue. Not merely teach, but persuade,
compel nations to become disciples of the Son of God.
—General William Booth

We have no hobbies…unless it be a hobby to want to save the
largest number of souls with the highest possible salvation in the
quickest space of time by the best imaginable methods. That is the
sum and substance of our mission.
—Commissioner Frederick Booth-Tucker

Without excuse and self-consideration of health or limb or life,
true soldiers fight, live to fight, love to fight, love the thickest of the
fight, and die in the midst of it.
—General William Booth

In his old age, the world recognized Booth's heroism:

Placing his top hat on a chair and bending down, the
General washed his hands in a workman's bucket. He was
then ready to visit the head of the British Empire.

The General was delighted to be able to speak of the
work of his people in 49 countries. The King complimented

him and asked how the churches viewed his work. "Sir," replied the 75-year-old warrior, "they imitate me."

The King was amused and requested him to write in his autograph album.

> *Some men's ambition is art.*
> *Some men's ambition is fame.*
> *Some men's ambition is gold.*
> *My ambition is the souls of men.*[16]

Part of the success achieved in primitive Salvationism is attributable to a single passion—to win the world for Jesus. Such was the effectiveness of their efforts that Catherine Booth could assert the following and not get run out of town:

> There is no record since the Apostles of a body that has so encompassed the Divine idea, all its members being taught to make all other objects and aims of life subservient to the one grand purpose of preaching the Gospel to every creature and striving to win every soul with whom they come in contact to its salvation.[17]

The one thing was not evangelism but world winning. Although evangelism is certainly an integral part of that, so is discipleship. General William Booth affirmed: "The objects for which this Army exists…are, in brief, to seize the slaves of sin and not only set them free and turn them into children of God but as far as possible in each case to make them soul winners."[18]

World war against sin was the sole, abiding passion of the primitive salvationist:

> And what is our work? To go and subjugate the world to Jesus, everybody we can reach, everybody we can influence, and bring them to the feet of Jesus.[19]

> My business is to get the world saved. If this involves the standing still of the looms and the shutting up of the factories and the staying of the sailing ships, let them all stand still. When we have got everybody converted, they can go on again.[20]

This Hero Army did not settle for numerical growth, not for favor, not even for good meetings. A corporate one-track mind resolved always to accomplish mission:

> The Army, by its very success, is ever in danger of drifting away from the great ungodly mass for whose Salvation it was expressly raised up, and to whom it is essentially sent.

The only remedy is attack. The gulf must be crossed, and re-crossed, and crossed again. Aggression is the key to the indispensable, nay, the only means of conquest. To overcome, there must be skilful, persevering, systematic, desperate aggression…. We must go to the people. We must attack. New methods must be invented if the old ones do not bring us into contact with the godless crowds. For, no matter what the cost, we must get at them. We must attack.[21]

THE DARING, RECKLESS, DETERMINED STANDARD

They wanted to win the world for God. They sacrificed outrageously to do it.

Commissioner Railton laid down the law of "an open-air service and an indoor service—at least one of each—at every station, every night."[22]

We naively believe that today we can accomplish more than our primitive forebears because of the improvement in technology. After all, we possess the Internet, television, radio, and airplanes. The 19th century Hero Army had none of these things. And yet the expectations for them were much higher than any of us would think of imposing on ourselves or others today. William Booth instructed, "Under ordinary circumstances a *daring, reckless, determined* Commanding Officer can make himself known to 30,000 people in less than three days."[23]

How do we measure up to the daring, reckless, determined standard of primitive Salvationism? How likely is it that we'd see this report in a current mainstream Christian publication?

My heart is cheered. We are making the devil mad. Victory will come! Look out for some martyrdom here in the near future—it is to come, for sure. Well, we are saved to die, and don't care much where our bones are buried.[24]

How likely is it that we'd email this short-term plan to our superior, as Captain Albert Brice telegrammed Commissioner Thomas Coombs in the heat of persecution in 1887: "Expecting to go to Glory Wednesday night."[25] He was expecting martyrdom.

Catherine and William Booth's rebukes to the churches of their day are appropriate for many parts of the Church today:

We have to subdue everybody to Christ. Nobody will be subdued if they can help it. We have neither arms, learning, worldly influence nor money with which to subdue others and would not and could not use any of these to procure a single professed convert if we did. We have to do it simply by the power of the Holy Ghost working through us.[26]

These people stand in these paths of traditionalism and routinism just where their forefathers left them, occupying all their time admiring the wisdom and benevolence and devotion of their forefathers instead of IMITATING THEIR AGGRESSIVE FAITH, and MARCHING ON TO THE CONQUEST OF THE WORLD.[27]

But this opinion was borne out by those outside the Army. Isak Dinesan, the author of *Out of Africa*, wrote home from that continent in 1911:

For some it suffices to find adventure enough in learning to drive a car or attend Mrs. Zahle's school, but there are others who must take a different road and lose themselves in a war, become explorers to the North Pole or join *The Salvation Army*. It is the destiny of some mothers that their children were fated to take such paths.[28]

Mission-Crafted System

Talk of systems and organization seems vulgar in juxtaposition with discussion of passion and fire. Yet it remains a truth that we must structure to handle revival. The 19th century Hero Army organization was organized for success. Salvationist structure was even a part of its definition:

We are an army of soldiers of Christ, organized as perfectly as we have been able to accomplish, seeking no church status, avoiding as we would the plague every denominational rut, in order perpetually to reach more and more of those who live outside every church boundary.[29]

This 19th century manifestation of this Hero Army did not just adopt military jargon. The Christian Mission actually became The Salvation Army, filled with soldiers organized as perfectly as possible.

The media preferred to call it a "cold-blooded system."[30] Of the first Orders and Regulations one reporter noted, "It is shrewd enough to have been written by Machiavelli…the book is clever in the most worldly sense."[31] Catherine Booth didn't entirely deny it, testifying:

We believe that all rational measures, all the measures which men use with respect to the world, if they are lawful and good, may be transferred by the sanctification of the motive, by the transposition of aim, to the Kingdom of God…. Yea, we are bound to it.[32]

Change, adaptation, and novelty were persevering principles of primitive salvationism.

AN UNLEASHED HOLY SPIRIT

Clearly this Hero Army of the 19th century was a holiness movement with holiness as the theological glue that bonded it all together. It was the experienced blessing of a clean heart, of perfect love, and of eradicated inclination to sin that powered the movement. But the Booths were also willing to tie the success of The Salvation Army to the work of the Holy Spirit in their midst:

> What unkind things have been said of The Salvation Army, because people have fallen on their faces under the convicting power of the Holy Spirit at our meetings; but you see, this is Apostolic.[33]

In response to criticism, Catherine Booth asked, "How is it that wherever we go as an organization signs and wonders are wrought?"[34]

THOROUGH REPENTANCE

The prevailing problem then and today in evangelism is the tendency to ask Jesus into our hearts without repenting of sin. Catherine Booth explained:

> They try to believe; they want to follow Him, but they are kept back by the right hand and the right eye which the Holy Spirit has told them they must cut off and pluck out before He will receive them. They will not do it, so they are ever learning, and never able to come to a knowledge of the truth. You must renounce evil in your will. You must will to "obey the truth." You must say "yes Lord."[35]

The primitive Salvation Army fought through long battles while the Holy Spirit convicted men and women of the guilt with regard to sin, righteousness, and judgment and brought a godly sorrow, which brings repentance that leads to salvation and leaves no regret. Many then outside and, ironically, many within the Body take offence at what conviction, godly sorrow, and repentance can look like. Here is an extended critical description of a Hero Army all night of prayer by a newspaper correspondent during which all of these things occurred:

> So great was the commotion in the centre of the room, so terrifying was the din that this incidence (four rows tipping over), which would have thrown an ordinary congrega-

tion into uproar, passed almost unnoticed…Several figures are bent double near the platform, groaning and wringing their hands. The "Hallelujah Lasses" have surrounded them; the tall figure of the proprietor of the "Hallelujah Fiddle" gyrates around them; the sweep is dancing and shouting "Glory be to God;" and the "General" is smiling placidly and twiddling his thumbs.

Penitents! Are these penitents who kneel on the form and wring their hands? Or are they persons struck with the contagion of over-wrought enthusiasm?

As may be seen from what I have written, until penitents "throw themselves at the feet of Jesus," as it is called, a meeting of The Salvation Army is a tolerably sane affair. The fat is at once in the fire, however, when penitents come forward.

Half a-dozen crop-headed youths are praying vociferously, with their faces towards me. Did I say praying? It was vociferous shouting, with closed eyes. Their bodies sway to and fro; their hands are lifted, and brought down again with a thump on the form; they contort themselves as if they were in acute agony.

The converts retire to their seats with red faces. Let us follow one of them. He is a broad-faced, shock-headed youth, of about twenty. A few minutes since, he was foaming out of a well-developed mouth. Now he is dancing about the floor, shouting "hallelujah" and wringing the hands of all those who will yield their arm to him. Anon he will mount one of the forms, and shout his experience into the middle of a hubbub, which condemns him to remain unheard. Then he will waltz round again, alternately laugh and cry, and go through a new course of hand-shaking. He has in fact been converted.[36]

Primitive Salvationism emphasized repentance of sin. In William Booth's effective salvation tract, How to Find God, five of the seven steps deal with sin. You can't get through it without completely repenting of sin. If all our converts today, whatever stripe, experienced this heart-searching process, whether or not it is accompanied by the manifestations described, we'd likely create more warriors for the Hero Army.

PERSECUTION

Hot on the heels of The Salvation Army was another Victorian creation, this one born not in the imagination of God, but in the schemings of the devil. The Salvation Army actually took its name in 1878. Within three years the opposing Skeleton Army was organized at Weston-super-Mare.

The Christmas War Cry of that year states that "the chief officers of the Skeleton Army raised to oppose us at Exeter were converted." This marked the beginning of the popular use of the term. For 15 years, The Salvation Army's Blood and Fire standard was often challenged in the open-air meeting by the Skeleton Army's Skull and Crossbones.

A "Bethnal Green Eastern Post" newspaper report in November 1882 exposed the purposes behind this untimely birthed counter-army:

> A genuine rabble of "roughs" pure and unadulterated has been infesting the district for several weeks past. These vagabonds style themselves the "Skeleton Army".... The "skeletons" have their collectors and their collecting sheets and one of them was thrust into my hands...it contained a number shopkeepers' names.... I found that publicans, beer-sellers and butchers are subscribing to this imposture...the collector told me that the object of the skeleton army was to put down the Salvationists by following them about everywhere, by beating a drum and burlesquing their songs, to render the conduct of their processions and services impossible.... Amongst the skeleton rabble there is a large percentage of the most consummate loafers and unmitigated blackguards London can produce...worthy of the disreputable class of publicans who hate the London school board, education, and temperance, and who, seeing the beginning of the end of their immoral traffic, and prepared for the most desperate enterprise.
>
> The skeleton armies carried flags usually bearing a "skull and crossbones," no doubt inspired by the prominence given to piracy in contemporary "penny dreadfuls" for boys. Variations included the addition of two coffins and the motto "blood and thunder"! Others decorated theirs with monkeys, a devil, and rats. Another had a yellow banner with three B's—beef, beer, and "bacca"![37]

Listen to this re-enactment of the invasion of Coventry, England:

"This blessed drum is our pulpit and penitent-form," said Sister Mrs. Caroline Reynolds. "Friends, as many of you know, Sister Burrell and myself have been sent by William Booth...to open fire for our blessed Redeemer."

At that, hoodlums set up a howl of midnight wolves intent on a kill and readied themselves, armed with fish, vegetables, eggs, and butcher bones in every stage of decomposition, but Sister Reynolds lifted her arms to heaven and sternly commanded, "Stay! The King's business must be spoken clearly, me lads. After prayer we'll call on Mistress Katie Docker for a word o' testimony. She's a precious brand plucked from the burnin' who radiates the love o' Jesus."

"Cheers for Katie Docker!" Bawled a hooligan and up shot a string of Hip! Hip! Hoorahs! Though one bawdy voice screeched, "Go home, Katie Docker! Go home!" The two women and about 50 recruits knelt in the snow while Sister Reynolds prayed.

"God of creation, convict Coventry! Bring this Babylon of 60,000 souls to desolation then raise it up in Jesus to such a revival as converts every wayward Tom, Dick, and Harry within sight an' sound. Hinder an' hamper an' make 'em agonize until they throw aside every weight that so easily bests 'em and jump into the fountain o' Your love. Then kiss 'em and hug 'em and send 'em after their strayin' mates. Oh, sweep the city streets with us, Your consecrated brooms, and send revival! Send us results that from this very spot the world will be set afire wi' Your love. In the precious name o' Jesus, amen!"

Katie Docker stood forward, a worn Bible in her mittened hands. She had not so much as opened it when two ruffians, black woolen caps close around their pocked noses, began to jostle her.

"Katie, stan' back! Jimmy Docker vows e'll smash yer 'ead in if ye speak ou' once more! We're sent t' persuade ye."

It was pure honey, the smile Katie gave them before she opened her Bible. Calmly she proceeded: "The wages of sin is death, but the gift o' God is eternal life through Jesus Christ our"

Like fury arrows, the roughs sped toward the marketplace where Jimmy Docker loitered...known for a good half of his thirty odd years as the most notorious villain in many a county.... Now, before Katie had done, a yowl went up that could be heard halfway to the tower of London. "Ye-ow! Ye'ow!" A string of oaths, enough to make a walking stick curl pierced the air as Jimmy came whirling through the snow, swinging an axe handle, a dozen mischiefmakers pounding behind him. "Ye-ow! Ye-ow!" They rushed the Hallelujahs, slammed the preaching women in the snow, scattered the screaming crowd like feathers and, stomping, hissing, yapping, confronted Katie, who still read her Scriptures. Clogs spread, axe handle high, Jimmy Docker bellowed, "Katharine, wife o' James Docker, step for'd an' follow thy legal master an' mate!"

There was a pause.

"Come not, an' we'll bash the lot!"

Bestowing on him one pleading look, Katie recommenced: "The people that walked in darkness have seen a great light; they that dwell in the land of the shadow of death, upon them the light…"

"Katie Docker come willin'!" screamed Jimmy, "er I'll—I'll—" He lunged.

"Sir," Eliza shouted, "to reach Katie, you must first pass me. Bash away!"

Docker was so surprised at the miniature rebellion he stepped back, heaving.

The preaching ladies squeezed in front of Eliza.

"I'm in command, Mr. Docker," stated Sister Reynolds. "Bash me before you touch a hair of Katie's head."

"And me. Bash me!" dared Sister Burrell, a somewhat portly duplicate of Sister Reynolds, with much bolder features.

Jimmy Docker and his mates bashed away. The Hallelujahs, dozens of them, piled up in the snow, bloodied and broken as rank on rank they confronted the Docker brigade, refusing either to take the offensive or to defend themselves.…

That afternoon, March 8, 1878, seventeen constables were enlisted to subdue one James Docker, with a law enforcement officer having a good part of his right ear bitten off for his devotion to duty. Hate and gore were hardly more in evidence in the Crimea, several veterans observed that afternoon,

recounting that the Docker onslaught was uncontested as the
Hallelujahs preached passive nonviolent resistance to evil.[38]

The punch line to this true story is that in September 1878, newly converted Jimmy Docker marched down the aisle in a fresh black suit with a red jersey, shined shoes, and a poled placard that proclaimed, "GLORY!"[39]

These gangs of loosely organized hooligans, often mobilized with the reward of free whiskey by pub owners whose businesses were threatened by the effectiveness of the Hero Army's gospel at converting their customers, wreaked havoc through England until 1892.

In the early years of the Canadian campaign, Corps buildings were routinely burned down.[40] The most notorious confrontation, "The Battle of the Basilica," November 24, 1887, confirmed the Army's fears of the insistent and sinister opposition of Quebec to the gospel. Fully 5,000 marchers assembled against the Army, smashing the Army buildings, fighting with soldiers and police, and forced a test-case in the courts that found the Army guilty.[41]

Not all the persecution was physically violent. In 1886, one pioneer Salvation Army 18-year-old soldier gave this report after a night of "pub booming" in *The Black Cat*, in Johannesburg, South Africa:

> The barmaid was truly a "black cat." She caught me and locked me in her room and used the most filthy language to me. I sat on a chair and she started to undress. I just put my head in my hands—prayed...she began to write the most filthy letters to the officer, what I had done and what I did not do. That lasted until 10 pm, closing time. Then a man came and let me out and paid for my War Crys. Then I had to dodge the Skeletons and walk three miles home.[42]

But the pub owners were not alone. Eastbourne's mayor declared that it was his intention to "put down this Salvation Army business," and if necessary the town council would call on the Skeleton Army to help them. He did, and the collusion of the government with the Skeleton Army resulted in the brutal assault of defenseless Salvationists. At first London's Metropolitan Police turned a deaf ear to the appeals made for protection for Salvationists. Their leader, Sir Edmund V. Henderson, even denied the existence of what was alleged to be taking place. In Canada, arrests were commonplace, and on one occasion, "practically the whole Corps was thrown into jail," in Lindsay, in 1887, "into ONE SMALL DARK CELL."[43]

Before 1892, when the tide of British public opinion had turned and serious conflicts with the police had resulted in drastic legal measures being taken, the Army suffered greatly. Among thousands of beatings, the female

Corps officer at Guildford was kicked into insensibility, not 10 yards from the police station, a woman soldier was so injured that she died within a week, and at Shoreham, a woman captain died through being hit by a flying stone.[44]

Often opposition came from high society and the Church. T.H. Huxley, who labeled Salvationism "Corybantic Christianity" after the raving rituals of that dead religion, was simultaneously one of the most respected and most vicious critics of the Hero Army and its General. He declared:

> Few social evils are of greater magnitude than uninstructed and unchastened religious fanaticism; no personal habit more surely degrades the conscience and the intellect than blind and unhesitating obedience to unlimited authority.[45]

From another source came criticisms of:

> Histrionic services and the multiplicity of genuflexions...of The Salvation Army, amongst whom scarcely a vestige of religious awe, or even of decorum touching things reverenced by their neighbours, can be traced.... The stillness of Heaven itself is broken to our ears by vile talk of "rows," "Hallelujah gallops," and "jolly" prophets ascending in "fiery vans."[46]
>
> The daily papers continue to be filled with letters complaining about the doings of the most noisy of recent additions to the copious and variegated hortus siccus of dissent. From day to day somebody writes to ask whether this lasts growth of vanity and vulgarity is to be allowed to obstruct traffic and endanger life in the streets. For the benefit of the people who require to have everything written out for them in large capitals, we may observe that we are speaking of The Salvation Army. It is just as well to avoid any risk of being misunderstood, or else we might speak of these latter-day flagellants as this hideous or this blasphemous buffoonery without calling them "out of their name."[47]

It is during this period that The Salvation Army experienced some of the most explosive spiritual growth in the history of the world. But no matter the era or the time zone, whether opposing the symptoms of fallen humanity manifest in oppression, exploitation, cruelty, and injustice, or the root of fallen humanity, the conversion of the heart, persecution always confronts the tip of the spear.

THE CONQUEST OF DEVIL'S ISLAND!

Devil's Island was notorious before the imprisonment of French Army captain Alfred Dreyfus, of "Dreyfus Affair" fame, at the penal settlement there in 1895, and before the classic movie *Papillon* nearly a century later. Conditions were horrendous. "The prisoners were forced to work in water up to their waist, assaulted by malarial mosquitoes, baked by the sun. They were underfed and overworked."[48]

Failure to meet their daily wood-cutting quota meant only dry bread to eat that day and the left over quota the next.[49] "Men were dying of fever, leprosy was rampant, good food unknown, beatings commonplace."[50]

Degradation was the order of the day. To minimize escape attempts (limited by piranhas, army ants, clouds of malaria-bearing mosquitoes, and cannibals), convicts in the punishment camps were made to work naked except for shoes and straw hats.[51] Once their sentences were complete, prisoners had to stay and get jobs to pay off the "costs" of their imprisonment and earn passage home. Only a quarter of the 56,000 prisoners ever returned to native France. *Crime* magazine calls it the most infamous prison in history.[52]

The Salvation Army invaded the Islands. Led by Major Charles Pean, they determined to bring life and purpose to the hopeless captives.

This hero improved the living conditions, trained the prisoners, treated the sick, provided homes for those who had completed their sentences, preached the gospel with integrity, created jobs, generated international export businesses, and transformed the whole society.[53] He shut down the injustice and cruelty. He ravaged the evils of the penal colony. He shut down Devil's Island prison!

And the result is that the whole island was converted. Once called Devil's Island, it is now, to this day, called Salvation Island!

CHAPTER SEVEN

IN DARKEST ENGLAND
AND THE WAY OUT

Salvationism means simply the overcoming and banishing from the earth of wickedness.

The Army of the Revolution is recruited by the Soldiers of Despair.

Go for souls and go for the worst.

—William Booth

It is often said that, one year, early in the 1900s, when wireless telegraphy was in its infancy, William Booth sent a one-word message, "Others!" by telegram to encourage his officers around the world. *Others!* was Bramwell

Booth's motto for the year 1895, and it was also the title of the Army's annual report for 1894-95.

When the *Empress of Ireland* went down with 130 Salvation Army offi- cers on board (May 29, 1914), 109 officers were drowned, and not one body that was picked up had on a life-belt. The few survivors told how the Salvationists, finding there were not enough life-preservers for all, took off their own belts and strapped them upon even strong men, saying, "I can die better than you can"; and from the deck of that sinking boat they flung their battle-cry around the world—*Others!*[1]

Just two years earlier, on May 9, 1912, at the Royal Albert Hall in London, the old warrior William Booth preached his last. He said good-bye to his comrades, and, explaining that he was going into dry-dock for repairs, concluded:

> While women weep, as they do now, I'll fight; while lit- tle children go hungry, as they do now, I'll fight; while men go to prison, in and out, in and out, as they do now, I'll fight; while there is a drunkard left, while there is a poor lost girl upon the streets, while there remains one dark soul without the light of God, I'll fight—I'll fight to the very end![2]

William Booth, with masterstrokes, paints the picture of the status of the fighting:

> The man who walks with open eyes and a bleeding heart through the shambles of our civilization needs no…fantastic images of the poet to teach him horror. Often and often, when I have seen the young and the poor and the helpless go down before my eyes into the morass, trampled underfoot by beasts of prey in human shape that haunt these regions, it seemed as if God were no longer in this world, but that in His stead reigned a fiend, merciless as hell, ruthless as the grave.[3]

Common sense suggests that saving and sanctifying the world's pop- ulation will change the nature of the world. Holiness is, here, the solution to every problem. William Booth saw societal transformation as both a necessary cause *for* and an indicative measure of progress *in* the mission to win the world for Jesus. Using sociological terms, it was necessary but not sufficient. That is to say, meeting the essential needs of the very poor enabled them to actually listen to the gospel. It was necessary for them to hear it—but it wasn't sufficient for them to be saved. Booth characterized it this way: "No one ever got saved on an empty stomach." And societal alteration was an indicative measure of progress. If people were actually being saved, you'd notice it by changes in lifestyle.

It is difficult for us to conjure up images of the pre-social welfare society. Picture Dickens if you will. There was no safety net. The poor, who, along with coal and innovation largely powered the Industrial Revolution, suffered appalling conditions at home and at work.

> The plight of the poor in the 1880s was caused by the administration of the Poor Law. The State accepted responsibility for providing shelter and food for every man, woman and child who was destitute but they fulfilled this responsibility in such a way that poverty became a stigma. Those temporarily without a home were provided with shelter at a casual ward. There they were made to pick oakum or break stones—the traditional task of prisoners. The necessity to complete the required task caused great strain on those who were often weak with hunger. The principle seemed to be to make life for the poor so intolerable that they would seek employment more diligently. The fact that most of the paupers would have liked nothing more than a secure job escaped the notice of the authorities. Only those with nothing left but the clothes they wore were allowed a place in the workhouse. It was a dubious honor—the conditions there brought many to despair.[4]

Booth was no proponent of a social gospel. He hadn't even succumbed to the relative ease of feeding the lost instead of saving them, or of housing them instead of discipling them. In fact, he insisted on charging a man for a meal, something looked at with disdain today. Inspired by God, he and Catherine developed a massive, brilliant, ambitious plan to rescue the "submerged tenth" of society, the lowest of the proletariat.[5] Booth depicted the worst of the population of those living in extreme poverty, in abject destitution, as:

> "...the 'Submerged Tenth' because the actual number represented 10-percent of the country's population [much of the rest lived in conditions we describe as deplorable]— a number he said was 'scandalously high.' This segment of the population, Booth contended, was nominally free but actually enslaved."[6]

Booth's battle charge was, "God for souls and go for the worst." His plan was called *In Darkest England and the Way Out*, and it has proven the basis for the social welfare systems of the world.

Despite the efforts of revisionist historians to remake it into a trendy, relevant machine of its age, the 19th century Army was anything but! In fact, one editor of the day assured readers that, "There is no more startling paradox in the modern history of England."[7] This does not mean that the Army wasn't innovative. It pioneered the use of automobiles and film for evangelism. It means that it was not a servant of the culture. The intent went beyond cultural relevance to cultural influence.

Yet Booth was quick to use the culture for his purposes. The *New York Herald* sent renowned African explorer Sir Henry M. Stanley to what he called "darkest Africa" to find Dr. David Livingstone. Booth's best-selling account that followed, *Through the Dark Continent*, caused quite a sensation.[8] Booth effectively played off the conditions of darkest Africa and the emotions of Victorian Britons to capture their hearts, their resolve, and their funds.

Right from the preface of this controversial book, Booth emphasized his purposes:

> It will be seen therefore that in this or in any other development that may follow I have no intention to depart in the smallest degree from the main principles on which I have acted in the past. My only hope for the permanent deliverance of mankind from misery, either in this world or the next, is the regeneration or remaking of the individual by the power of the Holy Ghost through Jesus Christ. But in providing for the relief of temporal misery I reckon that I am only making it easy where it is now difficult, and possible where it is now all but impossible, for men and women to find their way to the Cross of our Lord Jesus Christ.
>
> Time, experience, criticism, and, above all, the guidance of God will enable us, I hope, to advance on the lines here laid down to a true and practical application of the words of the Hebrew Prophet: "Loose the bands of wickedness; undo the heavy burdens; let the oppressed go free; break every yoke; deal thy bread to the hungry; bring the poor that are cast out to thy house. When thou seest the naked cover him and hide not thyself from thine own flesh. Draw out thy

soul to the hungry—Then they that be of thee shall build the old waste places and Thou shalt raise up the foundations of many generations" (Isaiah 58:5-6).

The Cab Horse Charter

A master communicator, Booth summarized the plan with his "Cab Horse Charter," and demonstrated the principles for success with "Lights in Darkest England."

What, then, is the standard towards which we may venture to aim with some prospect of realization in our time? It is a very humble one, but if realized it would solve the worst problems of modern Society. It is the standard of the London Cab Horse. When in the streets of London a Cab Horse, weary or careless or stupid, trips and falls and lies stretched out in the midst of the traffic there is no question of debating how he came to stumble before we try to get him on his legs again. The Cab Horse is a very real illustration of poor broken-down humanity; he usually falls down because of overwork and underfeeding.

If you put him on his feet without altering his conditions, it would only be to give him another dose of agony; but first of all you'll have to pick him up again. It may have been through overwork or underfeeding, or it may have been all his own fault that he has broken his knees and smashed the shafts, but that does not matter. If not for his own sake, then merely in order to prevent an obstruction of the traffic, all attention is concentrated upon the question of how we are to get him on his legs again. Tin load is taken off, the harness is unbuckled, or, if need be, cut, and everything is done to help him up. Then he is put in the shafts again and once more restored to his regular round of work. That is the first point. The second is that every Cab Horse in London has three things: a shelter for the night, food for its stomach, and work allotted to it by which it can earn its corn.

These are the two points of the Cab Horse's Charter. When he is down he is helped up, and while he lives he has food, shelter and work. That, although a humble standard, is at present absolutely unattainable by millions—literally by millions—of our fellow-men and women in this country. Can the Cab Horse Charter be gained for human beings? I answer, yes. The Cab Horse standard can be attained on the Cab Horse terms.

The Cab Horse Charter shamed the public and galvanized support for his immense project. Booth followed this up with a well-publicized success to demonstrate the viability of the plan. He tackled and transformed the match industry in England.

LIGHTS IN DARKEST ENGLAND

A mother and two children under nine years old, were found to be working 16 hours a day, without lunch or tea breaks, making matches in abysmal conditions for only two shillings [equivalent purchasing power is $11.84 USD 2002, less than $0.75 an hour[9]].

The matches were made from yellow phosphorus, a poisonous substance often causing necrosis or "phossy jaw" in the matchmakers. Phossy jaw was a severely painful, terminal disease that ate into the bone of the jaw.

In response to this brutal situation, The Salvation Army opened a clean, airy, well-lit factory where harmless red phosphorus was used in the match making process. Booth called the matches "Lights in Darkest England." Tea making facilities were made available and the 100 workers received decent wages—more than one third above the rate in other factories.

Concomitantly, the Army launched a nationwide "British Match Consumers League" whose members were urged to, "Worry their grocer, oilmen or other shopkeeper, who does not at present stock or sell these matches, at least twice a week, until such time as he does do so."

Soon retailers were stocking safety matches exclusively, and commercial match factories were forced to not only improve working conditions, but also to switch over to the safe red phosphorus in their factories.

Having achieved his original purpose "to raise the wages of the matchmakers, to fight against sweating, and to help the poor to help themselves by labor" The Salvation Army closed shop.[10]

He appealed to the public for £100,000 ($11.9 million US Dollars, 2002[11]) to start his scheme and a further £30,000 per year ($3.57 million US Dollars 2002[12]) to maintain the program. The first edition of *In Darkest England and the Way Out* sold out, all 10,000 copies, on the first day. The second and third edition sold out within weeks. A year later, 200,000 were sold. Editions followed into the 1970s. Nine years after the first edition, The Salvation Army had served 27 million cheap meals, lodged 11 million homeless people, traced 18,000 missing people and found jobs for 9,000 unemployed people.[13] Spiritual revolution has social consequences.

Farthing breakfasts for children, midnight soup kitchens, midnight work among women (prostitutes), street-cleaning brigades, traveling hospitals, refuges for street children, asylums for moral lunatics, hostels, sheltered housing, prison ministry, missing persons (family tracing), poor man's bank, poor man's lawyer, and accommodations for the elderly are all programs existing in various forms today through the innovations of the Darkest England Scheme.

Booth invested nine chapters of *In Darkest England* in describing the plight of the submerged tenth. In turn, he depicts the squalor of the homeless, the out-of-works, those on the verge of the abyss, the vicious, the criminals, and the children of the lost. He asserted, "The Scheme of Social Salvation is not worth discussion which is not as wide as the Scheme of Eternal Salvation set forth in the Gospel."[14] He clarified that the planned social upheaval had nothing to do with the conventional understandings of revolution:

DELIVERANCE

In his chapter entitled "Stupendous Undertaking," Booth outlines the essentials of success. They have little to do with the remnant theology of much of the 20th century. They have nothing to do with the small plans of mice and men. Here is one of them:

> Any remedy worthy of consideration must be on a scale commensurate with the evil with which it proposes to deal. It is no use trying to bail out the ocean with a pint pot. This evil is one whose victims are counted by the million. The army of the Lost in our midst exceeds the numbers of that multitudinous host which Xerxes led from Asia to attempt the conquest of Greece. Pass in parade those who make up the submerged tenth, count the paupers indoor and outdoor, the homeless, the starving, the criminals, the lunatics, the drunkards, and the harlots—and yet do not give way to

despair! Even to attempt to save a tithe of this host requires
that we should put much more force and fire into our work
than has hitherto been exhibited by anyone. There must be
no more philanthropic tinkering, as if this vast sea of human
misery were contained in the limits of a garden pond.[15]

There are three components to the Darkest England Scheme: the City
Colony, the Farm Colony, and the Colony Across the Sea.

Although the plan was never fully implemented as envisioned, most of
it was established to some degree. Snippets of some of the plans suggest the
extent to which this Scheme anticipated much welfare reform and even
recent environmental and recycling concerns and efforts.

THE CITY COLONY

Despite a lack of immediate funds Booth decided to put his plan into
action. In June 1890, Booth established the first employment bureau. In the
first seven years, 70,000 of the 80,000 men who registered found employment. Twenty years later the British government followed The Salvation
Army's example.[16]

The Army's famous slum officers lived in the worst locations and made
them beacons of light to the hopeless.[17] They established beachheads called,
in Britain, Goodwill Centers, and deployed soldiers in "cellar, gutter, and gar-
ret brigades."[18]

This was front-line warfare. Unemployed, destitute, drunk, criminal,
prostitute, ne'er-do-well—all were targets of the Army's modus operandi,
"Capture, Train, Deploy." All contributed shining examples of "trophies"
saved by grace, captured from the enemy, and won to Jesus. This 19th century Hero Army was effectively implementing God's big idea, that invisible
people can become People people through an encounter with God.

The Army established City Industrial Workshops. As the plan explains:

These workshops are open for the relief of the
unemployed and destitute, the object being to make it
unnecessary for the homeless or workless to be compelled
to go to the Workhouse or Casual Ward, food and shelter
being provided for them in exchange for work done by
them, until they can procure work for themselves, or it
can be found for them elsewhere.

Booth, the visionary, also scooped environmentalists by about a century,
in his creation of "The Household Salvage Brigade." He describes it in his
own words:

There is one material that is continually increasing in quantity, which is the despair of the life of the householder and of the Local Sanitary Authority. I refer to the tins in which provisions are supplied. Nowadays everything comes to us in tins. We have coffee tins, meat tins, salmon tins, and tins ad nauseam. Tin is becoming more and more the universal envelope of the rations of man. But when you have extracted the contents of the tin what can you do with it?

Huge mountains of empty tins lie about every dustyard, for as yet no man has discovered a means of utilizing them when in great masses. I see in the old tins of London at least one means of establishing an industry which is at present almost monopolized by our neighbors.

Most of the toys which are sold in France on New Year's Day are almost entirely made of sardine tins collected in the French capital. The toy market of England is at present far from being overstocked, for there are multitudes of children who have no toys worth speaking of with which to amuse themselves. In these empty tins I see a means of employing a large number of people in turning out cheap toys which will add a new joy to the households of the poor—the poor to whom every farthing is important, not the rich the rich can always get toys—but the children of the poor, who live in one room and have nothing to look out upon but the slum or the street. These desolate little things need our toys, and if supplied cheap enough they will take them in sufficient quantities to make it worthwhile to manufacture them.

A whole book might be written concerning the utilization of the waste of London. But I am not going to write one. I hope before long to do something much better than write a book, namely, to establish an organization to utilize the waste, and then if I describe what is being done it will be much better than by now explaining what I propose to do.

I refer to old newspapers and magazines, and books. Newspapers accumulate in our houses until we sometimes burn them in sheer disgust. Magazines and old books lumber our shelves until we hardly know where to turn to put a new volume. My Brigade will relieve the householder from these difficulties, and thereby become a great distributing agency of cheap literature. After the magazine has done its duty in the middle class household it can be passed on to the reading-rooms, workhouses, and hospitals. Every publication issued from the Press that is of the slightest use to men and women will, by our Scheme, acquire a double share of usefulness. It will be read first by its owner, and then by many people who would never otherwise see it.

We shall establish an immense second-hand bookshop. All the best books that come into our hands will be exposed for sale, not merely at our central depots, but on the barrows of our peripatetic colporteurs, who will go from street to street with literature which, I trust, will be somewhat superior to the ordinary pabulum supplied to the poor. After we have sold all we could, and given away all that is needed to public institutions, the remainder will be carried down to our great Paper Mill, in connection with our Farm Colony.

The Household Salvage Brigade will constitute an agency capable of being utilized to any extent for the distribution of parcels newspapers, &c. When once you have your reliable man who will call at every house with the regularity of a postman, and go his beat with the punctuality of a policeman, you can do great things with him. It will be a universal Corps of Commissionaires, created for the service of the public and in the interests of the poor, which will bring us into direct relations with every family in London.

It does not require a very fertile imagination to see that when such a house-to-house visitation is regularly established, it will develop in all directions; and working, as it would, in connection with our Anti-sweating Shops and Industrial Colony, would probably soon become the medium for negotiating sundry household repairs, from a broken window to a damaged stocking. If a porter were wanted to move furniture, or a woman wanted to do charring, or some one to clean windows or any other odd job, the ubiquitous Servant of All who called for the waste, either verbally or by postcard, would receive the order.

There seemed to be a program aimed at every imaginable sin of the city. But the City Colony was just the beginning.

The Farm Colony

General Booth purchased a farm where men could be trained in certain types of work and at the same time gain some self-respect, because often when men had been unemployed for some years their confidence needed to be restored.

Although far more than a mere geographical cure, this resettling away from the easy temptations of the city did provide a physical and social second chance to go with the spiritual new birth. Away from the bustle of the metropolis, and supported by the disciplined structure and schedule of Colony life, the "down and out" developed skills and character traits that provided a framework for the new life that the Holy Spirit had generated within them.

The rigorous training and demands were augmented by a healthy diet of Salvation Army meetings that featured lively music, first-person testimony, and fiery appeals from the Bible.

The Overseas Colony

From this farm colony, men could be further helped through emigration to an overseas colony, where laborers were few. Whole families could be helped to a much better standard of living.

Although Booth underestimated the disdain of the British Colonies for his Overseas Colony plan, records show that almost 250,000 people were helped to emigrate through the program.[19] In our province there is a town, Coombs, named after the Army's first national leader. It was originally an Overseas Colony.

This ultimate extrapolation of the geographic solution, the emigration from England and resettling in overseas colonies offered an opportunity that is difficult for Western readers to comprehend. These invisible people, the butt of the Industrial Revolution, were the grunts on whose backs capital was created, and yet they bore the negative ramifications of industrialization discussed above, while reaping few if any of the benefits. These invisible people, given dignity by God and transformed into People people, were given tracts of land to work and build a new life. Those who had been near-slaves became landowners, which in England comprised the nobility! What a revolution! They'd already been morphed from spiritual slaves of satan into children of the King of Kings, joint-heirs with Christ, part of an eternal nobility. And now occurred some semblance of this change in the physical. From slave to nobility, both spiritually, at conversion, and now socially, through the Darkest England Scheme.

The promise is attached to the land. The Israelites' blessing was in the Promised Land. Today in northern Canada, the indigenous Nsga'a people have signed a treaty that gives them their own land. It is highly spiritually significant that the Overseas Colony gave land to those who received the social lift of the gospel. It is one of God's ways of making invisible people into People people.

PROMOTED TO GLORY[20]

God's strategy worked in Victorian England. Today The Salvation Army is the world's largest social service provider after the UN.[21] In early 2004 the Army is still the most popular (judging by, among other measures, the $1.5 billion donation to build and operate community centers it received from the widow of the founder of McDonalds, Joan Kroc—enough to buy 645 million Happy Meals).[22] Though General Booth was much maligned throughout most of his earthly warfare, he became a "*wildly* respected international figure fighting poverty," in his later years.[23] He was known as "the world's best-loved man," and "the Archbishop of the World."[24]

Fully 150,000 people passed by his casket. The funeral was held at London's Olympia, drawing 40,000, including Queen Mary, who sat next to an ex-prostitute, a convert of General Booth's, and Queen Alexandra.[25] The heart of London stood still for nearly four hours as his funeral procession of 10,000 marching Salvationists, led by 40 brass bands, marched through the downtown streets, 2,950 on-duty policemen respectfully watching.

His 47-year-old Army consisted of 21,203 officers (vocational leaders) and 8,972 mission stations, working in 58 countries preaching the gospel in 34 languages! It is estimated that Booth traveled 5 million miles and preached 60,000 sermons in his 60 years of ministry.[26] Parts of the earth were changed as the hearts of its people were transformed. Booth promoted invisible people to the status of People people. He was a hero to the Submerged Tenth, and an example for us today.

SECTION THREE

CHAPTER EIGHT

WHO ARE THEY AND WHERE DO THEY COME FROM?

The suffering of children is the greatest proof against the existence of God.
　　　—Ivan Karamazov, a character in Fyodor Dostoyevsky's,
　　　　　　　　　　　The Brothers Karamazov

There are 2,103 verses of Scripture pertaining to the poor. Jesus Christ only speaks of judgment once. It is not all about the things that the church bangs on about. It is not about sexual immorality, and it is not about megalomania, or vanity. It is about the poor. "I was naked and you clothed Me. I was a stranger and you let

Me in." This is at the heart of the gospel. Why is it that we have
seemed to have forgotten this? Why isn't the church leading this
movement?

—Bono

END-TIME HARVEST?

Regardless of the accuracy of Bono's exegesis or his number on judgment, Jesus is all about the poor. And it is highly probable that the poor—women and children at risk—will be the final and choice recipients of God's grace at the end of the age.

The prophets of the Bible speak of a great end-time harvest. While in exile late in his life, the apostle John was allowed to see into the future to the end of time. He recorded in the Apocalypse what he saw.

After this I looked and there before me was a great multitude that
no one could count, from every nation, tribe, people and language, standing before the throne and in front of the Lamb. They
were wearing white robes and were holding palm branches in their
hands. And they cried out in a loud voice: "Salvation belongs to
our God...and they fell down on their faces before the throne and
worshiped God.... Then one of the elders asked me, "These in
white robes—who are they, and where did they come from?" I
answered, "Sir, you know." And he said, "These are they who
have come out of the great tribulation; they have washed their
robes and made them white in the blood of the Lamb"
(Revelation 7:9-14:9).

Both the question and the answers are important for us.

The question concerns "a great multitude that no one could count, from every nation, tribe, people and language, standing before the throne and in front of the Lamb." Specifically, "These in white robes—who are they, and where did they come from?"

Answering his question, the heavenly elder explains, *"These are they who have come out of the great tribulation; they have washed their robes and made them white in the blood of the Lamb."*

The vision and answer implies two important points.

1. The harvest is global—it involves every people group
   on earth.
2. The harvest is future—they come out of the great
   tribulation.

FIRST, THE HARVEST IS GLOBAL

There was a great multitude that no one could count, from every nation, tribe, people, and language, standing before the throne and in front of the Lamb.

Before Jesus returns, His gospel will be preached throughout the whole earth, and all peoples, nations, and languages will worship Him (see Daniel 7:14). This hope has been a favorite theme of the prophets since Abraham. Almost 2,000 years before Jesus walked the earth, God called one man and said, Abram:

> Leave your country, your people, and your father's household and go to the land I will show you. I will make you into a great nation and I will bless you; I will make your name great, and you will be a blessing. I will bless those who bless you, and whoever curses you I will curse; and all peoples on earth will be blessed through you (Genesis 12:1-3).

Paul, writing to the Galatian Christians some two millennia later, explains, "The Scripture foresaw that God would justify the Gentiles by faith, and announced the *gospel* in advance to Abraham: 'All nations will be blessed through you' " (Gal. 3:8).

The most famous of prophets, Isaiah, noted that both Israel as well as a coming special chosen servant were to have Yahweh's Spirit on them, "And He will bring justice to the nations.... In faithfulness He will bring forth justice; He will not falter or be discouraged till He establishes justice on earth. In His law the islands will put their hope.... I will keep You and will make You to be a covenant for the people and a light for the Gentiles" (Isa. 42:1, 4, 6).

And again:

> He [God] said to me, "You are My servant, Israel, in whom I will display My splendor...and now the Lord says: It is too small a thing for you to be My servant to restore the tribes of Jacob and bring back those of Israel I have kept. I will also make you a light for the Gentiles, that you may bring My salvation to the ends of the earth (Isaiah 49:3, 6).

A Light to the Gentiles

God's plan to save the entire world was to single out one man and through him build a nation that was to ultimately become a light to the world. Through Israel was also to come the anointed deliverer—the Christ—who would, in fact, be the mysterious suffering servant of Isaiah's prophecies (see Isa. 11:1-3; 42:1-9; 49:1-9; 50:4-11; 52:13–53:12; 61:1-4). This same

Christ was actually Daniel's "son of man" (Dan. 7:13), the "rock that became a mountain" (Dan. 2:35), and "the Anointed One," the ruler, that was coming to be cut off (Dan. 9:25-26). It was all so mysterious that even the disciples couldn't understand it initially. That God would choose a special nation through whom He would birth His own Son—"The Suffering Servant"—who would become the ultimate sin sacrifice making it possible for anyone—the "whosoever will"—to come to God, was just too stupendous for them to fathom.

Paul describes this as the "mystery of the gospel" (Eph. 6:19), the mystery that has been kept hidden for ages and generations, but is now disclosed to the saints (Col. 1:26). So, in Jesus, the work was fulfilled and the commission was given. The scope was that the message of salvation in Christ was to go, as the prophets had said, to the whole wide world—every tribe, tongue, and nation.

> He [Jesus] told them, "This is what is written: The Christ will suf-
> fer and rise from the dead on the third day, and repentance and
> forgiveness of sins will be preached in His name to all nations,
> beginning at Jerusalem" (Luke 24:46-47).

Again, Jesus said, "And this gospel of the kingdom will be preached in the whole world as a testimony to all nations, and then the end will come" (Matt. 24:14).

Though this commission of Jesus was never fully realized by the early Church, the force of this prophecy was enough to propel a believing people to evangelize a good portion of the earth. Patrick Johnstone writes, "It is possible that in the space of those first 45–50 years nearly 30% of the world's population at that time had been exposed to the Good News.… By the end of the fifth century this had risen to about 40% (with approximately 20% of the earth being Christians)."[1]

This was an admirable feat on the part of the early Church, all without the modern benefits of travel, pervasive law and order, technology, and mass communication. Yet for all the heroism of this massive thrust it didn't fulfill the words of Jesus. Sadly, after the 5th century the Church lost ground for the next 13 centuries.[2]

War Report

Before we can gauge where we stand in light of this prophecy we need to agree on terms. Trying to arrive at any semblance of consensus on what it means to be a *true* "Christian" is a very difficult task. Thankfully the Bible includes both the first use of the term and its definition. It states, "So for a whole year Barnabas and Saul met with the church and taught great numbers of people. *The disciples were called Christians first at Antioch"* (Acts 11:26). The Bible is clear: Those who were disciples—actual adherents to Christ and His teaching—they were called Christians.

Today there are many self-professed "Christians" who lack Christian experience and do not adhere to Christ or His teachings. Society, both religious and irreligious calls this second group "nominal" Christians. This would be like someone who says, "I'm Catholic, but I'm not really practicing right now." It's like one is saying, "I am American, but I'm not very patriotic right now."

Jesus simply said it this way, "Not everyone who says to Me, 'Lord, Lord,' will enter the kingdom of heaven, but only he who does the will of My Father who is in heaven" (Matt. 7:21). On top of that, there are the cults—those whom Christ Himself called false prophets (see Matt. 7:15). Thus, in an effort to clarify our intent, some missiologists have coined the title "great commission Christians" (Matt. 28:19-20), as opposed to others who merely claim some sort of allegiance to a Trinitarian faith in God the Father, God the Son, and God the Holy Spirit.

Still, within the larger professing sector of Christianity, it is impossible for us to determine the proportion of "great commission Christians" from "nominal" or "lip service Christians." And only God knows those who are truly His.

Looking further into definitions, there are also two schools of missiologists. One school takes people's word for their confession of faith. The other looks for some support to the claim. As a result, there are two groups of very different statistics concerning the size and growth of the international Church of Jesus.

For the purposes of measuring growth it doesn't matter so much which school you attend as long as you take all your classes there. That is, be consistently in one school or the other for statistical analysis. And the good news is that, proportionately, both schools report accelerated growth.

The inclusive school claims that Christianity has just more than 2 billion adherents of every stripe.[3] The other group records 11 percent of the world population as "Great Commission Christians."[4]

What is even more exciting is that since 1974 the proportion of the world's population not within reach of the gospel has decreased from one half to one third.[5] What does that mean? It means that we're in shooting range. It means that we don't need to have the gift of faith to see that we can actually fulfill the great commandment to preach the gospel to every person (see Mark 16:15). We can cover the whole globe!

Obviously, numbers of this magnitude aren't precise but the statistical evidence is overwhelmingly positive. The Church's growth dwarfs the world population growth of 1.6 percent each year.[6]

GREAT COMMISSION BELIEVERS—PROPORTION OF WORLD POPULATION

FIGURE 2

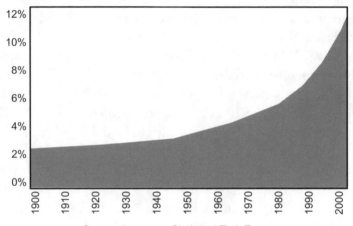

GREAT COMMISSION BELIEVERS - PROPORTION OF WORLD POPULATION

Source: Lausanne Statistical Task Force

It took 18 centuries for dedicated believers to grow from 0 percent of the world's population to 2.5 percent in 1900, only 70 years to grow from 2.5 to 5 percent in 1970, and just the last 30 years to grow from 5 to 11.2 percent of the world population. Now, for the first time in history, there is one Great Commission believer for every nine people worldwide who aren't believers. The inclusive school statistics are up 20 percent but show the same growth rate.

Things are accelerating. If you don't gear up soon, you may miss the whole shooting match!

"The Universal Religion"

What must be noted as a modern-day phenomenon is the historic acceleration of the Church since Israel became a nation. The secular news world has largely ignored the greatest advance of the gospel in history. Philip Jenkins notes that, at the end of the century, even *Christian History's* "100 Most Important Events in Church History" disregarded all of Africa, except to note the British abolition of slavery there.[7] This is a continent in which the Christian population exploded from 10 million to 360 million.[8] The accelerated growth of the Body of Christ went without comment.

A century ago there were no Christians in Korea. Today nearly 50 percent of the population is Christian.[9] Missiologists Ralph Winter and Bruce Koch enthuse:

> We are in the final era of missions. For the first time in history it is possible to see the end of the tunnel, when there will be a church movement within the language and social structure of every people group on earth.[10]

Christianity has been the primary motivation for the translation of more than 3,800 languages. The Bible is usually the first thing translated. Although there are still 3,000[11] of the world's languages still lacking written Scripture in their native tongue,[12] speakers of 5,580 languages can listen to the gospel.[13] Not only that, the New Testament was translated into all languages spoken by over 500,000 people by the end of 1998.[14] *Every Home for Christ* has systematically distributed almost 2 billion multi-page gospel messages globally, each with a decision card, in languages spoken by 95 percent of the world's population.[15]

Jesus Film has been translated into 848 languages[16] with 226 more in progress.[17] The film, seen by 5.6 billion people, has been viewed in 236 countries, 176 of which showed it on television.[18] And more than 195.2 million people have indicated decisions to accept Jesus after watching the film.[19] Respected Missiologist Patrick Johnstone writes, "I reckon that there are now about 3,000,000 congregations of all kinds in the world today."[20]

FIGURE 3

THE SPREAD OF CHRISTIANITY-TWO MILLENIA OF EVANGELIZING THE WORLD

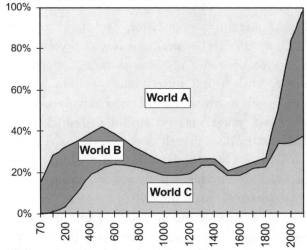

Patrick Johnstone. THE CHURCH IS BIGGER THAN YOU THINK. 1998. p67.

This isn't an indefinite exercise. World A is that part of the world that hasn't heard the gospel and lacks a viable church within its culture from which to hear it. World B consists of people who live where it is likely they will hear the gospel in their lifetime. World C is Christian. Note that by 2050, Patrick Johnstone figures that there will be an effective church in every culture, thereby enabling everyone to hear and believe!

The Wycliffe Bible Translators state: "By the year 2025, together with partners worldwide, we aim to see a Bible translation program begun in all the remaining languages that need one."[21]

This is not a pipe dream. There are currently more than 434,000 "alien" missionaries.[22] The "Back to Jerusalem Movement," birthed by a vision in 1920, intends to send 100,000 missionaries, more than one fifth of the grand total today, from China to fulfill the Great Commission in the "10/40 window" between China and Jerusalem.[23] This is an astounding story.

Jesus in Beijing

Chinese Christianity itself is extraordinary. In 1949, on the eve of the communist takeover, the population of China was approximately 550 million. The Christian Church was just getting a foothold, with 3 million Roman Catholics and fewer than 750,000 Protestants. Then came the forced communization of Mao's red death, and the ensuing persecutions and systematic murder of over 40 million of the Chinese people. At the top of Mao's hit list were political dissidents, religious persons, and the intellectual elite.

Today China boasts of a population of 1.3 billion people. And still, persecution goes on. To be sure, it is not as severe as under Mao, but it continues with sporadic persistency. Most remarkable is that within this bloody soil, the Church has blossomed and bloomed. Reliable estimates such as those from David Aikman, former Beijing bureau chief for *TIME* magazine and author of *Jesus in Beijing*, report that the Roman Catholic Church has grown to 12 million, the approved "3 Self Patriot Church" (i.e. the State Church) has grown to 15 million plus, and the underground non-sanctioned house church movement has grown to 55 million.[24]

We're talking about an astounding 2000 percent increase in 55 years, during which time the population grew by just over 100 percent. The government in China has come to view the house churches similar to the way the Egyptians viewed the Israelites in captivity, "The more they were oppressed, the more they multiplied and spread; so that the Egyptians came to dread the Israelites" (Exod. 1:12).[25] Senior statesmen such as Loren Cunningham of YWAM and C. Peter Wagner of Global Harvest[26] predict that China is on the verge of emerging as one of the dominant Christian nations of the world.

It is the leaders of this same house church movement that are committed to the completion of the Great Commission task. China believes that it has been chosen by God to evangelize the most difficult area of the world: the 10/40 window. When a number of underground house church leaders were asked what they wanted to do to commemorate the 200th year anniversary of the first Protestant missionary Robert Morrison in 2007, they answered that they would like to respond with 100,000 Chinese missionaries who will take up the "Back to Jerusalem" (BTJ) call.

"BTJ refers to a call from God for the Chinese Church to preach the Gospel and establish fellowships of believers in all the countries, cities, towns, and ethnic groups between China and Jerusalem"[27]— traditional strongholds of Islam, Buddhism, Hinduism, and communism. BTJ comprises 100,000 believers, who believe at least 1 in every 10 of them will be martyred, but who are determined to see the path of the ancient silk roads evangelized among the most unreached people of the world.

So impressive has been the explosion of Christian faith around the world that one of the great historians of the missionary movement, Stephen Neill, concluded, "In the twentieth century, for the first time, there was in the world a universal religion—the Christian religion." Stop for just a moment and thank God...you are now living in the first generation in 2,000 years where the mandate of Jesus' words will actually be fulfilled.

SECOND, THE HARVEST IS FUTURE

Again, take a look at this verse: "And this gospel of the kingdom will be preached in the whole world as a testimony to all nations, and then the end will come" (Matt. 24:14).

What end? The words *and then the end will come* (Matt. 24:14) should cause even the most casual Bible reader to sit up and take notice. "The end will come"—it sounds so ominous, so final. What does it mean?

Of course people have been warning of "the end" (of the world) in every generation. But things are different now. The gospel has never gone to the whole world before like it has in this last generation. Say it one more time. *"And this gospel of the kingdom will be preached in the whole world as a testimony to all nations, and then the end will come"* (Matt. 24:14).

Could it be that all that the prophets say in the future is about to happen in our time? Many believe it is.

What is evident from the New Testament is that both Jesus and the apostles knew that what they were living was not the final fulfillment of what the prophets had prophesied.

After the death of Jesus, the disciples thought the work of their Messiah was over, and their reaction was that they were hopelessness and despairing (see Luke 24:21,17). Their reasoning was obvious: "The chief priests and our rulers handed Him [Jesus] over to be sentenced to death, and they crucified Him; *but we had hoped that He was the one who was going to redeem Israel"* (Luke 24:20-21).

What they were hoping for was different than what they were experiencing. To get into the mind of a 1st century Jew—and to comprehend his understanding as to what he was expecting Messiah to do and how God was going to redeem Israel—is to enter a very involved belief system. How could the Messiah suffer and reign at the same time? What about the restoration of all things (see Acts 3:21)? What about...what about...what about?

What Were the Disciples Expecting?

The Jews of Jesus' day expected:

- God to come and establish His Messiah (Christ, anointed one) and set up a Kingdom with no end (Dan. 2:31-45; 7:13, 14; 26-28; Mic. 4:1-8; Zech. 9–14).
- Sin to be dealt with (Isa. 4:2-6; Isa. 53).
- Salvation to touch the whole body; the sick will be healed (Isa. 33:24; 53:4-6).
- That there would be a universal outpouring of the Spirit (Joel 2, Jer. 31:31-37).
- That God would re-establish Israel in the land that He gave them. Israel, as a people, would not be oppressed; God would deal with the oppressor (Zech. 9-14).

- God Himself to establish worldwide peace—a God Utopia (Isa. 2:4; 9:2-6; 11:1 -19).
- The dead to rise (Dan. 12:1-3)!

For any disciple it didn't take much discernment to know that though much of this was started, none of it was fulfilled. None of this happened in totality. In fact, what is worse, Israel, as a nation, rejected her Messiah, and the judgment of God came upon her.

Just Before Jesus' Passion

> As He approached Jerusalem and saw the city, He wept over it and said, "If you, even you, had only known on this day what would bring you peace—but now it is hidden from your eyes. The days will come upon you when your enemies will build an embankment against you and encircle you and hem you in on every side. They will dash you to the ground, you and the children within your walls. They will not leave one stone on another, because you did not recognize the time of God's coming to you (Luke 19:41-44).

Based on Israel's rejection of Jesus as Messiah there was nothing left but judgment. The Romans would demolish them in A.D. 70, destroying the land and slaughtering the people. Historian Josephus reports that, "The number of those that perished during the whole siege...eleven hundred thousand!"[28] Survivors, the 97,000 known as the *diaspora*, were flung into the ends of the world.[29]

The New Testament provides four major clues, called the "untils," that help us understand the events preceding Christ's coming again.

> For I tell you [Jerusalem], you will not see Me again **until** you say, "Blessed is He who comes in the name of the Lord" (Matthew 23:39).

> They will fall by the sword and will be taken as prisoners to all the nations. Jerusalem will be trampled on by the Gentiles **until** the times of the Gentiles are fulfilled (Luke 21:24).

> I do not want you to be ignorant of this mystery, brothers, so that you may not be conceited: Israel has experienced a hardening in part **until** the full number of the Gentiles has come in (Romans 11:25).

The last one is most enlightening:

> He must remain in heaven **until** the time comes for God to restore everything, as He promised long ago to the prophets (Acts 3:21).

After Jesus rose from the dead Luke writes:

> *After His suffering, He showed Himself to these men and gave many*
> *convincing proofs that He was alive. He appeared to them over a*
> *period of forty days and spoke about the kingdom of God (Acts 1:3).*

Jesus began to teach His disciples again after the resurrection to explain the confusion. He taught about the Kingdom. Luke continues:

> *On one occasion, while He was eating with them, He gave them*
> *this command: "Do not leave Jerusalem, but wait for the gift My*
> *Father promised, which you have heard Me speak about. For John*
> *baptized with water, but in a few days you will be baptized with*
> *the Holy Spirit" (Acts 1:4-5).*

As they waited in Jerusalem, Jesus appeared again to them and continued teaching on the Kingdom. What is especially insightful is the disciples' question. The record states:

> *So when they met together, they asked Him,* **"Lord, are You**
> **at this time going to restore the kingdom to Israel?"** *He*
> *said to them: "It is not for you to know the times or dates the*
> *Father has set by His own authority. But you will receive power*
> *when the Holy Spirit comes on you; and you will be My wit-*
> *nesses in Jerusalem, and in all Judea and Samaria, and to the*
> *ends of the earth" (Acts 1:6-8).*

It's amazing to see that, even after crucifixion and resurrection, the disciples are still fixated on the whole topic of when Jesus the Messiah is actually going to "restore" the kingdom to Israel. To them, this is of paramount importance. Deftly, Jesus sidesteps the question and says, "I'm not going to tell you when I am going to restore the kingdom to Israel, but what I will say to you is this, you are going to have power to be witnesses of the message."

Peter's second message, after the occasion of the miraculous healing of the lame man, in Acts 3, highlights the point.

> *Repent, then, and turn to God,*
> **so that** *your sins may be wiped out,*
> **that** *times of refreshing may come from the Lord,*
> **and that** *He may send the Christ, who has been appointed*
> *for you—even Jesus.* **He must remain in heaven until the**
> **time comes for God to restore everything, [How?] as He**
> **promised long ago through His holy prophets....** *Indeed,*
> *all the prophets from Samuel on, as many as have spoken,*
> *have foretold these days (Acts 3:19-24).*

In other words, somewhere between Acts 1:6 and this incident after Pentecost in Acts 3, Peter knew something he didn't know before. That is, if Israelites would hurry up and repent, they would be forgiven, have a time of refreshing, and God would send the Christ back—even Jesus must remain in heaven **until** the time comes for God to "**restore everything**," just like God promised long ago through His holy prophets (see Acts 3:20-21).

Peter finally understood that God will actually answer all the promises of the Old Testament prophets when the world has heard about Jesus. Times of refreshing (revival) will happen everywhere, and just before Jesus returns—then God will restore the Kingdom back to Israel.

This is future. This is the return of Christ and the day of the Lord. This is the end of the age. The fanatical zeal of the early Church was an effort to bring Jesus back.

Concerning Jesus' second coming and the prophets' forecasts of the end of the age, Jesus says:

> And this gospel of the kingdom will be preached in the whole world as a testimony to all nations, and then the end will come (Matthew 24:14).

His next words warn of desolation, tribulation, and the kind of end He foresees:

> Therefore when you see the abomination of desolation which was spoken of through Daniel the prophet, standing in the holy place (let the reader understand)... For then there will be a great tribulation, such as has not occurred since the beginning of the world until now, nor ever will (Matthew 24:15,21 NASB).

Paul writes it this way:

> Concerning the coming of our Lord Jesus Christ and our being gathered to Him [the rapture], we ask you, brothers, not to become easily unsettled or alarmed by some prophecy, report or letter supposed to have come from us, saying that the day of the Lord [the rapture] has already come [see Rev. 16:1]. Don't let anyone deceive you in any way, for that day [the day of the rapture] will not come until the rebellion occurs and the man of lawlessness is revealed, the man doomed to destruction. He will oppose and will exalt himself over everything that is called God or is worshiped, so that he sets himself up in

God's temple [see Matt. 24:15], proclaiming himself to be God And then the lawless one will be revealed, whom the Lord Jesus will overthrow with the breath of His mouth and destroy by the splendor of His coming [see Rev. 19]. The coming of the lawless one will be in accordance with the work of Satan displayed in all kinds of counterfeit miracles, signs and wonders [see Rev. 13] (2 Thessalonians 2:1-9).

And again:

But immediately after the tribulation of those days the sun will be darkened, and the moon will not give its light, and the stars will fall from the sky, and the powers of the heavens will be shaken [compare Rev. 6:13-16; Isa. 24:1,23; 2 Pet. 3:10; Joel 2:30-32; Acts 2:19-20], and then the sign of the Son of Man will appear in the sky [Luke 21:27], and then all the tribes of the earth will mourn [Zech. 12:10; Rev. 1:7], and they will see the Son of Man coming on the clouds of the sky with power and great glory [Dan. 7:13-14]. And He will send forth His angels with a great trumpet [1 Cor. 15:51-52] and they will gather together His elect from the four winds, from one end of the sky to the other (Luke 24:29-31 NASB).

Notice the text: immediately after the tribulation of those days—the great tribulation—Jesus will come. The term "great tribulation" comes from two Greek words: *thlipsis*, meaning anguish and persecution, and *megalee*, meaning exceedingly great.[30] So it's the "mega tribulation"!

The main point of all this is that the Old Testament prophecies are not null and void. Their fulfillment continues and will be ultimately completed just prior to the return of Christ. This will happen when the gospel has gone to every nation and people of the earth and after the mega tribulation immediately preceding the return of Jesus. It is from out of this great tribulation that the great multitude is coming (see Rev. 7:13-14).

WHO ARE THEY AND WHERE DO THEY COME FROM?

We can now read Revelation 7 with new eyes and a new application. If we were to ask the same question of the great multitude and apply it to us we might answer differently than John.

[This] *great multitude… These in white robes*—who are they, and where did they come from? *These are they who have come out of the great tribulation; they have washed their robes and made them white in the blood of the Lamb* (Revelation 7:9,13,15).

When John saw this multitude, he was asked two questions: *"Who are they…and where did they come from?"* (Rev. 7:13). Not wanting to give the wrong answer, John simply said, "You know." Then he was told that "these are they who have come out of the great tribulation"! But since we are the first generation to come within range of fulfilling the words of Jesus, we should ask ourselves the same question. What if Jesus were to come back in the next 50 years? The specifics of the harvest are integral to the mission. Who are they, and where do they come from?

Who are they? They are the poor—women and "children at risk"! Where do they come from? They come from the developing nations!

Who Are They and What Do They Look Like?

Of the 95 percent of the masses who don't live in North America, most are poor. If we were to take the world and make it into a pie, at least three quarters, 75 percent, would be poor.

FIGURE 4

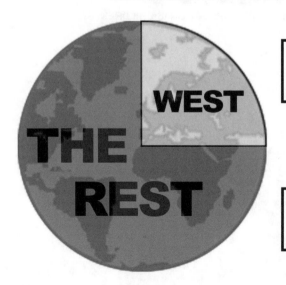

THE WEST VS. THE REST

CONSIDER THIS: 75% OF THE WORLD IS POOR!

The average Gross National Income (GNI) of a quarter of the world is approx. $27,000 USD per person.

The average Gross National Income (GNI) for the rest of the world is approx. $450 - $2,500 USD per person.

Looking at the world from a different angle, half of the world's population, 50 percent, are women. Everyone knows that when the going gets rough, it's the women who suffer more than the men.

FIGURE 5

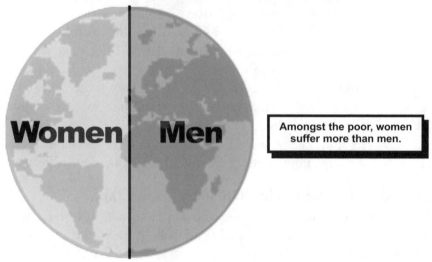

WOMEN VS. MEN
50% OF THE WORLD'S POPULATION ARE WOMEN.

Women   Men

Amongst the poor, women
suffer more than men.

In addition, if we took the world and assessed it by age category, we would find out that about a third are children under the age of 15. In a suffering world, the only ones to endure more than the women are the children.

FIGURE 6

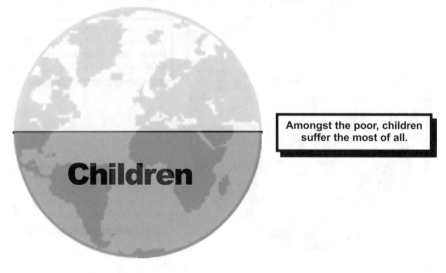

CHILDREN
40% OF THE WORLD'S POPULATION IS CHILDREN.

Children

Amongst the poor, children
suffer the most of all.

Thus when God pours His Spirit out on all flesh, He will land primarily upon the poor who don't live in the West—and who are made up of women and "children at risk."

Reaching "children at risk" and their poor mothers (if they have them) is how the glory of God will cover the earth. Consider this: Of the 1.1 billion people who live on under $1.00 a day, or the nearly half the world (2.7 billion people) existing on less than $2.00 each per day,[31] virtually none of them live in the West. In fact, the average per capita income in America is $35,000, with 35 million (12.1 percent) rated in the poverty zone ($18,392/year for a family of four). Of course, poverty in any country is not fun, but Western poverty is not even close to that of the 1.9 billion children who will be born in the next 10 years—95 percent of them to houses earning less than $1.00 a day! They will all be "children at risk"!

A significant proportion of the world's population, 1.8 billion people, is under the age of 15.[32] UNICEF produced a composite depiction of the global child:

Who Is the Global Child?

There are 2.1 billion children in the world, accounting for 36% of the world's population. Some 132 million children are born each year. One of every 12 children dies before they reach five, mostly from preventable causes.

Of every 100 children born in 2000...

- 53 were born in Asia (19 in India, 15 in China).
- 19 were born in sub-Saharan Africa.
- 9 were born in Latin America and the Caribbean.
- 7 were born in the Middle East and North Africa.
- 5 were born in Eastern Europe, CIS and Baltic States.
- 7 were born in the industrialized nations of Western Europe, USA, Canada, Israel, Japan, Australia and New Zealand.

If social conditions remain unchanged, the following will most likely be their fate:

Birth Registration

- The births of 40 out of every 100 will not be registered. These children will have no official existence or recognition of nationality.

Immunization

- 26 of every 100 will not be immunized against any disease.

Nutrition

- 30 will suffer from malnutrition in their first five years of life.
- Only 46 will be exclusively breastfed for the first three months of life.

Water and Sanitation
- 19 will have no access to clean drinking water.
- 40 will live without adequate sanitation.

Schooling
- 17 of the children will never go to school. Of these, 9 will be girls.
- Of every 100 children who enter 1st grade, 25 will not reach the 5th grade.

Child Labor
- 1 of every 5 children between the ages of 5 and 14 in the developing world will work.
- Half of those who work will do so full time.
- 9 of the 24 children born in Africa will work.
- 11 of the 53 children born in Asia will work.
- 1 of the 8 born in Latin America will work.

Life Expectancy
- These children will live to an average of 63 years.
- In the industrialized world, they will live 78 years.
- In the 45 countries most affected by HIV/AIDS, their average life expectancy is 58 years. In Botswana, Malawi, Mozambique, Rwanda, Zambia, and Zimbabwe—countries heavily affected by HIV/AIDS—life expectancy is less than 43 years.[33]

Where Do They Come From?

We know who they are. They are the poor. But *"where do they come from"* (Rev. 7:13)? We believe that the great multitude is emerging from the masses of humanity in the developing nations.

A simple comparison of populations will show that the bulk of humanity who will make up the great multitude that no one can count, from every nation, tribe, people, and language, do not live in the wealthy West. This is hard for us who live up here in the peaceful Dominion of Canada (so named to signify that God shall have dominion from sea to sea—Ps. 72:8) to comprehend. Here, on the second largest country of the world, dwell a meager 30 million people—most of which are hugging the U.S. border to keep warm. (The bulk of Canada's population lives within 100 miles of the American border.) Yet, consider the following illustration.

The city that I (Wesley) live in is a resort city (Kelowna, BC) known as a tourist capital of the nation. It boasts a population of 100,000. We have over 100 churches, some of which range between 1,000 and 2,000 members. If we are honest, we mostly tend to fixate on our local churches as we try to reach the rest of the city for Jesus, spending most of our budgets on ourselves.

In contrast, I think of the time we traveled through Tokyo, Japan. I was shocked to learn that there were apartment buildings with over 100,000 people in each building. I couldn't believe it. Single apartment buildings were bigger (had more people) than my whole city, and that is in a nation in which the Christian population is less than 3 percent!

At another time we were part of a year-long revival in Mexico City. All the leaders were quick to boast that the population of greater Mexico City was around 28 million, making it the largest in the world! I was shocked to find that in this one *city* there were almost as many people as were in our whole *country!* Even the mighty United States has a population of only 290 million—one-twentieth of the population of the earth.

When these numbers are compared to the staggering populations of China (1.3 billion), India (1 billion), or sub-Saharan Africa (665 million), we cannot help but be confronted with the obvious—the masses don't live here! When God's Spirit is poured out on *all* flesh, there will be a whole lot more flesh in China, India, Southeast Asia, and Africa on which this holy fire will be poured out.

COMPARING GEOGRAPHICAL LOCATIONS AND POPULATIONS

The maps clearly demonstrate the world's regions by population, wealth, and religion. This graphically portrays the enormous disparities.

FIGURE 7

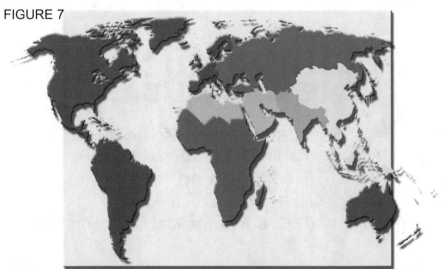

Regions of the World
Population of the World: 6,314,000,000
Nations of the World: 193

FIGURE 8

Western World
Population: **909 Million**
Gross National Income, sum per capita (USD):
$26,950.00
Main Religions & / or Beliefs:
Christianity and Secular Humanism

(Mostly the 24 Western Developed Nations)

INCLUDING 7 OF THE 25 MOST POPULOUS NATIONS:

USA, Japan, Germany, France, UK, Italy & South Korea

FIGURE 9

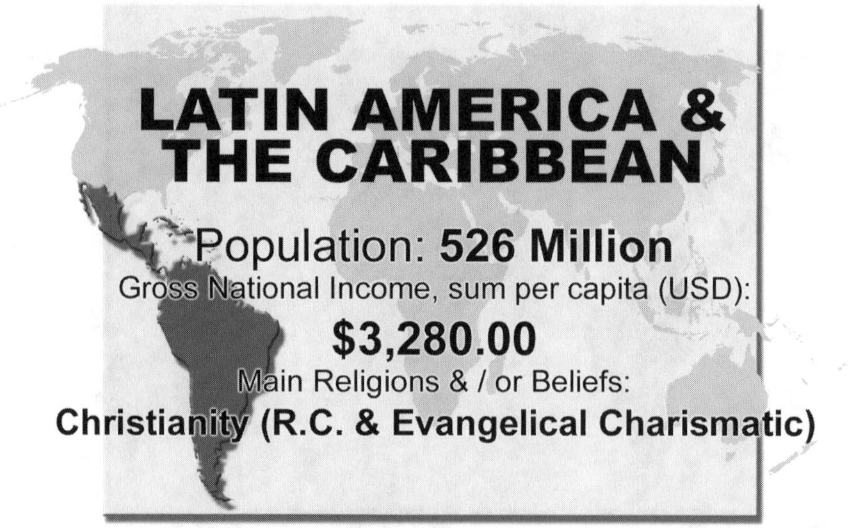

LATIN AMERICA & THE CARIBBEAN
Population: **526 Million**
Gross National Income, sum per capita (USD):
$3,280.00
Main Religions & / or Beliefs:
Christianity (R.C. & Evangelical Charismatic)

(30 Developing Nations)

INCLUDING 2 OF THE 25 MOST POPULOUS NATIONS:
Brazil & Mexico

FIGURE 10

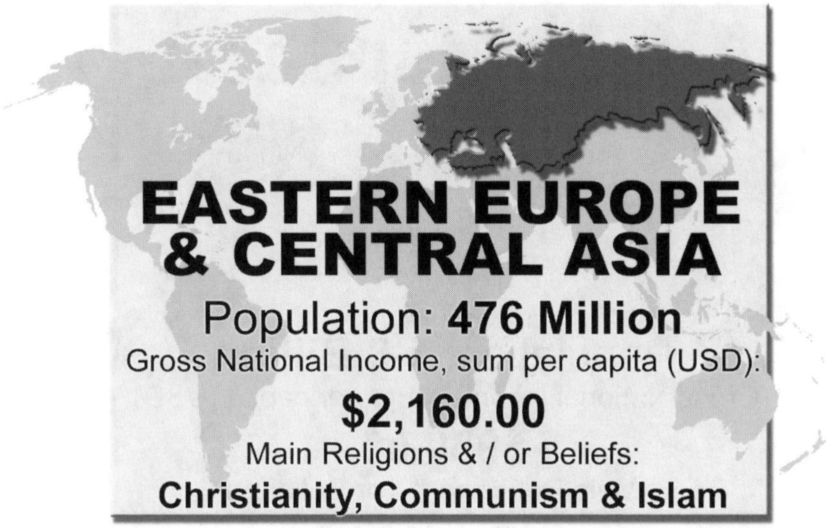

EASTERN EUROPE & CENTRAL ASIA

Population: 476 Million

Gross National Income, sum per capita (USD):

$2,160.00

Main Religions & / or Beliefs:

Christianity, Communism & Islam

(30 Developing Nations)
INCLUDING 2 OF THE 25 MOST POPULOUS NATIONS:
Russia &Turkey

FIGURE 11

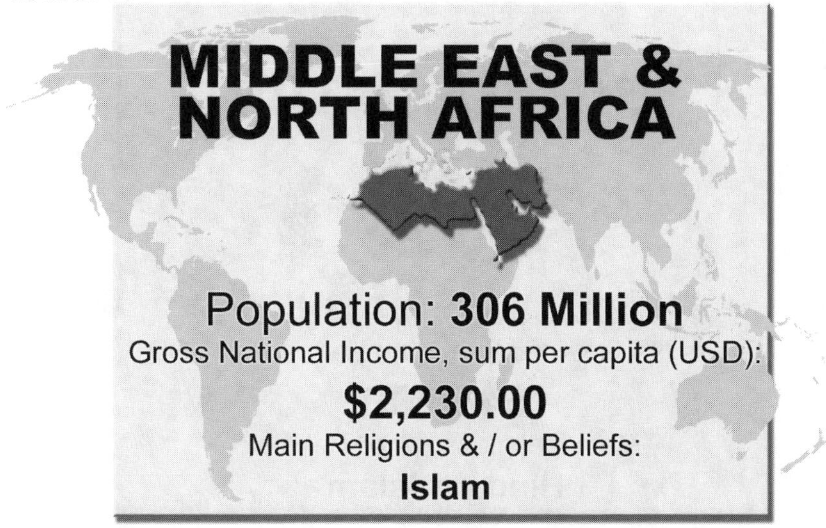

MIDDLE EAST & NORTH AFRICA

Population: 306 Million

Gross National Income, sum per capita (USD):

$2,230.00

Main Religions & / or Beliefs:

Islam

(15 Developing Nations)
INCLUDING 4 OF THE 25 MOST POPULOUS NATIONS:
Egypt, Iran, Saudi Arabia & Yemen

FIGURE 12

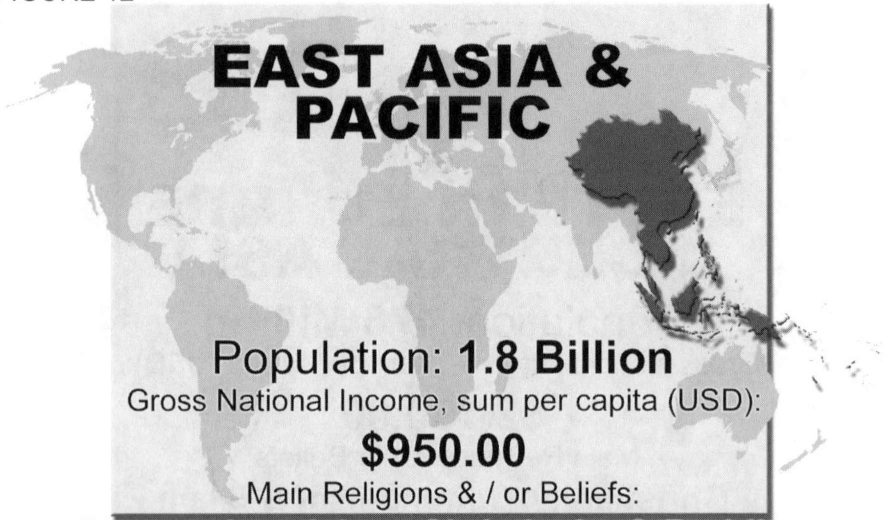

EAST ASIA & PACIFIC

Population: **1.8 Billion**
Gross National Income, sum per capita (USD):
$950.00
Main Religions & / or Beliefs:
Communism, Islam, Christianity & Buddism
(24 Developing Nations)
INCLUDING 4 OF THE 25 MOST POPULOUS NATIONS:
China, Indonesia, Philippines & Vietnam

FIGURE 13

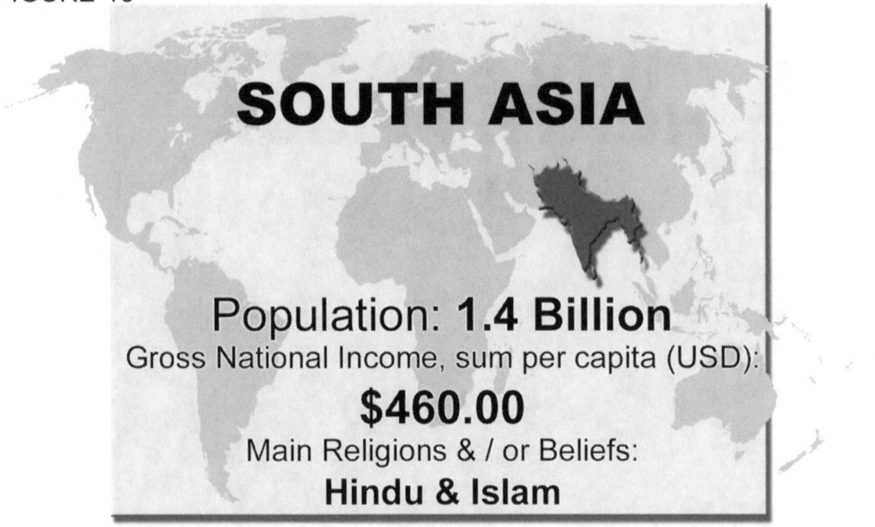

SOUTH ASIA

Population: **1.4 Billion**
Gross National Income, sum per capita (USD):
$460.00
Main Religions & / or Beliefs:
Hindu & Islam

(Indian Sub-Continent - 8 Developing Nations)
INCLUDING 3 OF THE 25 MOST POPULOUS NATIONS:
India, Pakistan & Bangladesh

FIGURE 14

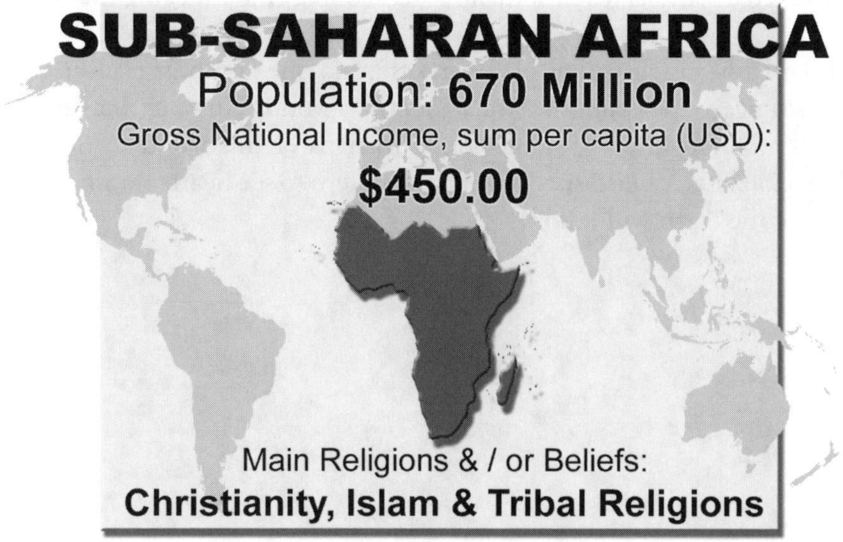

SUB-SAHARAN AFRICA
Population: 670 Million
Gross National Income, sum per capita (USD):
$450.00

Main Religions & / or Beliefs:
Christianity, Islam & Tribal Religions

(48 Developing Nations)

INCLUDING 3 OF THE 25 MOST POPULOUS NATIONS:
Nigeria, Ethiopia & Congo Democratic Republic

NOT AT RISK?

It's one thing to decry the current state of things and things to come. It's quite another to diagnose the problem and prescribe a solution. Viva Network founder Patrick McDonald argues that there are seven essentials that, when present in a child's life, will effectively neutralize the seven deadly sins to which we will shortly introduce you.

What a child needs in order to *not* to be at risk include the following seven essentials in their growth:

1. at least one loving parent
2. good health
3. safety
4. equipping with marketable skills (beginning with school)
5. an opportunity to serve others
6. an opportunity to hear and understand the gospel
7. an opportunity to be part of a Christ-centered worshiping community.

Whenever one of those seven doesn't exist, there's trouble. We believe that God wants every child to have an opportunity to become all He intends and the seven essentials will inform any local strategy for attacking the seven deadly sins.

If our Father is clear that He desires that no one perish, it is clear that we need to engage the young and the poor of this world. This is a trumpet call to the 680 million Great Commission Christians of this world to rise up. Mobilize. Catalyze. Metastasize. Begin to take steps to see hearts transformed. The face of the earth will follow.

CHAPTER NINE

SEVEN DEADLY SINS

I was hungry and you gave Me something to eat; I was thirsty and you gave Me drink. I was a stranger and you invited Me in; naked and you clothed Me; I was sick and you visited Me; I was in prison and you came to Me (Jesus, in Matthew 25:35-36).

This is pure and undefiled religion in the sight of our God and Father, to visit orphans and widows in their distress, and to keep oneself unstained by the world (James, in James 1:27).

Righteousness and justice are the foundation of His throne (Psalm 89:4).

Heroes of revival bring a new order that, in the civil realm, is founded on social justice. Revival is characterized by faith that transforms society.

There is no dichotomy between righteousness and justice. They are twins in the biblical understanding of social interrelations.

What follows is a contemporary primer on social justice followed by an attack plan. To strategize effectively we must know the lay of the land, the social conditions of the world. There are seven scourges in millennium three, seven deadly sins if you will, that the end-time harvest must address as the Hero Army accomplishes a righteous revolution. Sins, in this case, are not things of which the people are guilty, but things of which they are victims. Our Seven Deadly Sins are sins against humanity:

- Dirt Poor
- Children in Chains
- Orphans of the Street
- Sex and the City
- AIDS and Plagues
- War-Affected Children
- Religious Persecution

Granted, there is much overlap with several of these categories, as children are orphaned by parents with AIDS, as poor children are sold into slavery, or as wartime conditions cause famine. But the conditions described are enough to shake the peace of anyone seeking to satisfy God with righteousness alone. Yes, righteousness, first, but not righteousness alone.

There is no biblical dichotomy between righteousness and justice.

> He has showed you, O man, what is good. And what does the Lord require of you? To act **justly** and to love mercy and to walk humbly with your God (Micah 6:8).

As we've described in outlining God's big idea of transforming invisible people into People people through three essential actions—justice, righteousness, and compassion—the Hebrew word rendered "justly" is mishpat, which means "the way prescribed, the rightful action, or the appropriate mode of life."[1] Throughout the Bible mishpat justice is closely related to righteousness. As Isaiah reports, "This is what the Lord says, 'Maintain justice and do what is right, for My salvation is close at hand and My righteousness will soon be revealed' " (Isa. 56:1).

In fact, God's rule is based on these virtues:

> Righteousness and justice are the foundation of Your throne. Love and faithfulness go before You (Psalm 89:14).
> But let justice roll on like a river, righteousness like a never-failing stream (Amos 5:24).

Holiness is the solution to every problem. This is true in that as the righteous revolution spans the globe, as an increasing portion of the population establishes God's standard by God's Spirit in their lives, the social inequities will disintegrate. Each of the seven scourges will be overturned as the world's population comprehends the truth that holiness is the solution to every problem.

The mission is not compromised. It remains the goal to win the world for Jesus. But, as respected missionary Amy Carmichael noted, "Souls are more or less attached to bodies."[2] And so, out of the natural overflow of a sanctified heart saturated with compassion, we obey William Booth's exhortation to, "Go and do something!" And the face of the earth will change as the hearts of its people are transformed.

But look at the statistics: The 10/40 window contains 1.3 billion people with little chance to hear the gospel. Fully 85 percent of the world's poorest countries are here, and 40 percent of these populations are children. Tragically, only 1.2 percent of Christian mission dollars go there.[3] Gerald Coates, "March for Jesus" co-founder, says: "The predicament of such children is a barometer for the state of humanity at the brink of a new millennium."[4]

We've got to agree by now that righteousness and justice are not mutually exclusive, that the hearts change the face. And, even if we have to look farther than outside our kitchen window, we can imagine that all is not well on the face of the earth. How bad is it?

The unofficial shadow economy is estimated to be $9 trillion (USD), compared with the 1998 global GDP as tabulated by IMF to be $39 trillion (USD).[5] There are no regulations or law to protect the marginalized from barter, bribe, and illegal activities that include illicit drugs, street children, child labor, sexual exploitation, and more. The shadow economy rides the backs of poor children.

We know that there are 1.3 billion Chinese. But now there are also 1 billion Indians.[6] The world population is exploding, and with it the seven deadly sins comprise a spreading Hydra-headed pandemic. Know thy enemy.

Warning: This may be numbing to your senses. Please don't turn off emotionally. Read carefully. This chapter will introduce you to our version of the seven deadly sins.

DEADLY SIN #1—DIRT POOR

- *I was hungry and you gave Me something to eat; I was thirsty and you gave Me drink… I was naked and you clothed Me.*

—Jesus

- *However, there should be no poor among you, for in the land the Lord your God is giving you to possess as your inheritance, He will richly bless you, if only you fully obey the Lord your God and are careful to follow all these commands I am giving you today* (Deuteronomy 15:4-5).

- *Give generously to him and do so without a grudging heart; then because of this the Lord your God will bless you in all your work and in everything you put your hand to. There will always be poor people in the land. Therefore I command you to be openhanded toward your brothers and toward the poor and needy in your land* (Deuteronomy 15:10-11).

Every year our grade seven students line up for a long needle from the health nurse that immunizes our children from a laundry list of diseases. Every day 6,000 kids in a very different part of the world where the grade seven students don't wait in those lines die because they don't.[7]

A partner in Africa watched a little boy he knew called Zachary playing all day with twigs underneath a tree. Eventually the priest wandered out to see Zac, on the way picking a mango from the tree for him.

While they chatted, the boy played with the mango. Finally the priest said to Zac: "Well go on, eat it." Zac replied: "I can't Father, it's not my turn to eat today." That little boy was living the reality of many, many people in the poorest countries who have so little food that they have a rota to decide who eats on which day.[8]

Jesus called it hunger (in its rawest form)—famine. Without food, a person dies. It is not inconsequential that the Christian world has led the response to famine. *World Vision, Christian Children's Fund, Tear Fund*, and others have struggled to meet the challenges of a starving two-thirds world in the company of a first world that lives in the lap of luxury.

Even secular organizations are fueled by a Christian worldview inasmuch as they recognize that there is something sacred about humanity. It is not the Hindu, nor the Confucianist, nor the Islamic philosophies that have spurred this important work, but the Christian worldview. So it is incumbent upon Christians to become acquainted with what in the world we are doing, and how each of us can help.

Poverty is something that affects us all. No one who has experienced revival can turn a deaf ear to the poor. They are everywhere. We're talking about the real poor here. There are some who are poor by Western standards and who have access to social mechanisms that facilitate the basic needs such as food, shelter, and clothing.

There are others, who through addictions and other personal life choices find themselves on the street, and exclude themselves from even these social nets.

But there is another face of the real poor about which many in the West know nothing.

This is the world poor—the real poor—people who can do nothing to change their situations. They need our help.

A modern option is to raise up entrepreneurs for social justice. We can help to create work and capital along the vision of William Booth. His vision became the social net for the Western world.

We must go farther, to the rest of the world.

What we take for granted in our social welfare system emerged from the application of this same principle by Christians, whether the Benevolent Empire or the primitive Salvation Army. With the advent of the global village we are obliged to let our compassion bleed beyond our borders to help our neighbors, halfway across the world.

There is a call to the marketplace apostles who are not leading churches, who are not planting mission stations, and are not doing evangelistic campaigns. These marketplace apostles are no less apostolic than the more familiar gifts of the Body. They are akin to the Old Testament righteous kings who used their wealth, expertise, and authority on behalf of the poor.

Where are the business leaders, who themselves manage multi-million dollar endeavors, who will raise up these entrepreneurs for the poor?

Holy Cow!

North American journalist Paul Harvey commented on the relationship between people's religious beliefs and poverty. "There is no way that you and I are ever going to comprehend a society that feeds cows and starves babies," Harvey writes, speaking of the land of India and his understanding of the Hindu religion's sacred cows.

But one wonders which culture, India's or affluent Western nations, has the most "sacred cows." While our sacred cows are not part of recognizable religious traditions, American families feed their cattle 1,800 pounds of protein-rich grain in order to produce 250 pounds of meat for our dinner table.[9]

Even if this seems improper so close to your dinner table, it might help to hear the way *TIME* magazine reports it: This industry is so big that in Texas, 18 kg. of cow manure per Texan per day is created.[10]

Setting the Stage

The following cold numbers welcome us into the inequities of the two-thirds world, where there are so many quality of life casualties, and, in which, most people are dirt poor. Read sensitively, the statistics are breathtaking.

In 2001 UNICEF estimated that 1.2 billion people live in poverty, and the number is increasing. These people earn less than $1 per day.[11] Half the world—nearly 3 billion people—lives on less than $2 a day.[12] By October 2003, a new UNICEF study concluded that more than 1 billion children around the world are suffering from the debilitating effects of poverty.[13] One third of the world population is under 15, and 80 percent of these live in the third world.[14]

In fact, the Gross Domestic Product of the poorest 48 *countries* is less than the wealth of the world's three richest people. Or, to expand the comparison further, a few hundred millionaires now own as much wealth as the world's poorest 2.5 billion people.[15] Twenty percent of the people in developed nations, that's most of us reading this, consume 86 percent of the world's goods.[16] Bluntly put, we're pigs. In 1960, the 20 percent of the world's people in the richest countries had 30 times the income of the poorest 20 percent—in 1997, 74 times as much.[17] Let us correct ourselves, we're rich pigs.

It is incumbent upon those of us living in the Western world to ante up to mitigate the inequities. And yet our track record, as the "holy cow" comparison intimates, stinks.

Added to that embarrassment, the wealthiest nation on earth had the widest gap between rich and poor of any industrialized nation.[18] America is not the model to follow. Disastrously, the developing world now spends $13 on debt repayment for every $1 it receives in grants.[19] And here's a similar travesty: the poorer the country, the more likely it is that debt repayments are being extracted directly from people who neither contracted the loans nor received any of the money.[20]

What are the repercussions?

Here are a few:

- 2 million children die each year because they have not been immunized[21];

- "The lives of 17 million children were needlessly lost in 2000 because world governments have failed to reduce poverty levels"[22];

Have you ever had diarrhea? So have 300,000 poor children. They died of it, this year.[23] Almost 11 million children under age 5 died in 2000, mostly from preventable diseases.

Stop, read that again. Nearly 11 million under the age of 5 died in 2000, mostly from preventable diseases.[24] The Boeing 747-100SR airplane seats 550 people. It is like stacking a 747-100SR full of kids and then downing it into the ocean, every 24 minutes, every hour, every day, every week of the year.[25] Have a nice sleep tonight.

How do we know that it's not getting any better? Because 97 percent of the world's population growth takes place in the developing world.[26] This is true despite the sad fact that the infant mortality rate per 1000 births is 7 in northern Europe, 51 in South America, and 108 in Eastern Africa.[27] And, as if to help the odds, China has begun officially acting to enforce the baby-limit law, aborting 20,000 babies in one summer month of 2001.[28] The tragedy is that these abortive measures are celebrated by the United Nations Population Fund's Beijing representative Sven Burmester for having, "achieved the impossible. The country has solved its population problem."[29]

Responsibility

The Church will understand we are called not just to give to the poor, but to be in relationship with the poor. Casual giving to soothe our consciences will be replaced by vital action, where our lives will intertwine with the poor, and we will see we have lessons to learn that only they can teach us.[30]

Today, you woke up, ate breakfast, worked a long day, and settled back for some light reading. On this day, according to the Kids AIDS Site, 1,800 children were infected with HIV.[31] In the time it has taken to read the last couple of pages, 5 people between the ages of 10 and 24 have acquired the virus.[32]

Yes, we already have a section on AIDS. Yes, it is a lifestyle issue. But don't be deceived. It is very largely a poverty issue. The fact is, 95 percent of people with HIV live in the developing world.[33] Every day 400 to 500 Zambians are infected with the AIDS virus.[34] In 1995, Action International estimated that by 2000, 2 million people would be infected with HIV. But

182 BE A HERO

NETAID reports that in 1999 alone, 5.4 million people became infected with HIV! This is an accelerating plague.[35]

NETAID also reports that 2.8 million people died of AIDS in 1999. There are 10 million children orphaned in sub-Saharan Africa by AIDS. In some countries, 10 percent of the children under 15 have been orphaned by AIDS. *TIME* magazine estimates that there may be 30 million more by 2010.[36] Early in the new millennium, experts predicted that *more people will die of AIDS in the next decade than have died in all the wars of the 20th century.*[37] The vast majority of these people are living in the two-thirds world. They are poor.

How poor are they? Read the last two sentences of the last paragraph again. Okay, during that time, someone died of hunger. In fact, according to The Hunger Site, every 3.6 seconds someone dies of hunger—75 percent are children.[38] A child born today in the developing world has a 4 out of 10 chance of living in extreme poverty.[39]

The United Nations estimates that 800 million people live in the condition of chronic, persistent hunger and malnutrition, about 100 times as many as those who actually die of it every year.[40] Several countries, such as Benin, Burkina Faso, Central African Republic, Chad, Ethiopia, Guinea, Mali, Nepal, Niger, and Sierra Leone, are comprised of populations more than half of which are living in poverty.[41]

> Rural populations are driven further into poverty as they compete for scarce natural resources. Women and children now on average spend four to six hours a day searching for fuel wood and four to six hours a week drawing and carrying water… Worldwide, the number of such "environmental refugees" from the survival economy may be as high as 500 million today and the figure is growing.[42]

Over the last 20 years, as the world economy increased exponentially, the number of people living in poverty grew to more than 1.2 billion, or one in every five persons, including more than 600 million children.[43]

And even in the great USA, in 1999, a year marked by good economic news, 31 million Americans were food insecure, meaning that they were either hungry or unsure of where their next meal would come from. Twelve million of these were children.[44]

According to the UN Poverty Report 2000, "The foundation of poverty reduction is self-organization of the poor at the community level—the best antidote to powerlessness, a central source of poverty. Organized, the poor can influence local government and hold it accountable."[45] However, this is made increasingly complicated by lack of education.

Nearly a billion people entered the 21st century unable to read a book or sign their names.[46] "Tell them to go to school!"

More than 20 percent of primary school-aged children in developing countries are not in school,[47] and 130 million of these are primary school age children who have no access to education.[48] What can we do? Here's an idea: Less than one percent of what the world spends every year on weapons was needed to put every child into school by the year 2000.[49] Less than one percent!

So, for example, using statistics provided by PRAVDA, as of May 3, 2001, let's take the number of Submarine Launched Ballistic Missiles (SLBM) that USA and Russia have at the ready: 3,616 and 2,024 respectively.[50] As far as SLBMs are concerned, the Americans would just need to cut 362, while the Russians only need to reduce by 202. That would still leave them with a combined 5,076 SLBMs aimed at each other. That should be enough.

There are many related concerns, such as stunted babies due to malnourished pregnant mothers, and the millions of children who give birth every year in a state of ill-preparedness economically and socially to raise children.[51] But clearly we, as humans, let alone Christians, are obliged to fight to win the war against poverty, so as, if for no other reason, to live out the love with which Jesus infuses us and maintain integrity in our evangelistic efforts. We must, "Give a damn."[52]

A Hero Army will see to it that this heinous monster is confronted and vanquished in the power of the Holy Spirit. The silver and the gold is Yahweh's, and He is the Commander of the Army. He will release resources and change wills such that the poor will receive biblical justice, righteousness, and compassion, being transformed in the process into People people.

DEADLY SIN #2—CHILDREN IN CHAINS
The World's Most Endangered Species

> *The Israelites groaned in their slavery and cried out, and their cry*
> *for help because of their slavery went up to God. God heard their*
> *groaning…God looked on the Israelites and was concerned about*
> *them* (Exodus 2:23-25).

This is Shankar, a child in bondage at 6 years old:

> *I was very small and I am still small. I used to have to*
> *handle the heavy instruments to cut the knots in each carpet.*

Many times, my thumbs and fingers were injured when the cutter slipped. Then I would cry for my mother, but the Master would only beat me. He never took me to the hospital or gave me any medicine. What he used to do was, to take a match stick and fill the cut with the match stick powder then he would set fire to it with another match so that my skin and blood would bond together. I would cry for my mother, and he would beat me again.[53]

It's a global village.[54] And so the recent price war between the multinational chocolate bar manufacturers impacted all of us. Some of us benefited; others were hurt. I benefited. I could get sale prices on my favorite chocolate bars and go on a bit of a binge. Victor didn't benefit.[55] While I binged, he was conscripted into child slavery, slogging long hours in the cocoa fields of Ivory Coast. He literally slaved to support my habit. And it paid off, too, royally, at least for his "owners," who, along with other perpetrators of this crime against humanity, raked in $7 billion last year.[56]

One third of the world population is under 15.[57] That is 2.1 billion people. Any world-transforming revival is going to be youth-flavored. And yet, this is the world's most endangered species—its least protected species. Children are under attack from all sorts of forces and all sorts of places.

Statistics vary on the magnitude of the problem of child labor. *UNICEF* estimates that between 100 and 200 million children are forced to work, worldwide, some as slaves, and some to support families.[58] *ChildHope* concludes that, "As many as 300 million children under the age of 15 are being exploited for their labor worldwide."[59] And 27 million of these are plain slaves.[60] It seems apparent that the crisis is growing.

6 Cents A Day

John Miller, senior advisor on international slavery to the Secretary of State, says, "Gary Haugen is one of the heroes of our time."[61] International Justice Mission founder Gary Haugen, puts a name and a face on one invisible person:

Take the case of another child, named Shawna. When she was 7, she was living with her very, very poor family in a village in India. Her mother was giving birth to her baby brother and needed about $25 to pay for a doctor. The only way they could get $25 was from the local moneylender, who demanded that the family sell Shawna to him. She was made to roll cigarettes by hand six days a week, 12 hours a day, sitting in one place on the floor. If Shawna didn't roll 2,000 cigarettes a day, she was beaten. She was paid about six cents a day.

After three years, when we met her at 10 years of age, she was not one penny closer to paying off her debt. This is bonded slavery. While it is illegal in India, we believe there are some 15 million children in such circumstances there, rolling cigarettes, making jewelry, making fireworks, and breaking rocks with little hammers.[62]

And three years is nothing. Haugen's International Justice Mission (IJM) freed a man who was a child when he took a debt of $4.00, **58 years ago!**[63] His children had been enslaved for their whole lives, toiling to help their father pay off that miniscule debt. It is a pandemic, affecting several areas of the world. IJM and other worthies are fighting to bring hope in a hopeless situation. World Vision reports that "60% of all children in Asian cities are full-time wage earners. Child prostitution is one of the principal means of making money."[64] In Africa, estimates are that 25 percent of the children between the ages of 10 and 14 are involved in labor.[65]

Reports are that children comprise 17 percent of Africa's labor force.[66] Estimates for India show that as many as 126 million children are child laborers.[67] The government reckons it to be 18 million![68] An estimated 12 million children work in Nigeria alone,[69] and 153 million children work in Asia, 80 million in Africa, and 17.5 million in Latin America.[70] Prostitution and trafficking of women and children is the third largest income-earner globally. The only two bigger are drug-trafficking and arms sales.[71] These are mind-boggling figures. Let us help you put some flesh on them. Meet a sugar-cane worker, named Rosie.

> I am Rosie Baroquillo. I started working on the sugar cane field when I was seven years old. Now I am nine and I still work in the field. I stopped going to school because my family could not afford to spend the money. My father is already dead.
>
> The money I earn is not enough to buy food. I am tired and hungry doing my work in the field. I wish I could have soup to go with the rice I eat because without soup it is hard to swallow.[72]

Persons sometimes are sold into virtual slavery. Many boys from India, some of whom are as young as four years, end up as riders in camel races in West Asia and the Gulf States, especially to the United Arab Emirates, or begging during the Haj.[73]

Drop Dead Prices

Soccer is the world's favorite sport. Dirt-poor fans all over the earth pay small fortunes to catch some of the world's richest people kick around a ball hand-stitched by children. In Pakistan, a recent study by *Save the Children Fund* found that more than 15,000 children are used to stitch footballs by hand. In India, an NGO report released last year suggested that upwards of 10,000 children were being used, but the sporting goods industry claims to only know of 70 child laborers.[74] "Far off in Asia, most of the world's soccer balls are being produced under fear and exploitation. Under the tight control of their employers, children and adults in Pakistan and India are made to stitch footballs at drop dead prices."[75]

The Cost of a Coffee

As you might imagine, numbers like these generate enormous opportunities for profit in the black market, so the child labor market is a bullet growth industry. *Newsweek* recently reported that in 2000, the Chinese government crackdown caught dozens of traffickers and freed 110,000 women and 13,000 children.[76] Some 200,000 children are trafficked every year in West and Central Africa. These children are employed on fishing vessels and farms, in prostitution and sweatshops.[77]

The number of trafficked children being intercepted at the Benin border has risen from 117 in 1995 to 1,081 two years later.[78] In 1997, Benin police arrested five West Africans caught preparing to ship 90 child slaves to Gabon after they had bought the youngsters in Benin and Togo for as little as $1.50—the cost of a coffee. The situation is so bad that CNN reports that on April 17, 2001, UNICEF spokesman Alfred Ironside asserted, "The slave trade never stopped in West Africa."[79]

American Cigarettes

There was a time when American cigarettes were made by slaves. Today, there is a trendy teen cigarette made with triple the nicotine of regular cigarettes and rolled in leaves, complete with sweetener in chocolate and bubble gum flavor. These American cigarettes are made by slaves—today. CBS's *60 Minutes* exposed the child slave system in India that forces children as young as five to roll quotas of up to 1,000 of these *bidis*, as they are called, every day for no recompense and with only the threat of beatings as incentive.[80] Think of that during your next drag.

"Eating My Flesh, Drinking Our Blood"

The most infamous scandal of the early third millennium was coined "The Chocolate Slaves." On May 4, 2001, BBC News reported that the Ivory Coast government blamed international chocolate companies for artificially sustaining low cocoa prices, and, in so doing, forcing some farmers in poverty to use child slave labor. Prime Minister Pascal Affi N'Guessan outright blamed them.[81]

More than 90 percent of cocoa from Ivory Coast—the world's biggest producer of cocoa—is procured by the sweat of child labor, according to *Slavery*, a documentary broadcast on British television. When the documentary filmmakers asked the former slave, known as Victor, if he had ever tasted chocolate, he said "no." When they asked him what he would say to the millions of Britons who ate chocolate daily, Victor answered: "If I had to say something to them it would not be nice words. They buy something I suffer to make. They are eating my flesh."[82] Or, as Sali Kante, director of Save the Children in Mali put it: "People who are drinking cocoa or coffee are drinking their blood."[83]

It truly is a global village. Our behavior, for good or for evil, affects everyone. Invisible people must be made to be People people. Victor was created to be more than a slave for our passions.

How do we initially respond to that? Don't buy Easter eggs and tell your children why.

DEADLY SINS #3—ORPHANS OF THE STREET

I was a stranger and you invited Me in.

—Jesus

It's a wet cold. Whatever that means. To me it means adding a scarf, a toque, and mitts to my thick overcoat. To Red it means scaring up another cardboard box, the thicker the better, to bolster the cardboard hut that surrounded the massive vents on Queen's Park in Toronto. You know that it shoots up warm air from the subway system. The trick is to be airtight, not to allow that warm air out. It is a goal that constantly evades Red and friends. The costs of failure are high. On a particularly frozen night, it meant death for one of his friends who fell asleep with incomplete coverage. It's just another statistic—another invisible person no longer a strain on our welfare rolls.

One third of the world population is under 15.[84] And the world is getting younger! It is anticipated that between 1998 and 2025, 4.5 billion children will be born.[85] Not surprisingly, these babies are not being born in the affluent Western world. Of all the children born today, 80 percent live in developing countries in Asia, Africa, and some parts of Europe where extreme poverty is prevalent.[86] The urgency of the hour is punctuated by the newly minted 4/14 window—85 percent of Christians get saved between age 4-14.[87] While these kids should be getting saved at camp and in Sunday school they are scrounging for discarded food from garbage dumps in our mega-cities.

"Throwaway" Culture

At least 100 million children worldwide are believed to live at least part of the time on the streets.[88] According to the *New York Times*, the U.S. government believes that its country contributes about half a million under-age runaways and "throwaways" to this total.[89] "The present day numbers of street children in single cities like Calcutta may be equal to the total population of those cities in the [19th] century."[90] Homeless children in Brazil number around 12 million.[91] That is a city the size of Mexico City nearly filled with homeless children!

> *Enkhbold, now 10, lived on the streets for more than three years. Ekhbold's mother left when the children were young. His father was imprisoned for theft. Enkhbold, aged 6, and his sister, aged 13, ended up running away.*
>
> *He was wandering alone on the city streets, cold and bored, when another boy asked him to join his group in an underground tunnel. Enkhbold was the youngest and smallest of the 10 children in the tunnel so they nicknamed him "Youngst." Although the tunnel was cramped, dark and stinking, it was still the best option for him. Enkhbold made a living by begging and using the money to buy bread and ice cream, and sometimes a candle to light his way in the tunnel.*
>
> *One winter's day, social workers from World Vision provided the group with hot meals. Soon they asked if he would like to live in the street children's centre. Enkhbold thought, "I don't know what the centre is like, but as I do not like living in this hole, I better go with them." So he did and the Light House became his new home.[92]*

Worldwide we're talking about one child in every classroom who lives on the street. Of course, most of these kids never see the inside of a classroom. Their lives can be close to hell on earth. "In Western and Third World countries, sexual abuse is a chief reason why girls turn to life on the street."[93] Of Latin America's 40 million street children,[94] half are estimated to be addicted to inhalants.[95] It is estimated that as many as 130,000 street children exist daily in Nairobi, often high from snorting glue, who sleep in the streets and in alleyways, who panhandle and scavenge for food, shoeless and barely clothed.[96] There are about 200,000 orphans in Rwanda as a result of the civil war.[97]

> Sunil was 12, a carpenter's son. He lived with his parents and seven brothers and sisters in Jayaprakashnagar, the shanty-town nearest to Union Carbide's pesticide factory.

> As the clock on Bhopal's distant railway station struck 1 a.m. on 3rd December 1984, the family woke in their small house, with their mouths and throats burning and their eyes stinging.

> The family ran outside to find a panic-stricken crowd stampeding through the narrow, dimly-lit alley.

> The force of the human torrent wrenched the children's hands from their parents' grasp. The family was whirled apart. Sunil heard his mother calling their names, then she was gone.

> The toxic cloud was so dense and searing that people were reduced to near blindness. As they gasped for breath, its effects grew ever more suffocating. The gases burned the tissues of their eyes and lungs and attacked their nervous systems.

> People lost control of their bodies. Urine and faeces ran down their legs. Some began vomiting uncontrollably, were wracked with seizures and fell dead. Others, as the deadly gases ravaged their lungs, began to choke, and drowned in their own bloody body fluids.

> Sunil woke in terrible pain to find himself in Hoshangabad. His body had been brought there by a truck. To his joy he found Kunkun. But their mother and father were dead.[98]

What is the end of most lives that are lived without parental love and guidance, without education, in the context of sexual abuse, without hope, and caught in addictions of various sorts? We don't have to guess. In Bogota,

Columbia, 85 percent of all street children die before they turn 15.[99] These are lives snuffed out before the kids really get an opportunity to live.

The infamous Twin Towers attack not only snuffed out the lives of thousands of Americans in New York City. The economic vibrations from those physical collapses shook the world and the final death toll, could it ever be tallied, would probably include nearly 40,000 of these orphans.[100]

How can this happen? How can we let children live and die in the streets while we have the resources to make a difference? Captain Sandra Ryan of The Salvation Army is convinced that if every evangelical family in Toronto opened its home to homeless, there would be no homeless problem in that city. Surely religious America can do even more.

These are children for whom Jesus died. This is part of the harvest waiting to be reaped. They don't need to remain invisible people. These are our people, our children. These are souls with whom we will be able to enjoy eternity in heaven, if we can reach them in time.

DEADLY SIN #4—SEX AND THE CITY, THE AWFUL HORROR OF THE SEX TRADE

Come, let us build for ourselves a city (Nimrod and friends, Gen. 11:4).

Ra Ratt is a frail 14-year-old whose vagina has been stitched up more than five times so that clients would think she was a virgin.

Her owners forced her to take clients well before her wounds healed, so that the men would believe that the bleeding was from her torn hymen.

"It was so very painful," she said with a shudder.

Last year, she followed a neighbour from her home in Preah Vihear, 200 km north-east of Phnom Penh, to look for work in the city to help her mother, three sisters and brother. Her father had died.

In the city, she was left in a house with promises that work at a restaurant would begin the next day.

But that evening, she found she had been sold for US$1,000.

For a year, she saw many clients—Koreans, Japanese, Singaporeans, Malaysians, Taiwanese, and Caucasians.

"I cannot remember most of them—as soon as one leaves, another comes in," she said.

She worked from 8:30 a.m. to 10 p.m. and there were beatings if she could not meet the quota of clients.

Often, she was taken to a doctor who would put her under anaesthesia and stitch up her vagina.[101]

The world is moving to the city. It is the loneliest place in the world. Its architects neglected to build community into the design. It offers a perverse sense of anonymity, a lack of accountability that draws out the worst in some people. The psyche of anomie emerges at massive gatherings of lonely people, where, like at the million-person Berlin city rave, all restraint can be abandoned without any fear of personal repercussions—or so they think. It is the place where the evangelists of wickedness (see 2 Tim. 4:3-4) congregate.

We're living in a world in which pedophiles can surf the net and choose from a menu of children in countries in Central America. They scout out their targets from the comfort of their own homes. They can take virtual tours and plan their trips. They can pay online with credit cards. And then they can fly down to their vacation destination to commit their indecencies. "Today's Internet has also become the new marketplace for child pornography," explains U.S. Attorney General John Ashcroft.[102]

There are a growing number of pedophiles who are deliberately stalking the young on the net, sometimes posing as children to develop trusting relationships. In 1996, 16 men from the United States, Finland, Canada, and Australia who were part of an online pedophile group called the Orchid Club were indicted in the United States for their illicit activities. Its members shared homemade pictures, recounted sexual experiences with children and even chatted electronically as two of the men molested a 10-year-old girl.[103]

The New Terrorism

Commercial sexual exploitation has now been defined as terrorism by UNICEF. UNICEF Executive Director Carol Bellamy asserted, "Millions of children throughout the world are being bought and sold like chattel and used as sex slaves."[104]

In describing a 2001 Canadian case, B.C. Supreme Court Justice Kathryn Neilson noted that it "demonstrates how the Internet can be used for the anonymous and clandestine sexual exploitation of young people," and then turned around and let off a former member of the B.C. legislature convicted of trying to buy sex with an 11-year-old girl over the Internet.[105]

The second Bush administration in the U.S. has prioritized the child sex trade "at the top" of its policy ranking.[106] U.S. Secretary of State Colin Powell asserts:

> It's the worst kind of human exploitation imaginable. Can you imagine young children, learning their ABCs or whatever the equivalent is in their language, being used as sexual slaves for predators? It is a sin against humanity, and it is a horrendous crime.[107]

Let's get one thing straight here, though. You don't even have to fly to Thailand or the Philippines or Latin America to find kids working the streets. In 1990, ChildHope estimated that there were about 150,000 child prostitutes in the United States.[108] By 1997, American field workers were estimating that number to be 300,000 child prostitutes, male and female, under the age of 16.[109] Can you grasp that? According to the 2000 U.S. Census data, we're talking about 1 out of every 207 children being a street prostitute![110] Put another way, it is 41 under-16 street prostitutes for each of the 20 largest cities in America![111]

The Living Dead

Worldwide, the figures are even more staggering. World Vision estimates that 10 million children are caught up in the sex industry; child prostitution, sex tourism, and pornography.[112] According to UNICEF, a further 1 million children enter the child prostitution racket every year![113] And it is a tragic sight. "Nothing compares to the deadness in the eyes of a kid in a brothel," Gary Haugen, 40, says. "In Rwanda, the dead were already gone. In the brothels of Cambodia, they are the living dead."[114]

> *Sukan will break your heart. She is an eight year-old Cambodian girl, sold by her parents to help pay the expenses of raising the rest of their family. Spirited out of Cambodia into Thailand along with another little girl, she was sold again. New "owners" and a false passport got the two to Toronto's Pearson International Airport and through customs. After a day of pornographic photography, they sat on a stool and watched a dozen white men pull out cash from their wallets and pass it to their "owner." The two who ponied up the highest amount got the "honour of deflowering the two virgin children."*
>
> *"After being robbed of their childhood by the two wealthiest men, the little girls were subjected to a series of rapes lasting through the night." The next morning they were taken across the*

Windsor border in the United States. Stripped, each was given a number on her back right shoulder blade with a black felt marker and pushed into a large room behind the stage in a club. They weren't alone. Sukan and her partner were overwhelmed by the sight of 19 8-10 year olds, all naked, all numbered with the black felt marker. This night was to be a slave auction.

After being paraded out in a cattle call, and submitting to a litany of instructions—jump, turn, bend over, strike alluring poses—they were herded backstage. Then each was brought out alone to be auctioned off. Sukan was reserved to the end. She'd been told that the health of her family and her own future prospects hinged entirely on her performance. She determined to excel. She danced, hopped, twisted and turned like her very life depended on it. A heated bidding war escalated as Sukan tried even harder—spiraling, arching, bending, smiling—anything to increase her value. Finally the auctioneer called those time-honoured words—"going once, going twice, sold!'

"Sukan's eight-year-old life was hawked for forty-two thousand dollars—the highest price ever paid for a prostitute at this site."[115]

As Young As Five

And Sukan isn't the youngest. IJM Anti-Trafficking Unit head, Sharon Cohn, testifies, "Our investigators came into Svay Pak, and within ten minutes pimps came up saying 'Do you want small-small? I can get small-small.' It was unbelievable—kids as young as five."[116] Here is the classic way that the seven deadly sins interbreed. The child slave trade has a large prostitution component. Children in war situations are often forced to become prostitutes for the adult soldiers. Poverty influences some to prostitute themselves. Many children rescued from brothels are infected with HIV.[117] And for those living on the streets, it becomes a way of life, a way to survive. And how do they get on the street in the first place? One of the main reasons is sexual abuse.[118]

In a now-dated study, David Finkelhor found that 19 percent of American females had been abused.[119] R. and J. Goldman, in a similar study, put the figure for Australia at 28 percent.[120] One in five American girls and one in four Australian girls have been abused! And it is not getting better.

"Going to Disney World
or Something Like That"

You don't have to stretch to imagine the effects on children. In a Thai study of 1,012 adolescents and young adults being prostituted, 90 percent of respondents disapproved of prostitution and their role in it, 43 percent felt disappointed in themselves, hopeless and trapped, and 50 percent felt that society showed contempt for them.[121] International Justice Mission's chief investigator, Bob Mosier, comments:

> You have an 8-year-old...just looking at you smiling, realizing that you're going to, in just a few moments possibly, probably going to engage in a sexual act they're going to get money for, and they're smiling about it. I mean, I see a smile like that on my kids' face when they're finding out they're going to go to Disney World or something like that.[122]

What a messed up start to life!

Sex is an enormous industry. As of July 2003, there were 260 million pages of pornography online, up a staggering 1,800 percent since 1998.[123] Americans rent upwards of 800 million pornographic videos and DVDs a year. Nearly one in five video rentals is porn.[124]

A Carnegie-Mellon University study reported that "48.4% of all downloads from adult commercial [Internet] outlets are child porn."[125] One out of every two! Hollywood produces 400 feature films every year. The porn industry makes 11,000.[126]

Just numbers? Here are a few more. "Studies in the Philippines reveal that underage female prostitutes have been pregnant: once (48%), twice (33%), three times (15%), four times (5%)," and 31 percent have a child themselves.[127]

In Thailand, *Viva Network* estimates that 80 percent of the 1 million prostitutes are under the age of 16.[128]

How's this one: 50 percent of 8,500 schools involved in a recent study admitted that computer pornography has been available to their pupils, some as young as eight years old.[129]

In some countries, one of the problems is that,

> Religious practices in some countries make prostitution appear a noble lifestyle. For example, the *devadasi* girls of India...dedicated to the gods before the age of ten, are mostly from the lower "untouchable" caste. Parents are offered large gifts of silver and promised reincarnation as

high caste Brahmins for giving their daughters to the temple. "Married" to the temple goddess...sometimes the young child is possessed by satan. The *devadasi* is believed to *become* the goddess for the male customers paying to sleep with her. The number of *devadasis* eludes the records, but the Indian state of Kanataka alone has an estimated 100,000 *devadasis*.[130]

The travesty here is that the veneer of religiosity covers hardcore child sex slavery. And what's worse, it is perfectly legal, and the best customers are considered holy men! The more you "worship" the holier you are! Even the infamous Afghan Taliban, misunderstood to be morally prudish, was eagerly involved in twisting religion to sexually exploit women, according to the *TIME* exposé, "Lifting the Veil on Sex Slavery."[131]

One "secondary" effect of "free" sex is that in America and the United Kingdom, one third of all births now happen outside of marriage.[132] The fruit of this is a fatherless generation.

There are millions of faceless, fatherless, invisible people being abused and mistreated on our watch. A Hero Army will see to it that these children become People people by imposing justice, by embodying righteousness, and by exercising compassion.

DEADLY SIN #5—AIDS AND PLAGUES
I was sick and you visited Me.

—Jesus

> It is a social nightmare. Although politically incorrect, it is the hottest topic of conversation in the pubs and in the cafés. The scandal is that all the deaths seem caused by infidelity. Saucy stories spread like sweat on a July afternoon about who was having sex with whom, and when the other partners would die. It isn't just death, though some might prefer it to the other alternatives. Disfigurement is a dead giveaway, a stigma sometimes worse than death. Chronic illness is another sign of the plague. It is ugly. No, it isn't America in 2002. It is Europe in 1494. The plague is syphilis.

Some people conclude that all plagues are from God. Certainly there is biblical precedent. But regardless of the source, the victims of myriads of epidemics are specially hand-crafted by God and in need of our help.

Syphilis is still around. But it sure isn't the scariest anymore. According to an August 2001 report, there are 15 million new cases of STDs (Sexually Transmitted Diseases) in America annually, partly because of the false reassurances given by the Centers for Disease Control over the years.[133] After years of promoting "safe sex," says Congressman Dave Weldon, a physician from Florida, the Centers for Disease Control (CDC) has been forced to admit that there is little scientific evidence to back up the claims of their safe-sex messengers.[134] The only proven protection against picking up these diseases is abstinence.

A new report issued by the U.S. Department of Health and Human Services (HHS) finds that there is no scientific evidence that condoms prevent the transmission of most sexually transmitted diseases. The report was developed by a scientific panel that Congress had directed the Clinton administration to establish. The panel was co-sponsored by the National Institutes of Health (NIH), the Food and Drug Administration (FDA), the Centers for Disease Control and Prevention (CDC), and the U.S. Agency for International Development (USAID).

"For nearly a year the CDC has been fighting the release of the report," Rep. Weldon said in a July 20th statement. "The report concludes that there is no scientific evidence to support the claim that condoms provide universal protection against gonorrhea, chlamydia, syphilis, chancroid, trichomoniasis, and genital herpes. Clearly the CDC and the proponents of 'safe sex' have overplayed the effectiveness of condoms and tens of millions of Americans are living with the consequences of decisions they made based on faulty information, much of it paid for with their tax dollars."

Dr. Weldon noted:

Sixty-five million Americans suffer today from incurable STDs, and there will be 15 million new STD infections annually unless Americans are given the facts so that they can change behaviors. Most young people today have been misinformed and believe that condoms offer them significant protection. Unfortunately, millions of teenagers have been misled and given bad information which will result in their making decisions that will cause incurable infections, genital warts, scarring of fallopian tubes, ectopic pregnancies, pelvic inflammatory disease, cervical cancer, and perhaps even death. The CDC has downplayed these risks, but I believe if teenagers are informed that

these are the risks—even when using a condom—they will
make better decisions to protect their health.[135]

But the increase in AIDS and other epidemics is itself pandemic. "Why do we have so many new infectious diseases?" From the U.S. National Institutes of Health, Dr. Richard Krause replied, "Nothing new has happened. Plagues are as certain as death and taxes."[136] And we've gained an alphabet's worth of them through STDs, HIV, AIDS, and SARS. It appears something new has happened in the last 20 years.

Superbug!

The *National Post* headlines screamed, "AIDS researchers see rise of drug-resistant HIV 'superbug.' Treatments have failed."[137]

Martin Schechter, national director of the Canadian HIV Trials Network, said "The ability of HIV to become resistant to medications is a worldwide phenomena."[138]

"According to World Health Organization studies, STDs among young people have increased markedly in the past 20 years and are among the most common causes of illnesses."[139] What does that actually mean, in real numbers? How about this? Again, from the World Health Organization, there are at least 250 million new cases of sexually transmitted diseases in the world every year.[140]

"Could Have Been Prevented"

Some 3 million children each year die from vaccine-preventable diseases.[141] This is up a staggering 50 percent from just five years ago.[142] I know this is tough to get your mind around. So try this: in 1998 it meant that every day you lived, about 33,000 children under the age of five died of a disease that could have been prevented.[143]

These are haunting words. The United Nations Children's Fund calculated that the money spent by western Europeans on cigarettes every six months (£14.5 billion sterling) would effectively control all childhood diseases, halve the rate of child malnutrition, bring clean water to all communities, and provide most children of the world with a basic education.[144]

And malnutrition is a mammoth, complex problem. It accounts for 55 percent of all child deaths each year. Approximately 17 million children are dying annually because they are hungry and thus susceptible to death from usually non-fatal diseases.[145] We're talking about potentially 34 million grieving parents - a country the size of Canada with its future ripped away, its legacy destroyed- every year.

Malnutrition leads to disabilities as well. Joshua Malina, the former mayor of Bulawayo, Zimbabwe, crawled around on the floor of his mother's hut for the first 12 years of his life, uneducated, and isolated, until he was reached by a missionary.[146]

The AIDS epidemic is undermining basic learning in certain parts of Africa: diminishing funds for school fees, forcing young people into the work-force earlier, and claiming the lives of teachers well before retirement age. In Côte d'Ivoire (Ivory Coast), 7 out of 10 teacher deaths are due to HIV. In 1998, Zambia lost 1,300 teachers in the first 10 months of the year—equivalent to two-thirds of the new teachers trained each year.[147] "In Botswana, where about one in three adults are already HIV-infected—the highest prevalence rate in the world—no fewer than two-thirds of today's 15-year-old boys will die prematurely of AIDS."[148]

It's the innocents who are suffering the most from the scourge of AIDS in Africa. The men bring AIDS home to their wives and then the wives unknowingly pass it on to their children in birth. Such is the case of 4-year-old Irene who lives outside Kampala, Uganda.

Her father, a policeman, died first of AIDS; then her mother, a nurse, died. And now Irene is dying. As we entered her hut, we found Irene sleeping on a mat on the floor. The Christian Children's Fund home care providers were completing a practicum and training on how to teach others to care for their loved ones during the last stages of AIDS. That day, they had come to teach Irene's grandparents how to care for her in her last months and days.

As Irene slowly woke, they helped her sit up. Except for the wisdom in her eyes, Irene looks to be a child much smaller and younger than four. I put Irene's hand in mine. She made no effort to move her hand or grasp mine. Her hand is so small and light. Like a leaf on a windless day, it doesn't move.

Just days later, it is hard to comprehend how something that felt so light in my hand, now weighs so heavy on the heart and mind.[149]

But AIDS hasn't stopped in Africa.

In 1989, AIDS made a new inroad into the mainland, penetrating China around the Burmese border. The virus has since hitchhiked along a transportation corridor through

Sichuan and Gansu provinces northward to Urümqi, a city in the far western deserts of Xinjiang province. The disease's traveling companions are a familiar crew: drug users and traffickers, prostitutes and truckers, itinerant workers and salesmen. And wherever AIDS visits, it finds familiar accomplices to help it jump to the next town: official denial, public ignorance, discrimination, and poverty.[150]

The whole issue of AIDS and plagues is complicated by the hand-me-down character of most of the diseases. The ramifications are staggering. Take AIDS for example. Worldwide, 21.8 million people have died of AIDS since the beginning of the epidemic; 4.3 million of them were children.[151] But it gets worse. More than 36.1 million people are infected with HIV worldwide.[152] In 2000, 5.3 million people were newly infected with HIV. In 2000, 3 million people died of AIDS—500,000 (1,400 per day) of them were children.

And, though admittedly Africa is ground zero, the hypocenter of concern, the Western world is not immune. In the U.S., it is estimated that two young people (ages 13-25) are infected with HIV each hour.[153] Two classes of kids a day. That's 336 youth since this time last week!

Disposable, Rape Babies

Cape Town, South Africa, is reputed to be the most beautiful city in the world. However, the following report is from a part of town you won't see on your bus tour. (If you are squeamish, you may want to skip over this story.)

Through the demonic prophecy of a high-ranking South African witch doctor, satanic belief has saturated the country. Though this witch is now dead, her lie lives on as many men in South Africa believe that having sex with a virgin will cure HIV and AIDS.[154] Every day in 2000, 58 children were raped, or victims of attempted rape![155] Over 15 percent of all South African rapes occur against children under the age of 11.[156] That is about seven primary school-aged children each day.[157] But some aren't even old enough for kindergarten. They haven't even learned to talk:

> On November 11, 2001, a nine-month-old baby girl from Kimberley in the Northern Cape who survived a gang rape underwent a full hysterectomy and will require further surgery to repair intestinal damage, a hospital spokesperson said. The baby from Louisville was left unattended by her 16-year-old mother when six Upington men allegedly raped her. The baby had undergone a full hysterectomy

and she suffered extensive damage to her colon and anus as well. The six men, aged between 22 and 66, appeared in the Kimberley Magistrates Court on charges of rape and indecent assault.[158]

On October 31, a month-old baby girl was raped, allegedly by her uncles, in Tweeling in the Eastern Free State. Police spokesperson Loraine Kalp said the mother of the child had left the baby in the care of the men when she went to visit her mother-in-law. Upon her return last night, she found the baby crying and as she lifted her, she saw blood on her bottom. She then took the baby to a clinic where she was told the girl had been raped and sustained vaginal damage.[159]

In a typical situation, a man with AIDS will rape his infant niece and then dispose of her on the garbage dump. This tragedy has steamrolled at an alarming rate to reach epidemic levels![160] But Fiona Brophy, a social worker with a tiny Christian outfit called *Little Angels*[161] has had enough of this despicable practice. Little Angels rescue these babies from the garbage dumps, and they care for them, the ones that are still alive.

What of the nameless ones—the thousands of little bodies (as many as 5,000 a year in South Africa) in various stages of decay and decomposition, found eaten by maggots in desolate places or crushed beneath tons of waste, never to be discovered? *Gifts of life from God thrown away with the trash!*[162]

Fiona wanted to show some solidarity with these disposable, raped babies. So she moved, for a while, onto a garbage dump. She wanted to raise awareness of this deadly sin. She endured the stench, ugliness, strangeness, and utter desolation in a black garbage bag.[163] What would move someone to live on a garbage dump?

- Female infant, full-term in black plastic bag, in decomposed state, with long, uncut, fresh umbilical cord.
- Male fetus, found in bin in Long Market Street, Cape Town.
- Female infant, full-term, the remains consist of a badly scavenged, mutilated body of a newborn infant girl. Both arms are absent.
- Infant boy found wrapped in a plastic bag on a field. Lungs float in water, thus indicating that the newborn had breathed and thus lived.

- Female newborn infant, found in bush, wrapped in cloth, was alive when abandoned but died due to hypothermia.[164]

Fiona explains a bit of her ordeal:

> At times, because of the lack of food and the unbearable circumstances, I would lose perspective. I did not mind, as it was a way for me to perhaps venture closer to how it may feel to be an outcast in a lonely, forgotten, inhuman and dangerous place. My feelings ranged from an incredible expansive and emotional feeling of love for everyone and everything to terrible panic!
>
> I would question myself, "What am I doing here? I do not belong here! Nobody should be rejected!" I felt convinced that we need to start knowing that we are part of each other, not separate at all. As we lift up and help those who are outcast, we lift up and help ourselves. Each person who gives of themselves through their prayers and their empathy, i.e., "feeling" the pain of the other and through giving of their resources, becomes a part of the healing of the division—the separation that destroys us.

Fiona Brophy and Little Angels are lifting up the outcasts, feeling their pain, and rescuing them in Jesus' name. *They are heroes to disposable, raped babies.*

Clearly, the ancillary effects of AIDS are more frightening than its current status. One third of the children born to HIV-positive mothers are infected with the virus, and 80 percent of these die before they are five years old.[165] Life expectancy at birth in southern Africa, which rose from 44 years in the early 1905s to 59 in the early 1990s, is expected to drop to just 45 between 2000 and 2010 because of AIDS.[166]

Increased demand for health care for HIV-related illness is taxing overstretched health services. In countries from Thailand to Burundi, HIV-positive patients are occupying 40-70 percent of the beds in big city hospitals. At the same time, the health sector is increasingly losing its own human resources to AIDS. One study in Zambia found a 13-fold increase in deaths in hospital staff, largely due to HIV, over a 10-year period.[167] And the death count continues to rise.

A sickness reaches epidemic proportions at five percent of the population. Then it is officially a plague. In sub-Saharan Africa several countries have need of a new term to describe the intensity of this scourge.[168] The United Nations expects that 70 million people will die of AIDS by 2022.[169] It has reached biblical plague proportions. Perhaps we should use the term hyper-pestilence.

Nearly 20 years have passed since AIDS claimed its first Asian victim, believed to be a 48-year-old male Japanese hemophiliac who received a tainted blood transfusion. Despite advances in treatment, the scourge continues to bully its way into new regions and new demographics. Every day in Asia, 1,192 people die of AIDS-related diseases. Another 2,658 become infected, according to UNAIDS, a U.N. group that monitors the disease globally. Even countries such as Japan and South Korea, which responded aggressively to curb the threat at the outset, are seeing an upsurge in contagion. More than 7 million Asians contracted HIV or AIDS by the end of last year; new cases reported in 2001 totaled 1.07 million, up 17% from the previous year.[170]

Aside from the obvious physical and social impact of this hyper-pestilence, AIDS has enormous economic effects. In Britain, the health costs of treating AIDS totaled an estimated £250 million in one year.[171] On top of that, an estimated 45,000 productive years were lost due to premature death.[172] Each of the 1,500 AIDS deaths represented an average loss of at least £360,000.[173] And that is just from one year, in one country.

Until the turn of the century, little impact had been made.

Today, on the continent of Africa, nearly 30 million people have the AIDS virus—including 3 million children under the age 15. There are whole countries in Africa where more than one-third of the adult population carries the infection. More than 4 million require immediate drug treatment. Yet across that continent, only 50,000 AIDS victims—only 50,000—are receiving the medicine they need.[174]

Put crassly by Bono, "What we're on about is: Africa. Seventy percent of HIV/AIDS is in Africa. *We're talking about a continent bursting into flames while we stand around with watering cans.*"[175]

Worldwide, the United Nations was searching for $10 billion to address the crisis. In Abuja, Nigeria, U.N. Secretary General Kofi Anan appealed for setting up a multi-million dollar fund to fight AIDS in Africa. "We need between $7 billion and $10 billion for the fight against AIDS to be effective," said Anan. He added, "The war on AIDS will not be won without a war chest, of a size far beyond what is available so far."[176] Early 2002 saw the birth of the Global Fund for AIDS, malaria, and tuberculosis.[177] United States President George Bush promised $15 billion to attack it.[178]

World leaders recognize that they are in a war.[179] Tens of millions are dying because of AIDS and plagues. And Jesus died for each one of them. Among them, He died for Yufa.

AIDS or Starvation?

> *Yufa leans against the pink neon-lit doorway of a café. She's a farm girl who has been in the sex game for only two weeks. She's wearing an ill-fitting red gown, and her feet hurt. Her pale, exposed shoulders are a sharp contrast to her face, burnt from laboring in fields. She came from Sichuan to look for factory work in Urümqi after her young husband died, leaving her with two children "and only the sky overhead," she says. In Urümqi, there were no jobs. A stranger fixed her up at a roadside brothel where she sells herself for $3. "Sure, I know about the disease," she says. "But I'm not so pretty, and I only get maybe three clients a week. If they won't use a condom, fine. I'll do it anyway. What choice do I have? I can't let my children die of hunger."[180]*

We cannot stand by, blithely turning channels and pages until our minds will be teased. Tony Lawrence has not stood by.

Circumcise and Evangelize

Different cultures celebrate different rites of passage. From the *toga virilis* and *bar mitzvah* to "paradise by the dashboard light," young people graduate from childhood to adulthood through culturally accepted means. Here's one you may not have heard:

> *Pride fills the young men wearing rough blankets and sheepskin headbands as they near the end of their ritual initiation. A month ago, a traditional surgeon used a blade to circumcise them and mark their passage into manhood.*
>
> *"I am more than proud. I am a man," declares one of the "abakhwetha," the Xhosa word for initiates.*
>
> *"No one can speak for me. No one can tell me where to go," says the youth, his face painted a ghostly white with clay as a symbol of purity.*
>
> *Meanwhile, in Ward 14 at the nearby Cecelia Makawane Hospital lie a dozen recent initiates who have nothing to celebrate. They are the victims of botched circumcisions.[181]*

Twice per year in June/July or November/December, approximately 50,000 young male initiates in South Africa alone take an important step toward manhood by undergoing circumcision during a time of initiation and

204 BE A HERO

training based upon their ethnicity and tradition. Traditional values include respect, discipline, self-control, abstinence, leadership, gender equity, and moral principles.[182]

But what should be a glorious occasion for these teenagers often turns out to be a nightmare. One out of five boys end up with their genitals partially or fully amputated. Many of them are cross-infected with the HIV/AIDS virus and Hepatitis B, simply because the same implement is used on many different boys without being sterilized.

The boys are traumatized. Many suffer psychological problems both before and after the experience. There is no counseling to help them through the process. Most boys do not want to return home after the botched circumcision. Rather than living with the shame, some of these initiates—ordinary, fun-loving adolescents on the threshold of adulthood—commit suicide.

What's the solution? The Tara Klamp.[183]

The *Seize the Day Foundation* is rescuing these children in a holistic way. Among other things, Tony Lawrence and Seize the Day volunteers distribute a pack to each initiate. "A pack includes a circumcision device called the Tara Klamp, which eliminates the risk of cross-infections like hepatitis normally caused by inadequately sterilized instruments."[184] The Tara Klamp is a disposable circumcision device that cuts down on infection and disease. Lawrence's program includes training and certification of traditional circumcision practitioners via values based on the Word of God. Each student receives a Bible and the gospel. The solution is to circumcise and evangelize.[185]

We can all do something. As God mobilizes unlikely heroes to do unlikely exploits, a Hero Army will rise up to exercise spiritual authority to bring healing. It will unleash the wealth of the nations to bring to bear sufficient resources for health on these plagues, all in the name and power of Jesus. Justice, righteousness, and compassion will morph invisible sick people into People people.

DEADLY SIN #6—THE EXIGENCIES OF WAR?
WAR-AFFECTED CHILDREN

At the turn of the 20th century, 90 percent of war casualties were male soldiers. At the turn of the 21st century, 90 percent of war casualties are civilians, the majority of whom are women and children.[186]

A child captures a grown-up in the sights of his gun and slowly pulls the trigger. This is no water pistol and this is no game. Someone has fallen, and in the boy's eyes, something has died. The same cold brutality is reflected in the faces of 15,000 children in Liberia. Children who are handed AK-

47s and recruited to the killing fields of the eight-year-long
civil war. Children as young as six.[187]

The "exigencies of war" is a time-honored phrase. It is bandied about to mobilize patriotic sacrifice, trumpeted to defend the enormous costs of victory. Exigency is: "something that a situation demands or makes urgently necessary and that puts pressure on the people involved."[188] We title this section with a question mark intentionally. Are refugees, are landmines, are child soldiers really part of the exigencies of war? The world has concluded in the affirmative. And this conclusion is a deadly sin.

> "I was defiled by some older boys [could not remember how many] when we were being marched to the rebel camp. After returning from Sudan, I was the wife to one rebel commander, then another junior commander and then two 'older' rebel soldiers. I had one child who died when he was a few days old. I was a slave to the rebels for 19 months. I do not think I will marry again." (A now-18-year-old girl, abducted by the Lord's Resistance Army, a rebel group in Uganda)[189]

And a Child Shall Lead Them

In Uganda, the "Lord's Resistance Army" has been known to recruit children as young as five years old.[190] We're not talking about a few five and six-year-olds either. About a quarter of a million children actually fought between 1985 and 1995.[191]

The Lord's Resistance Army has a terrifying reputation, having abducted more than 20,000 children since its inception.[192] Many become the sex slaves of soldiers. The females, "Tend to have an average of three children while they are in captivity."[193]

The fighting figure exploded such that today, 300,000 children are fighting in armed conflicts in at least 31 countries.[194] The most notorious child soldiers are Luther and Johnny Htoo, 12-year-old ethnic Karen children in Myanmar, who lead "God's Army."[195]

"God's Army rebels are Christians in a predominantly Buddhist country. The twins have a fundamentalist bent, barring fighting, swearing, drugs and alcohol."[196] "God's Army, which at its peak had about 150 fighters, had provided minor resistance in a wider guerrilla war by ethnic Karen rebels fighting for autonomy in Myanmar."[197] The twin children are, "believed to offer their fighters divine protection in a crusade that blends elements of the Old Testament with Lord of the Flies."[198]

They acquired near-legendary status around 1997, when Myanmar troops came to their village during a sweep of Karen areas. The mainstream guerrillas group, the Karen National Union, reportedly fled while the twins rallied some local men and directed a successful counterattack. After that, the twins' followers said the boys—who are Christians—had powers from God. Their followers believed bullets couldn't hit them and mines wouldn't explode under their feet.[199]

God's Army isn't alone. The UN Children's Fund (UNICEF) estimates that Renamo used around 10,000 boys, some as young as six, in its bloody 16-year war against the formerly Marxist government in this vast nation.[200] At least 35 countries have used child soldiers in the past 10 years.[201] More than 500,000 children under 18 have been recruited into state and non-state armed groups in over 85 countries worldwide.[202] Some of the Tamil Tiger male soldiers are obviously underage because their voices have not broken yet. "They trained me to move forward while the battle was on and to take a gun apart and put it back together again," explained one such 13-year-old, in a squeaky voice.[203]

In the decade since the adoption of the *Convention on the Rights of the Child*, more than 2 million children have been killed and more than 6 million injured or disabled in armed conflicts. Tens of thousands were victims of landmines. Hundreds of thousands were forced into armed conflict as soldiers, sex slaves, or porters.[204] During the 1994 genocide in Rwanda alone, a quarter of a million children were massacred.[205]

Child soldiers are subject to ill treatment and sexual exploitation. They are often forced to commit terrible atrocities, and beaten or killed if they try to escape. They are subjected to brutal initiation and punishment rituals, hard labor, cruel training regimes and torture. Many are given drugs and alcohol to agitate them and make it easier to break down their psychological barriers to fighting or committing atrocities.[206]

Human Rights Watch chief researcher Alison Des Forges, a hero, records the testimonies of the traumatized survivors of Congo's horror—which is, in itself, traumatizing and dangerous work. Human rights activists have been abducted, tortured, and murdered. In late 2002, a Pygmy man told this story:

> *About 20 miles from Mambasa, the militia attacked a pygmy camp. A man called Amuzati who was hunting in the forest heard shooting. As he wasn't far from his camp he returned to see what was happening.*
>
> *About half a mile away from the camp he heard shouts and crying, and then there was silence. He came closer and saw several militiamen. He saw the corpses of his family, including his nephew who was five-years-old, with his stomach cut open. They were cutting the flesh and eating the victims...*[207]

Not surprisingly, "scores of millions have been scarred psychologically by the violence they endured or witnessed at intimate range, and countless others have died for lack of food or health service."[208] Here is one who was scarred:

> *They beat all the people there, old and young. They killed them all, nearly 10 people...like dogs they killed them...I didn't kill anyone, but I saw them killing...the children who were with them killed too...with weapons...they made us drink the blood of people, we took blood from the dead into a bowl and they made us drink...then when they killed the people they made us eat their liver, their heart, which they took out and sliced and fried...And they made us little ones eat.*[209]

At least 15 million children have been displaced within their countries or made refugees.[210] Between 1985 and 1995, 12 million lost their homes as a result of war.[211] In 1995 alone, 53 million people—1 out of every 115 people on earth—were uprooted from their homes, either displaced within their countries or refugees across borders.[212] Women and children usually comprise 80 percent of the refugee and displaced populations.[213] Now, 18.9 million people live as refugees.[214] And some just die—during the period April to October 1992, children killed in Somalia numbered 200,000.[215] In fact, more than one and a half million children have been killed in wars worldwide in the past decade.[216]

There are now about 11 million illegal immigrants in the USA[217] More than 2 million foreigners have intentionally overstayed their welcome.[218] Many more would like to live as refugees! Around 450,000 asked for sanctuary in 25 European countries in 2000,[219] and many, many more did not stop to ask. The CIA estimates that 900,000 slaves were sold across international borders last year, 20,000 into the United States.[220] Many come from war-torn situations. *TIME* magazine reports that every day in USA a Mexican dies trying to sneak into the country.[221] In March of 2001 the lone survivor of a ship trying to smuggle people into the country recounted how people on board had resorted to cannibalism to stay alive.[222] *They say "War is hell." It appears that even a lack of peace is unbearable.*

"No More Virgins"

Jennifer Adoch and Susan Oyella, arms linked, backs straight, hair tightly shaved, hiked dusty trails without shoes, their feet swollen and callused. They walked with thousands of other children, all rushing away from the danger of night-time rebel raids on their villages and toward the safety of the town center to sleep. Tiny boys in tattered clothing, girls with chubby cheeks clutching ragged dolls, others with foam mattresses balanced on their heads, others with nothing at all were walking.

Jennifer and Susan sang a marching song. "People in Gulu are suffering. Education is poor. Communication is poor. There are no more virgins in Gulu," the girls sang sweetly in English. "They were all raped. Hear us now: There are no more virgins in Gulu."

The children are called simply "the night commuters" or "night dwellers." About 15,000 young Ugandans trek every evening from more than 300 villages, some more than five miles away into the safety of Gulu, about 175 miles north of the capital, Kampala.[223]

Susan, sixteen years of age, captures the brutalization children suffer at the hands of the Lord's Resistance Army (LRA) in northern Uganda in the following testimony:

One boy tried to escape but he was caught. His hands were tied and then they made us, the other new captives, kill him with a stick. I felt sick. I knew this boy from before; we were from the same village. I refused to do it and they told me they would shoot me. They pointed a gun at me, so I had to do it...I see him in my dreams and he is saying I killed him for nothing, and I am crying.[224]

The emotional scars of war are more difficult to measure. A nationwide survey of 3,000 children in Rwanda in 1995 revealed the following: over 95 percent of the children witnessed massacres; over a third had seen family members murdered; almost all believed they would die; nearly two-thirds were threatened with death; and over 80 percent had had to hide to protect themselves, many for up to eight weeks or longer.[225] And even those who've survived war have persisting threats to life and health. In 64 countries, an estimated 110 million anti-personnel mines—hidden killers—one for every 20 children in the world—lie in wait for unsuspecting footfalls.[226] These cost between $3 and $10 to buy and between $300 and $1,000 to remove. About 800 humans die every month because of them, with thousands more maimed for life.[227] It is more than just numbers:

> *"I've seen people get their hands cut off, a 10-year-old girl raped and then die, and so many men and women burned alive. So many times I just cried inside my heart because I didn't dare cry out loud."* ("Grace," 14-year-old girl, abducted in January 1999 by the Revolutionary United Front, a rebel group in Sierra Leone)[228]

There is going to be a lot of blood on a lot of adults' skirts for the sin of allowing and forcing these types of horrendous experiences on children. God is calling you to step in with righteousness to offer "Grace" and her comrades compassion, mercy, and justice. God is calling to you be a hero.

DEADLY SIN #7—RELIGIOUS PERSECUTION

I was in prison and you came to Me.

—Jesus

Most overseas Christianity is being destroyed by non-Christians in crushing defeat and, like cattle, they are every day being murdered, and Christians are being exterminated.
—c. 1070, Pope Gregory VII to the German King Henry IV

...Men of whom the world was not worthy (Hebrews 11:38).

They could hardly recognize him. His face was gaunt, his skin stretched tightly over his cheek bones. His body was like a stick. As a result, his eyes appeared rather large, his lips protruded and hung open. He was unable to close his mouth so that two rows of yellow teeth could be seen. His hair fell onto his face and his beard had grown unkept. His face was covered in dried blood and his clothes were absolutely filthy. They could not help but wail loudly...To see this awful scene would bring tears to the most hard-hearted, callous person.[229]

Brother Yun is one of the heroic leaders of the house church movement in China. He has been arrested more than 30 times, electrocuted, in prison several times (he escaped from arrest), and been beaten, starved, manacled, urinated on, and tortured for years. His first imprisonment included 100 straight days in solitary confinement and concluded with 600 converts from the 800 prisoners.[230] Because he'd escaped so many times, he had his legs smashed by a sledgehammer so that, "only the flesh attached the feet."[231] His release from prison followed a miraculous 74-day fast. Today millions of Christians serve in the church network under his leadership.[232]

There is a murderous spirit dedicated to eliminating Jews and Christians. This spirit is an actor that wears different masks for different scripts. Yesterday it was the dogmatic communist mask. Today it is the militant Muslim mask. Tomorrow will it be the extremist Hindu mask? Who knows? But the outward appearances merely mask the identity of an evil presence committed to wiping out the light of the world.

To be sure, not all religious persecution is against Jews and Christians. Amnesty International's Report 2001 reports that, "At least 93 Falun Gong followers were believed to have died in custody and hundreds of Buddhist nuns and monks remained in detention in Tibet."[233] China's minister of public security, Jia Chunwang, is quoted in published internal government documents stating, "We need to work more, talk less to smash the cult quietly."[234] Despite the fact that Amnesty International overlooks the persecution of Christians in China, there are martyrs and heroes being made.[235] And it is not ancient history. *Newsweek* magazine reports the following. Of one six-month period this century, *Newsweek* reported,[236]

> Chinese communists demolished 1,500 houses of worship—most of them Christian…In…India, scores of Christians have been murdered and their churches trashed since the rise of militant Hindu groups. On Christmas Eve (2000) churches in nine Indonesian cities were bombed, killing at least 18 believers and wounding about 100 more. An additional 90 Christians were murdered for refusing to convert to Islam, and some 600 more are still being forcefully detained on the island of Kasiui.[237]

Terrorists drained 400 bullets in 10 minutes into a Pakistan church, killing 17 Christian worshipers. Their last word, to the benediction, was "amen."[238]

In early 2002, the Committee for Investigation on Persecution of Religion in China, which is based in New York, published a set of internal Chinese government documents describing in remarkable detail the suppression of unauthorized religious groups, including efforts to crush underground

Catholic churches, use of secret agents to infiltrate illegal Protestant congregations and orders for "forceful measures" against the banned Falun Gong spiritual movement.[239]

Nor is it just a passing phase. "One of every four people who have been martyred for Christ in all of history has died during this generation."[240] "The five most dangerous of all Christian vocations (over 3% murder rates) are: bishops, evangelists, catechists, colporteurs, foreign missionaries."[241]

And the prospects are not looking any better. According to Laussaune II Congress on World Evangelization researcher David Barrett, one in 200 Christians can expect to be martyred in his or her lifetime."[242] And the recent escalation of religious-based terrorism in the West augurs poorly for comfortable Western Christians.[243]

The seven deadly sins aren't committed in a vacuum. The victims live in unholy lands, regions struggling for peace amid tribalism in tension with globalization, gangsterism that ridicules international law, and terrorism opposing hegemony. They live in places where people kill and take and they believe their religion, politics, or simple might, makes it right. They live in lands under dictatorships and oppression. They live in situations in which basic freedoms and choices have been ripped from their hands.

20th Century Bloodshed

While wars killed millions, military violence was not the primary cause of death in the 20th century. Battle deaths from all conflicts are reckoned to be about 35,654,000. But totalitarian regimes have killed more of their own citizens. "Totalitarian communism, which on a per capita basis is at least 20 times deadlier than war, was responsible for the deaths of at least 95,153,600 people in this century."[244]

Many of these deaths were based on religious belief. The World Christian Encyclopedia estimates that 45.4 million Christians were martyred in the 20th century.[245] Editors David Barrett, Todd Johnson, and Justin Long even break down the violence:

Christian martyrdoms at the hands of…
- Atheists: 31,689,000
- Muslims 9,121,000
- Ethnoreligionists: 7,469,000
- So-called Christians (i.e., State Church – RC, Orthodox, etc. vs Evangelicals, etc.): 5,538,000
- Quasi-religionists 2,712,000
- Mahayana Buddhists: 1,651,000

- Hindus: 676,000
- Zoroastrians: 384,000.[246]

The 20th Century Atlas breaks it down even more for us:

- 1921-50: 15 million Christians in prison camps
- 1950-80: 5 million Christians in prison camps
- Orthodox: 14.5 million killed by Stalin; 2.7 million of them martyrs (1929-37)
- Roman Catholics (1925): 1.2 million martyrs
- Christians executed by Nazis in death camps: 1 million
- Nazis exterminate 0.5 million Gypsies
- Khmer Rouge slaughter 2 million (1975)
- Massacre of 40,000 Vietnamese Catholics (1970)
- And so on.[247]

Stalin takes the blame for upwards of 51 million, Mao Zedong for more than 44 million, and Hitler for 25 million plus another 35 million soldiers and civilians.[243]

Meanwhile, religious-tainted conflicts (mixed with tribal elements in some cases) in various countries killed millions more:

- In Kinshasa, Congo, since 1998, 3.3 million;
- In Nigeria (1967-1970), 3 million;
- In Sudan, 2 million;
- In Vietnam, 2 million;
- In Cambodia under the Khmer Rouge (1975-1978), 1.6 million;
- In Rwanda and Burundi (1959-1995), at least 700,000;
- In India and Pakistan (1947), 500,000;
- In Uganda, under Idi Amin, 300,000;
- In the Philippines, 120,000;
- In Eritrea-Ethiopia (1998-2000), at least 70,000;
- In Indonesia since 1999, maybe 9,000;
- In Northern Ireland through The Troubles, 3,506;
- And so on.[249]

Several regions are ripe for further persecution in our lifetime. Several hot spots, in which different religions vie for prominence, could boil over in the coming generation. Things are not static. Take Lagos, Nigeria, for example. It turns out that in 1950 Lagos was a "ramshackle port community," with a population of a quarter million. By 1990 there were about 10 million people in metropolitan Lagos. In a dozen years there could be 25 million.[250]

There are 20,000 people/square kilometer and the city "suffers desperately from congestion and pollution."[251]

The city and its country are divided by Islam and Christianity.[252] And yet the city has hosted some of the largest evangelistic campaigns in history.[253] So, this city has exploded in half a century. It is a significant regional center. It is the base of religious conflict. And it's infrastructure is terrible.

What a classic example of a place to invest our prayers, and pounds, and people! We need to cultivate a hardy strain of Christianity, strong in doctrine and mercy and social justice. Out of such cauldrons of persecution will bubble up heroes of the 21st century.

Nativity Naïve?

We cannot remain naïve about the intention of some enemies of Christianity. Militant Communists are aggressively persecuting Christians. In 1992, the Chinese state-run press noted that "The church played an important role in the change" in Eastern Europe and warned, "If China does not want such a scene to be repeated in its land, it must *strangle the baby while it is still in the manger.*"[254]

It is not just communists. "Militant Muslims believe that the problems in their society have been caused by departure from the strict tenets of Islam, and that this trend can only be countered by a return to Islam in its purity."[255] And so, in the world's largest Muslim country, Indonesia, organized *jihads*, or holy wars, have led to the destruction of hundreds of Christian villages by Muslim extremists.[256] Pastors are being hunted mostly because there is a $5,000 (USD) bounty paid for each one killed.[257]

In the diehard Muslim states of the Middle East, things are even more systematically repressive. For example, "a Christian Saudi citizen is assumed to be apostate from Islam, and therefore is automatically subject to death."[258] In Myanmar, the Government's State Law and Order Restoration Council explicitly attacks Christianity, stating, "Christianity must be destroyed by peaceful means as well as violent means."[259] And with the extension of "The Base's" Holy War into North America, Westerners will get a close up and personal view of the praxis of Islam.[260]

Molten Steel

Meanwhile, an estimated 6,000 Christians sit in notorious "Prison 15" in North Korea waiting to die because they are Christian.[261] The persecution is worse. Says one non-Christian former prisoner: "The torture and the worst ways of execution were most harsh on the Christians. They didn't give them clothes. They were considered animals. And in the factories, they killed them by pouring molten steel on them."[262] And in Sudan, "millions (are) affected by persecution."[263]

It is small comfort that this is to be expected. "All who desire to live godly in Christ Jesus will be persecuted" (2 Tim. 3:12). It is almost sacrilege for people in the West to even offer comment on the persecution that Christian brothers and sisters suffer as a regular component of their godly lives. Besides the *de rigueur* questions we must ask ourselves concerning why we are not being persecuted like our comrades, we must ask ourselves how it is that:

1. we aren't aware of these kinds of things happening in a global village; and,
2. we aren't already doing something about it?

We can take solace in the fact that while thousands of Christians are imprisoned and tortured in China with such tools as electric prods, bayonets, and metal bars, 25,000 people get saved daily.[264] God increases the fruit.

A Hero Army will see to it that God is freed to accomplish His will and that justice is met.

Cyrus, the Judas character in *The Matrix*, wanted to return to his old life. For him, ignorance was bliss. Having seen the real world and been blown away with the rigors of the sacrificial lifestyle, he hankered after the comfortable cocoon of the stereotypical weekly grind of a normal person. It didn't work.

It won't work for you either. You may try to go back to the weekend-to-weekend schedule that typifies your life. But you will be haunted by the pictures of Joseph Malina (AIDS and plagues), the 7th grade students (too poor to get their immunization shots), Victor (the chocolate slave), 100 million street kids, the 11-year-old girl propositioned for sex through the Internet, the Myanmar twins, and Brother Yun (religious persecution).

You can't go back. They are no longer invisible people to you and to us. We have seen them. Now we have to decide if God's big idea, to make them into People people, is a worthy enough cause for us to mobilize our hearts and resources to bring justice, righteousness, and compassion to bear on their situations.

A Hero Army will do that. It is now recruiting. It attracts its heroes in the strangest ways.

CHAPTER TEN

THIS BUD'S FOR YOU

Now this was the sin of your sister Sodom: She and her daughters were arrogant, overfed and unconcerned; they did not help the poor and needy (Ezekiel 16:49).

Then I looked again at all the acts of oppression which were being done under the sun. And behold I saw the tears of the oppressed and that they had no one to comfort them (Ecclesiastes 4:1).

God sees all of the oppressed. From His throne in heaven, He looks down and sees the young girl being raped, the child forced to watch his family shot, the children "bought" for the cost of a cup of coffee to be enslaved until they outlive their profitability. He looks around and can find no one to comfort them.

God wants us to experience some of the burden He feels, and to carry some of the pain. The difficulty is crossing over from our comfort to their discomfort. For every individual it is a personal challenge. It is a threshold question that is only one step away. Jesus Himself lived for a while within the confines and edicts of His religion. But when the Spirit of the Lord came upon Him, He determined that He must be about His Father's business. And that took Him to the prisons, the hospitals, and the slums (see Luke 4:18).

Jesus explained the theology of it when He responded to a clever Jewish lawyer who asked Him what the bottom line was in keeping the commandments of God. His blunt question to Jesus was, "What must I do to inherit eternal life?" (Luke 10:25) This is a "what do I have to do to get to heaven" question? The parallel accounts affirm that Jesus said that the **greatest** commandments and the **most important** were to, "Love the Lord your God with all your heart and with all your soul and with all your strength and with all your mind"; and to "Love your neighbor as yourself." All the Law and the Prophets hung on these two commandments (Matt. 22:40).

The lawyer knew that Jesus' answer left a great big loophole. How much is enough, how will I know, who is my neighbor? To justify himself he asked for clarification. "Who is my neighbor?"

To depict a neighbor, Jesus told the famous story of the beaten traveler. Mobsters beat the daylights out of him. A pastor avoided him in the ditch. A worship leader avoided him. But a Samaritan man went to him and helped. He dealt with the bloody mess and the cultural contradictions. He dealt with the inconvenience and cost. And he helped this beaten man.

In response to the lawyer's desired clarification on just who was his neighbor, Jesus explained His intent in the context of mercy and social justice: *justice* because the robbers beat the man and left him for dead; *mercy* because the good Samaritan came and attended to the wounds of the dying man. This was compassion extended in the natural sense—no miracles, no healing, no supernatural. Just plain old "sweat equity." It seems we rarely notice Jesus' final injunction, twice repeated: *"Do this and you will live"* and *"Go and do likewise"* (Luke 10:28,37).

Part of the application of the first commandment—loving God—is actually fulfilled by the second commandment—*loving your neighbor*. As Jesus said, "The second is just like the first" (Matt. 22:39). Often this Scripture is used as a proof text for either getting involved in inner-city ministries, or in the vague, pseudo-social application of the golden rule—"Do unto others as you would have them do unto you." Even more often it means "just be a good guy." Yet what about real dying people—the billion "children at risk" who are out there praying to God and dying to see someone show them mercy? Real kids dying in our global village cannot be ignored while we scurry off like the priest and the Levite (the pastor and the worship leader) to take care of our "more important" agendas.

Jesus asked the man, *Who, then, was a neighbor to the beaten man?* (see Luke 10:36). The lawyer acknowledged that it was the Samaritan. Now watch this. Jesus instructed, "Yes, now go and do the same."

How do I receive eternal life? "Go and do the same." It is not merely an addition to the gospel. It is part of the gospel.

Consider the parable of the sheep and the goats. How do you distinguish sheep from goats? The criteria is plain—what one does for the poor.

When the Son of Man returns:

> All the nations will be gathered before Him, and He will separate the people one from another as a shepherd separates the sheep from the goats. He will put the sheep on His right and the goats on His left. Then the King will say to those on His right, "Come, you who are blessed by My Father; take your inheritance, the kingdom prepared for you since the creation of the world. For I was hungry and you gave Me something to eat, I was thirsty and you gave Me something to drink, I was a stranger and you invited Me in, I needed clothes and you clothed Me, I was sick and you looked after Me, I was in prison and you came to visit Me."
> Then **the righteous will answer Him**, "Lord, when did we see You hungry…thirsty… a stranger…or needing clothes? When did we see You sick or in prison…?" The King will reply, "I tell you the truth, whatever you did for one of the least of these brothers of Mine, you did for Me" (Matthew 25:32-40).

Conversely, it was what the goats did not do that made them goats: "I tell you the truth, whatever you did not do for one of the least of these, you did not do for Me" (Matt. 25:40).

"Do and not do," it can't be much plainer. Yet the problem we face in the West is that any mention of ministering to the poor and needy automatically generates the stereotypical mature adult drug-addicted, homeless male in a back alley. Though prevalent, this image blurs the biblical description of who the poor are—the widow, orphan, and refugees—"children at risk." Although most Christians do not feel their eternal life hinges on their participation in street ministry, the issues explode with horrific impact by the frightening status of the seven deadly sins.

Can you still sit by and do nothing? Will that affect your salvation? Doing something means more than just sympathy or having a good cry with your prayer time. Most people get caught up in sentimentalism, in the emotion pervading the frightening status of the seven deadly sins. They are so overwhelmed; all they can do is hide their head in their hands.

Some people in the world are beginning to do more than feel the burden. The list includes more than just the Bill Gates and Ted Turners who can throw hundreds of millions at a problem.[1] It includes people like Craig Kielburger.

Shocked to read that a boy his age had been murdered in Pakistan for protesting the child labor laws, this suburban 12-year-old decided to do something about it. He says, "We can't become a generation of passive bystanders; we have to be a generation that acts." *Kids Can* Free The Children (FTC) is what he decided to do. Six years later, FTC boasts more than 100,000 members in 35 countries and has expanded its attention to other seven deadly sin-type issues. Among other things, FTC has built 375 schools in 40 countries and raised the money to build 100 more. It has distributed 200,000 "basic needs" kits and invested $6.5 million in medical supplies for children in 40 countries. FTC has also established two peace and leadership centers for youth—one in Kenya and another in Arizona.[2]

The lesson? You don't have to be one of the world's richest men to make a difference. You don't even have to be out of elementary school. And, apparently, you don't even have to be a Christian!

If unbelievers can make that threshold step, then how much more should we, as people who recognize and embrace Jesus' sacrifice on the Cross, and own some responsibility for the sufferings caused by the seven deadly sins, step out from our comfort and into their discomfort?

Saint Francis left an affluent lifestyle to walk among the marginalized. It all began with a God encounter. This wealthy Italian, the son of a "magnifico," grew up with the typical rich boy stereotypes, both concerning himself and those on the other side of the tracks. His pet prejudice was against lepers. They were gross. And he feared them.

While riding his horse, God threw Francis into the face of a leper. He had his God encounter and was never the same again.

For Paul it took a blinding light to throw him to the soiled ground for him to experience a God-encounter that transformed his life.

For Ralph Bromley, it was the words of a beer commercial.

THIS BUD'S FOR YOU

Ralph started and led a growing mercy ministry from Kelowna, B.C., Canada. One day he got a knock on his door from three older native gentlemen. They'd heard from a friend that Ralph was involved in finding homes for people and showed up looking for one! These three inebriates had a combined 60 years of experience in the country's corrections system. Ralph immediately went into referral mode—you know, "Who's a bigger fool than I am and will take in three drunk Indians."

Walking down the hall to dig up a phone book, basically stalling while he tried to expedite a gracious way out of this interruption, God stopped him in his tracks. "This Bud's for you!" God clearly instructed him. "Take them into your home." This was Ralph's God encounter. Soon, Ralph had all three of the brothers living in his renovated garage in the back yard. It resulted in Ralph being mentored in issues such as shallowness, incongruence between word and deed, and compassion—or "love with its sleeves rolled up"—by three aging, uneducated, unsaved First Nations men. *This is Isaiah 58, curbside.*

Ralph's mercy ministry is called *Hope for the Nations*. It has a creative way of doing things called the "Mercy Paradigm." They act as middlemen, uniting North Americans with national Christians in developing countries. Their niche combines foster parenting, childrens' homes, entrepreneurship, and micro-enterprise to fulfil Matthew 28 and Matthew 25 at the same time. They connect only in relationship, and with credible local leaders. Through relationship, they invest in the local leader, help him get settled and started in adopting an orphan and establishing a small business. This model is proving effective.

Hope for the Nations is not on the hook for ongoing expenses and yet the model is replicated as the local leaders naturally start new churches while spreading the gospel. This guerrilla-cells model is the look of the next Hero Army. One of its leaders is Simon.

SIMON

Simon is the Che Guevara of Sikkim! Sikkim is a small country geographically unfortunate enough to be a potentially strategic invasion corridor from China to India. Predictably, it has been a pawn in world power political machinations. It was annexed by India, and Simon became the leader of the freedom fighters. He was recognized as the biggest threat to the Indian cause, having the biggest price on his head. He blew up army barracks and bridges, and killed many people.

This is a man who literally dug his own grave at the point of Indian Army guns. As he dug, a Hope for the Nations national happened to be walking by on his vacation (You walk everywhere in that world—no cars.) and was able to convince the soldiers to spare his life!

Simon soon escaped. His goal was to get to Nepal and while avoiding Indian forces he hid out in an empty home. Exhausted, Simon fell asleep in a little girl's bedroom. As God would have it, the little girl came home to find him sleeping in her bed. Her parents happened to be at a Hope for the Nations conference that evening! She woke him up and told him about Jesus.

Simon ran away to Nepal but the message stayed with him! While in Nepal he heard that India had offered amnesty to all of the rebels so he returned to Sikkim.

What does a life-long terrorist do for a living? What transferable skills does a rebel possess? Simon went to Hope for the Nations! He got saved, got discipled, became an evangelist and church planter, and started an orphanage.

As he started his little orphanage he heard a horror story about a young girl who was forced to watch her parents and brothers chopped to death with a machete. This was the first girl he adopted.

YOUR GOD ENCOUNTER

Where are the Christian Craig Kielburgers and Bill Gates? Where are the Christian entrepreneurs for social justice?

The Commander of the Hero Army is the God of the Encounter. Have you had your encounter? It is just a step away. You'll need to cross over from the confines of religion and tradition into a divine mercy for the more fragile in our world.

Ask God to shave your callous heart, and compassion will bleed from the wound. You will have had your God encounter; your leper-kiss; your Damascus Road body-slam; your beer commercial.

Have your God encounter. Be a hero.

CHAPTER ELEVEN

WHAT IS A HERO?

Mobilizing Mercy and Justice for End-Time Harvest.

So, what is the answer? Be a hero!

In light of Jesus' direction from the example of the Good Samaritan to "Go and do likewise," in recognition of the prophetic timetable promising a great end-time harvest, in response to the world's desperation when faced with the seven deadly sins, we want to inspire and mobilize an army of 10,000 heroes.

First, a disclaimer.

I had just finished preaching at a prestigious Church of England congregation in Oxford. The next day the CEO of a Christian organization that bankrolls a yearly budget of $130 million USD in loans to 500,000 microbusinesses started amongst the poor said to me, "I have to say, I was a little bit put out at the thought of a bunch of people running out to start children's homes in poor places of the world. Starting a home is not the total answer to all the world's problems." Over the next two hours we had a better chance to talk.

Of course we know that you and 9,999 others who become heroes are not the total answer to the world's problems.[1] Yes, we need to start thousands of micro-enterprises to create socio-economic lift. Yes, we need to see political despotism eradicated from the earth, and the management of police forces capable of enforcing it. Yes, we must create accessible health care and education for every man, woman, and child. Yes, it is God's will that every human being become good overnight and worship the Lord their God. Yes, yes, yes!

Although we know the five-point action plan is not the total answer to the totality of the world's problems—yet, it is a start. What we can say with certainty is that this is a biblical response to the world's problems. It's a simple call for every Christian everywhere, to become exactly what Jesus told us to be—a Good Samaritan; just one true disciple who loves his neighbor as himself. To be a Christian—to be a hero!

In our scenario, a hero is simply one who takes action by:

1. *Praying* for the Poor - Pray the Bible
2. *Investing* in the Life a Child - Sponsor One
3. *Starting or Supporting* a Project Working with Children
4. *Becoming an Advocate* for the Invisible People
5. *Going to See for Yourself* - Hero Holiday

RECRUITING THE HERO ARMY

This army of 10,000 heroes will: *love mercy* and *do justice*. Every member of the Hero Army will actually become a hero in the life of another. A hero is a zealot who rescues the life of another. Take one of our heroes from the first chapter, Bono. At this point in his life:

> He has given up on music as a political force. He believes his work negotiating in political back rooms is more vital and effective than singing in sold-out stadiums. "Poetry makes nothing happen," the poet W.H. Auden once wrote, and Bono wistfully agrees. "I'm tired of dreaming. I'm into doing at the moment. It's like, let's only have goals that we can go after."[2]

The Hero Army is not focusing on what a person is, but what they do…because heroism is something you do. You can't be heroic sitting on your hands. Neither can you properly do it alone. Rambo and the Terminator are restricted to a screen. Real heroes work together in cells, in congregations, in churches, with accountability, training, and strategy.[3] Patrick McDonald's seven essentials to cure the seven deadly sins include "an opportunity to be a part of a Christ-centered worshiping community." What is essential for them is essential for us.[4]

FIVE CHARACTERISTICS OF A HERO

1. A Hero Prays for the Poor - Pray the Bible

Spirituality is the new currency of the millennium. Everyone is praying these days to some god or another, but Yahweh is the God over all gods, the Creator God. Prayer doesn't take place in a vacuum. Christian prayer occurs with the Christian God. It alone is biblical prayer.

A hero prays the Bible. Why? The Bible depicts the "Mighty God", the "Hero God" and His hero Son. It's all about the heroic. God epitomizes the heroic. The desire to be heroic is a noble impulse God has downloaded into our DNA. Heroism comes from God. Prayer glorifies God, disciples our own hearts, and brings His will on earth. Prayer is the beginning of the first commandment and it will inevitably lead you to the second.[5]

That being the case, the best way to pray is to pray the Bible. William Booth said, "The Bible is 'God's heart on paper.' " When you pray the Bible you know you are praying God's heart back to Him. A spiritual hero prays the Bible because prayer is the fuel of the hero.

For years we have been involved in teaching people how to pray. Though it sounds easy, and almost everybody prays, most people don't feel their prayer life is as effective as they would like it to be. They don't know what to say, their mind wanders, they're too busy. These are the common problems we all face as we determine to pray.

Thankfully God has not left us without help. As early as Moses and Joshua (c. 1500 B.C.) God gave a simple yet powerful method for prayer. To the nation of Israel God said:

> Be strong and very courageous. Be careful to obey all the law
> My servant Moses gave you; do not turn from it to the right
> or to the left, that you may be successful wherever you go. **Do
> not let this Book of the Law depart from your mouth;
> meditate on it day and night**, so that you may be careful
> to do everything written in it. Then you will be prosperous
> and successful (Joshua 1:7-8).

This key passage gives God's expectation and His promise of prosperity and success to those who do this. The method developed into the heart of Jewish prayer. Simply stated we are instructed in the:

- how—*meditate*—audible recitation;
- the what—*on it*—the Book of the Law;
- the direction is implied, to God;
- and the frequency commanded—every day and every night.

Hence, pray the Bible, out loud to God everyday!

It seems like everyone has a story of struggle with private prayer. That is why for thousands of years the faithful have always prayed the Bible. The testimony of David was that he *"delighted in the law of the Lord, and on His law he meditated day and night"* (Ps. 1:2). David spent so much time in daily meditation of the Law that he became passionate about the glory of God and what God loves. So it was that God's Spirit inspired him to write the Psalms and create a prayer language concerning the poor (see Ps. 9:18; 10:14; 2:5; 35:10; 68:5; 69; 72; 82; 74:21; 112:9; 140:12). Here is a classic case of an intercessor praying the Bible and growing concerned for the poor. This is true of all the prophets and ultimately of Jesus Himself.

Because the content of prayer is so important we have compiled a *"Praying the Bible: Book of Prayers"* containing 88 prayers from the eight genres of prayer:

- The Theophanies—Visions of God
- The Psalms
- The Prayers of Wisdom
- The Song of Songs
- The Prayers of the Prophets
- The Prayers of Jesus
- The Apostolic Prayers
- The Hymns of the Revelation

In this prayer book, we provide detailed definitions of each of the eight prayer genres, as well as instructions on how to pray them. Later in this section is a sample prayer taken from the section on "The Prayers of Wisdom."

Having dealt with the problem of what to say, the second problem is equally difficult—how do I keep my mind from wandering? It is for this exact reason that I always tell people everywhere, "Learn to pray out loud." Many people wonder about this. They ask, "Why?" and are expecting some profound answer.

"The reason for praying out loud is simple...so that you will know when you have stopped!" It usually takes a moment or two to sink in, and then they all laugh knowingly. It's true that we need to use our mouth to lasso our mind, to affect our heart. As our mothers used to say, "It's hard to think about something else while you're talking."

Of course God had this all figured out from the beginning. When the Lord commanded the Israelites to meditate on His Law, He was telling them to pray it out loud. The Hebrew word for "meditate" is *hagah*, which means "to imagine, meditate, mourn, mutter, roar, speak, study, talk, utter." The

International Standard Bible Encyclopaedia interprets it as, "to murmur, to have a deep tone, to sigh, moan," or *higgayon*, "the murmur or dull sound of the harp." This is the sound of biblical meditation. The word has the idea of "saying over and over again, of speaking, of muttering, of reciting, or expelling air out loud." There was to be physical involvement in this activity. The result would accomplish our end product of meditation.

In the case of Joshua, they were to *hagah*—say over and over again—the *Book of the Law* out loud to God. Remember that the 2 million Israelites coming out of Egyptian slavery couldn't read and all data was transferred orally by professional storytellers. On top of that, there was nothing to read even if they had been taught. Basically all the cultures were oral, as books hadn't yet been invented. For instance, just the Law of Moses alone (Exodus, Leviticus, Numbers, and Deuteronomy) would have taken about 80 feet of animal skins on which to copy the text and then it would take two grown men to roll it up into a large scroll. It's ridiculous to imagine any Israelite having his own personalized "Book of the Law." No, every consonant of the Torah is said to have a musical notation above it, so that the reader will know the tonal sound with which to say the word, and worshipers would all chant the Law in sing-song fashion. Almost an ancient form of Hebrew rap, if you will.

So it was, from Moses and Joshua onward, the people of God prayed the Law out loud.

Lastly, beat the problem of *busyness* by scheduling in your prayer every day. God instructs us to meditate on His Law *day and night*. Everyone knows that you learn to pray by praying. If you never show up, you never learn. How Israel understood *"day and night prayer"* is evidenced by how they lived it out. When Zacharias went into the holy of holies and "the time for the burning of incense came, all the assembled worshipers were praying outside" (Luke 1:10). How early this practice started we cannot know, but when Moses would go into the tent of meeting to talk to God, all of the Israelites worshiped at the entrance of their own tents (see Exod. 33:8-10).

By the time of David, we know that morning and evening prayers were becoming the norm within Tabernacle/Temple worship. David said, "But I call to God and the Lord saves me. *Evening, morning and noon*, I cry out in distress, and He hears my voice" (Ps. 55:16-17). David's prescribed pattern in the Temple was to have morning and evening prayer.

David believed the sacrifices should be accompanied with morning and evening prayers and he called for "the Levites to help Aaron's descendants in the service of the temple of the Lord…. They were also to stand every morning to thank and praise the Lord. They were to do the same in the evening" (see 1 Chron. 23:28, 30).

Daniel carried this practice to the point of obsession as a captive in Babylon where, under threat of death, he refused to break his habit of praying three times daily. *"Three times a day he got down on his knees and prayed, giving thanks to his God, just as he had done before"* (Dan. 6:10). Historians tell us that sometime after the 70 years of captivity in Babylon (c. 450 B.C.), Ezra determined that Israel would never again provoke God to such wrath. So, he mandated daily prayers, accompanied with readings from the Torah.

In time, it became custom for Jews to pray the 18 "Benedictions," coupled with readings from the Torah, over three set "hours" of prayer at the temple, synagogue, or home. This custom was firmly in place long before the birth of Jesus. Accordingly, Jesus, along with every righteous Jew, would have observed this practice daily. It is interesting to think that Jesus, his father Joseph, and Joseph's father, all would have prayed this way; that Peter, James, and John grew up praying set prayers every day; and that Paul was steeped in the model of Jewish prayer.

The evidence from the New Testament is that "night and day" prayer was practiced by the entire early Church, as well as by the God-fearers who had attached themselves to Judaism. Luke records, "Peter and John were going up to the temple at the ninth [hour], the hour of prayer" (Acts 3:1). Cornelius, a Gentile God-fearer, is called a devout man who "prayed continually." The next verse explains what continual prayer means: "About the ninth hour of the day [the hour of prayer] he clearly saw in a vision an angel of God who came to him, and said to him, 'Cornelius!'..."Your prayers and alms have ascended as a memorial before God.' " (Acts 10:2-4).

As you can see, both the Jews and the early Church prayed a minimum of three set times of prayer. The first hour ranged from 6:00 a.m. to 9:00 a.m., the second at noon, and the third somewhere between 3:00 p.m. and 6:00 p.m. Whether they felt like it or not, whether they knew how to do it or not, whether they felt inspired or not, as worshipers of God they were just called to show up. Jesus and the apostles did this, and like them, we are called to do it as well. Like them, we need to set a time, and make a place, to get face-to-face with God.

Here is an example of a biblical prayer that you can pray out loud to God:[6]

MERCY
Father in Heaven, You have said:
He who oppresses the poor shows contempt for their Maker,
but whoever is kind to the needy honors God.
Rich and poor have this in common:
The Lord is the Maker of them all.

So I will not exploit the poor because they are poor
nor crush the needy in court, for You will take up their case
and will plunder those who plunder them.
The righteous care about justice for the poor,
but the wicked have no such concern.
And You say, he who is kind to the poor lends to the Lord,
and He will reward him for what he has done.
Let me be like Job, who said:
I rescued the poor who cried for help,
and the fatherless who had none to assist him.
The man who was dying blessed me;
I made the widow's heart sing.
I was eyes to the blind and feet to the lame.
I was a father to the needy; I took up the case of the stranger.
I broke the fangs of the wicked
and snatched the victims from their teeth.
I chose the way for them and sat as their chief;
I dwelt as a king among his troops;
I was like one who comforts mourners.
(Proverbs 14:31; 22:2,22-23; 29:7; 19:17; Job 29:12-13,15-17,25)[7]

2. A Hero Invests in the Life of a Child

Be a hero in the life of a child. James 1:27 says that pure religion is to "visit the widows and the orphans in their distress as well as to keep ones self unspotted from the world." In his appeal for children Kofi Anan said, "for every dollar spent on a child, there is a seven fold return to society." So why don't we do it? Not long ago I asked myself if I actually took care of even one orphan or did I just talk about it. I realized it was only talk.

Today in many lands there are millions of homeless and orphaned children, as well as myriads of options for investing in the life of a child. In sub-Saharan Africa the population of orphans is now a staggering 10 percent of all children, or 1 in every 10 children is an orphan. There are many options, but a hero will focus on the poor, and the poorest of the poor are the homeless orphans. For less than a dollar a day, the price of a cup of coffee, you can make a huge difference in the life of a child. Imagine if hundreds of millions of Christians through out the world each invested in one child's life enabling that child to have a safe place to live, grow up and develop?

Decide to be a hero today, and for example, sponsor an orphan. Need an idea of what to do and how to pay for it? Look up Appendix 3 and www.beahero.org.

3. A Hero Starts/Supports a Project Working with Children

Isaiah said the chosen fast that God likes is this: "to divide your bread with the hungry, and bring the homeless poor into the house—when you see the naked, to cover him; and not to hide yourself from your own flesh" (Isa. 58:7). The intent is clear, *share your bread...invite them into your house...you cover him!*

The prophets are clear. Take the child into your home. But we know that the problem is that you live here and they live there. You cannot get them here to take them into your home. So, obviously, you must build your home there to take them into your home! That is why every hero starts or supports a project working with children. *Be a Hero* has a huge array of different options ranging from building children's homes to helping existing projects expand and help more children.

It seems so simple, and yet the overarching truth is that all the primary needs of every "child at risk" could be met in the arms of godly and loving houseparents who provide all the elements of nurture through the most basic of structures—the Christian home. Food is only the first of the basic needs of human care. Immediately after saying that God is a father to the fatherless, and a defender of widows, the Psalmist states, "God sets the lonely in families" (Ps. 68:6). Think of it, one children's home that you start or help to expand will provide the ongoing godly care that will circumvent hunger and malnutrition due to extreme poverty, lack of clothing, shelter, safety from exploitation (whether sexual or labor-related), medicine, schooling, and simple love.

In Zambia a recent study showed that two-thirds of all child prostitutes were AIDS orphans, and then they got AIDS themselves. Presently there are 11 million AIDS orphans in the Sub-Sahara and it is feared to reach 20 million by 2010.[8]

While writing this book and flying somewhere to speak on "children at risk," a thought popped into my mind. "What if your firstborn child were to die if you did not start a business in Africa this year?" I hated the thought. I tried to think about other things and pray against this morbid thought. But it wouldn't go away. Even reading a magazine wouldn't do it. Then after about 30 minutes the thought came back again, but only this time it was inverted. Basically what God said was this, "Wesley, if you don't start a business or home in Africa this year, someone else's firstborn will die."

Suddenly this made all the difference. Thirty minutes earlier it was theory, mind games. Thirty minutes earlier they were just "children out there." But now they had a face—the face of my child. I realized at that moment that if it were my sons and daughter who were on the streets in Rio de Janeiro, or Mumbia, or Cairo, or Bangkok, I would find a way to get them a home. Of course I would. Nothing could stop me. Why? Because they are my children. We have to come to the place where we recognize the great populace of children at risk as God's children, and someone's son or daughter.

Our thesis is simply this: if starting or supporting a project working with children would save the life of your own child, you would do this. So do it! *Be a Hero* exists to help you accomplish this great work. *Be a Hero* works in coalition with other expert organizations and ministries, who in turn work with nationals on the ground in developing countries ensuring that we can get the job done effectively and with accountability.

Everywhere we go, we encourage churches and even groups of friends to please God's heart by asking Him for the wisdom to start a children's home from scratch amongst the poorest of the poor—the orphans and street children. We call for those who are blessed with the resources and abilities to do something about children at risk and become like Job, who confessed, "*I rescued the poor who cried for help, and the fatherless who had none to assist him. I was a father to the needy; I took up the case of the stranger*" (Job 29:12,16).

Think of it, one children's home or expanded project will provide care for all the primary needs of children in that place who were previously at risk. This includes food, clothing, shelter, safety from exploitation (whether sexual or labor-related), medicine, schooling, and the added bonus of the gospel of Jesus Christ.

Of course, starting or supporting a project working with children is going to take organization and commitment, yet you must believe that this is absolutely do-able for you and a group of your friends. Just say "yes!" Then go forward together and do it.

What do you do?

Contact us today, and say, "Yes, I want to be hero, and I want to know how to start or support a project working with children." Whether a James 1 small hut for a widow and her own children and a couple others, or a more conventional children's home with 10-25 others, you will find a variety of options. In some cases it's an intervention project where aid workers have 20 minutes at the entrance points of the city, like train stations, buses, market squares, etc. where the obviously lost and bewildered children end up in the clutches of those who will hurt and abuse them. Intervention programs seek to find the child in five minutes and refer them to caring churches or organization that can help. Whether health clinics, day care, modified food and education or whatever, there are a host of options to choose from. The main point is that you do one.

Costs range from smaller projects for kids in middle and high school to bite-sized projects of $10,000 to $15,000 USD for adults.

In many cases, the default reaction is "I can't afford it," or "You can't be talking to me!" Before you get overwhelmed, just remember that you don't have to finance it all yourself. The best advocate to everyone you know is you! Most everyone in the developed nations wants to give. They just need to see and believe a credible cause.

For instance in 2002, Americans gave a whopping $241 billion[9] to 1.4 million charities.[10] More than $84 billion was religious giving,[11] but that means that over $150 billion was not given to religious purposes. No doubt, a large portion of both the religious and non-religious giving went to mercy projects just like these. Surprisingly, individuals give three-fourths of the staggering total, more than $180 billion![12] This is not corporate giving, or subsidies, or foundations but average working Joe's like you and me.

What is even more amazing is that 7 of the 10 people you work with, 7 of the 10 soccer moms you drive with, 7 of the 10 families you live with, give![13] Each household gives an average of $2,335 each year.[14] Remember two-thirds of those homes aren't yet giving to religious purposes.[15] If they knew about children at risk, they'd give. We figure that if you've made it this far in the book, you're included in these numbers. We are talking to you.

Once this thing captures your imagination it will not let go. It caught up with apostolic evangelists George Whitefield and John Wesley a couple of hundred years ago. They were prodigious preachers, in the peak of their energies, delivering several sermons a day over their lengthy active ministries. Their journals indicate their habit of taking up an offering for the poor after each sermon. In fact, Benjamin Franklin tells the story about going to hear George Whitefield preach. Whitefield was so persuasive that friends warned Franklin to empty his pockets before going to the meeting. Franklin forgot. As Whitefield began to preach Franklin thought he would give him all the copper coins he had with him. But soon into the sermon he changed his mind and determined to give him all the silver he had, and finally decided to give Whitefield everything he had. That's not all. The appeal came for the poor and Franklin's companion asked the person next to them if he could borrow money to give it to Whitefield![16]

In 1737 Whitefield was only 22 year old. His journal informs us that he was preaching about nine times a week.[17] In one season that year, he records offerings of nearly 1,300 pounds.[18] The conversion rate from pounds to USD in 1737 works like this: 1 pound back then equals $196.43 today.[19] So, 1,300 pounds is equivalent to more than $200,000 USD today.

Here are some snapshots of the month of October, 1740:

- October 3—Whitefield preached at Portsmouth and took an offering for orphans amounting to 97 pounds (about $16,985 USD today);
- Later that day he preached in Hampstead and took an offering for orphans amounting to 41 pounds (about $7,178 USD today);
- October 4—Whitefield preached at Newbury and took an offering for orphans amounting to 80 pounds (about $14,008 USD today)
- Later that day he preached in Ipswich and took an offering for orphans amounting to 79 pounds (about $13,832 USD today);
- October 5—Whitefield preached at Salem and took an offering for orphans amounting to 72 pounds (about $12,607 USD today);
- October 6—Whitefield preached at Marblehead and an offering for orphans totaled 70 pounds (about $12,255 USD today);
- October 9—Whitefield preached at Maulden and took an offering for orphans amounting to 200 pounds (about $35,010 USD today);
- October 10—Whitefield preached at Charleston and took an offering for orphans amounting to 156 pounds (about $27,302 USD today);
- Later that day he preached again and took an offering for orphans amounting to 51 pounds (about $8,924 USD today);
- October 11—Whitefield preached at Cambridge and took an offering for orphans amounting to 100 pounds (about $17,505 USD today);
- October 13—Whitefield preached at Concord and took an offering for orphans amounting to 45 pounds (about $7,873 USD today).[20]

How's that for a fortnight? While preaching the gospel in different towns daily, George Whitefield took offerings for orphans totaling $173,478 USD. These evangelists were devoted to the poor.

We can't all take up collections. But there are more ways to raise funds than you can shake a stick at. You can use some of your own funds. The phenomenal Phil Wall has a novel idea that carries the ethos of our micro-paradigm.[21] His leadership and personal development company, SIGNIFY, was built on this. Based on the parable of the talents (Matt. 25) Phil gives $10 pounds ($17.50 USD) to each person at a conference or seminar with a challenge: Multiply the funds by ten and return it to HopeHIV. All the funds go to South African orphans with AIDS.

You need to become a fundraiser on behalf of children at risk in your sphere of influence. For instance, what if you got serious? Consider the following:

FIGURE 15

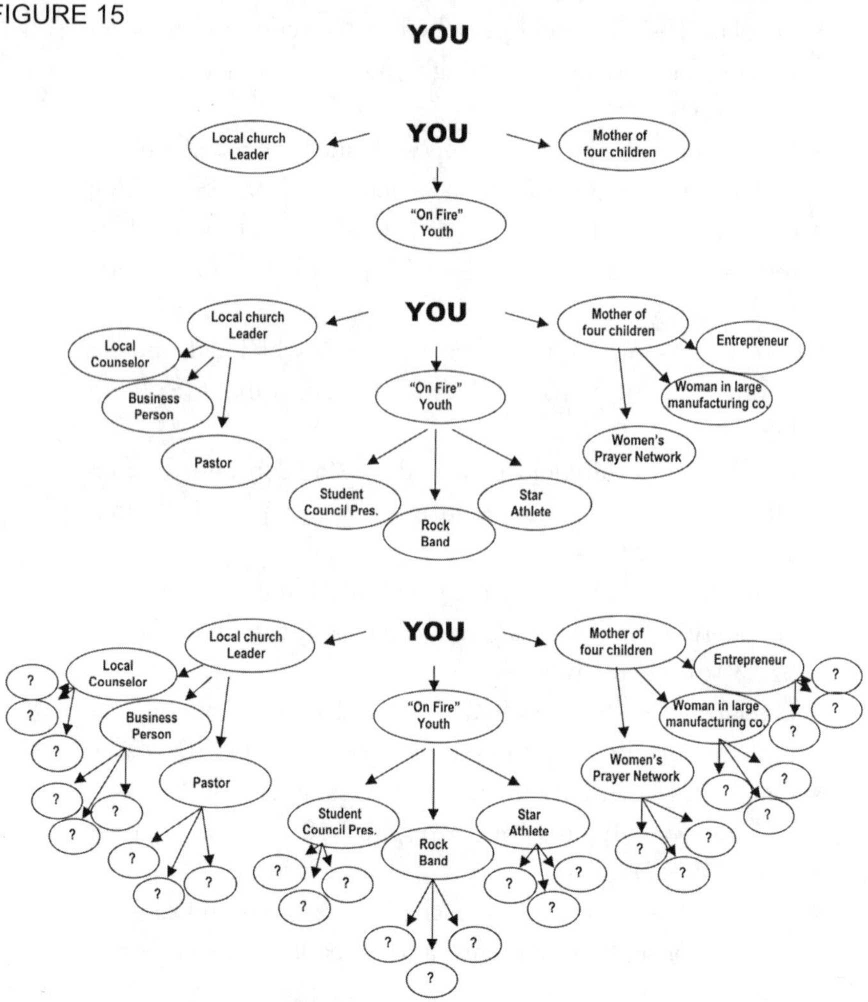

Start with your workplace. Next, consider your clubs, the organizations, to which you belong. What about your friends and neighbors? And, of course, don't forget your church—because every church needs a children's home. The Be a Hero organization exists to work with you to raise the funds to do children's homes. With you we will form a coalition of new partners that will ultimately establish homes or projects in places of need. The research has been done. The standards of care are in place. The workers are waiting. The children are praying. All that is needed is for you to say "yes"! Believe it. You… can…do…this!

By laboring to take the homeless child into your house that you start over there, you become a hero to them. Of course the added bonus is that children at risk who receive the care of Christians will also hear and be taught the gospel of Jesus Christ. Today we are seeing thousands of children who were previously exposed to every kind evil, laughing and filled with joy from being cared for and protected. They now experience God's love and know He has a plan for their lives. They have moved from the category of "children at risk" to children who are safe and saved.[22] Of course, starting a children's home from scratch is going to take organization and commitment, yet you must believe that this is absolutely do-able for you and a group of your friends. Just say "yes!" You can do this!

4. A Hero Advocates for the Invisible People.

When God looked at Israel, He was astonished that there was no one who would build up a wall and stand in the gap on behalf of the land so that He would not have to destroy it (see Ezek. 22:30). At that time there was no one who was an advocate for the poor, the needy, the fatherless, and the widow. There was no one like Job who said, "I took up the case of the stranger and those who had none to assist them" (Job 29:12).

A hero is one who becomes informed and from that knowledge becomes an advocate who agitates and organizes for mercy and social justice. A hero becomes aware of the needs of others, and then becomes a trumpet for those needs. The Bible says, "Rescue those being led away to death; hold back those staggering toward slaughter" (Prov. 24:11). To cry out for those who are unjustly treated is God's big idea. Invisible people are People people. Advocates are normal people like you and me who search out the case of the poor, the homeless, the exploited, and the dying, and then they advocate on their behalf. They make sure that invisible people—the widow, the fatherless, and the stranger—become People people. Publicize their case. Procure the help of power brokers. Raise up assistance. And, at times, lead civil disobedience. Become an advocate!

Advocacy

Heroes advocate. "Speak up for those who cannot speak for themselves, for the rights of all who are destitute. Speak up and judge fairly, defend the rights of the poor and the needy" (Prov. 31:8-9).[23]

Talk. Tell people what you know. You don't have to be an expert and if you've read through this far in the book, you know enough to blow people away with the crises around the world. Talk it up at work, at school, at the gym, in your cell group, in your church, everywhere.

For instance, once, at a conference, we met a lady who worked for Compassion International. I asked her, "How many people in your church now personally sponsor one child?" She said, "It's more like, 'How many don't?' The greater percentage of members all have one or more children they are sponsoring." I responded, "Tell me more."

Her pastor was very skeptical, as he had been burned once by writing to his supposed orphan and receiving letters only to later find out the child had died a few years earlier. He wanted nothing more to do with it. But then after gaining the pastor's trust and showing the credibility of Compassion International, which has sponsored over 1 million children in 30 years, the pastor was won back as an advocate for children. This one lady changed her church from a group who wasn't caring for children at risk to a whole church that does sponsor and care. You could do the same!

Join campaigns with which you agree. Jubilee 2000 scored 48 million signatures of people like you. Individually they probably couldn't get much of a hearing from international leaders, but together, 48 million of them convinced the G8 to forgive $100 billion of debt!

Change the way you do commerce. Use charity cards that send a percentage of your purchases to children at risk. Optimize the tax break given for charitable giving every year.

To Food for the Hungry, advocacy is simply a matter of sharing God's heart for the poor. FftH suggests sharing God's heart for the poor by establishing significant ministry links between your church and an impoverished community.[24] This is an exciting possibility, that can be enriched by sending short and long term mission servants, by establishing pen pals, by "adopting" families and sponsoring children, through educational exchanges, by donating needed items, and by praying intentionally. Organize the 30-Hour Famine with your church's youth group.

And there is more. You can write to government representatives expressing your concern and position on issues such as clean water for the poor.[25] And accompany it with community awareness-raising events. For example, a local Sydney group walked six kilometers carrying buckets to MP Brendan Nelson's office-the average distance African women walk each day to collect water.[26] That will draw attention (so much that we wrote about it and you're reading about it!).

For Refugee Advocacy, you can do most of the above-mentioned ideas. But you can also offer practical, personal assistance, befriending, tutoring, donating goods, hosting, etc.[27]

World Wide Day of Prayer

One thing to which we are calling every advocate is this: *Influence your congregation to participate in the World Wide Day of Prayer for Children at Risk.*[28]

Since 1996, the World Wide Day of Prayer for Children at Risk has been taking place on the first Saturday/Sunday of every June. Christians in more than 90 countries organize local prayer gatherings to intercede for children at risk. Early in March or April, try to get this day scheduled onto your church calendar. The minimum requirement for World Wide Day of Prayer for Children at Risk is that one prayer meeting is scheduled around it, and the mention of "children at risk" and prayer takes place on Sunday morning. It is even better if the pastor or minister actually speaks an entire message on the subject.

Viva Network has a "Day of Prayer" kit with materials to inspire informed prayer and to help with the planning of prayer events, as well as a sample message for the pastor and the notes and PowerPoint (see our viva.org web site).[29]

> Lift up your hands to Him for the lives of your children, who faint
> from hunger at the head of every street (Lamentations 2:19).

Don't be discouraged. You can make a difference in your own circle of influence. Remember the charts that demonstrate the potential reach of your advocacy. Six degrees of separation separate you from your national leader, your church leader, or Bill Gates.

Go and Do Something!

When William Booth wandered under a London bridge on the way home one night in the 19th century, he was shocked by the number of home-less people huddled in the modest shelter from the elements. He asked his son

236 BE A HERO

if he knew about their plight. Bramwell admitted that he did and was soundly rebuked and exhorted by his father, "Go and do something!"

That is Christian advocacy in a nutshell. "Go and do something!"

5. Go see it for yourself - go on a Hero Holiday

This is the concept of pilgrimage and encounter. In ancient times the Christian heroes went on a pilgrimage to holy sites. During their pilgrimage they often met God in a more profound and meaningful way. This is see, touch, feel. We advocate a pilgrimage to an unholy site—the poor.

Two of our friends were deciding what to do on their 25th wedding anniversary. After thinking about for a while they decided to go on a missions holiday and trek into an unreached people group located high in the Himalayas. Out of the holiday, they developed an ongoing Christian presence and started a children's home. Today churches exist in the region.

Go and see real poverty for yourself. Don't spend a week or two on a beach or skiing down mountains for your holidays, go and spend time with your brothers and sisters who have nothing. Feel, touch, smell, taste and listen to their world. Use your God given skills to go and do something amazing: you will not return unchanged. Go and work among the poor. Go and do what you can.

Pilgrimage

"Pilgrim": derived from Latin **peregrinum**—with idea of wandering over a distance.[30]

In 1990 1,500 pilgrims were trampled to death in Mecca.[31] These were Muslims.

You can see them from afar, a band of pilgrims on the road, raising dust.

They are easy enough to identify. They wear pilgrim clothes and emblems. Some are lame and sick. They carry votive offerings; they long for healing and spiritual nourishment at the holy shrine.

Far back in the distance, you spy other groups. (This pilgrim route gets busy at high season.) And between the groups you see occasional stragglers, shuffling towards their destination on their knees. They mortify the flesh now to ensure divine favor later.

Where are we, and when? Chaucer's pilgrims traveling to Canterbury? Or 13th century devotees on route to Santiago de Compostela in northern Spain? Could these, rather, be modern Christian pilgrims flocking to Lourdes? No. We are somewhere in

Gaul or Roman Britain. The date is A.D. 100. Trajan occupies the imperial throne at Rome.[32]

Christianity features a rich history of pilgrimage that reaches back to century one. Pilgrimages were born:

> ...in the instinctive notion of the human heart. For pilgrimages properly so called are made to the places where the gods or heroes were born or wrought some great action or died, or to the shrines where the deity had already signified it to be his pleasure to work wonders. Once theophanies are localized, pilgrimages necessarily follow. The Incarnation was bound inevitably to draw men across Europe to visit the Holy Places, for the custom itself arises spontaneously from the heart. It is found in all religions.[33]

Although the advent of Protestantism threw a wet towel on the passion for it, and today's Holy Land tours are often more recreational than spiritual, the "pilgrim impulse still animates" many Christians today.[34]

The Holy Land Pilgrimage and the Hero Holiday

Although there is much superstition tied to the history of Christian pilgrimage, and the reality remains that, as Augustine argued, "God is here and so we don't have to go there,"[35] the Holy Land pilgrimage still resonates in the hearts of many Christians today.

But for this last generation we're calling Christian heroes to alter the tradition. Instead of making a Holy Land pilgrimage, we who would be heroes ought to do an UN-Holy Land pilgrimage, visiting, as James exhorts us, "the orphans and the widows in their distress" (James 1:27).

ROUND UP

This is what we know.

God's big idea is that invisible people are *People* people too!

God's senses of compassion and mercy, justice, and righteousness are sharpened to the plight of the victims of the seven deadly sins.

Throughout biblical and post-biblical history, God has raised up heroes who can testify that the face of the earth changes as the hearts of its people are transformed.

There will be a great end-time harvest of souls, most of whom are poor and young, and live in the developing world.

Jesus is coming back soon.

God wants us to be involved.

Be a hero. Join a 10,000 strong army of heroes to please Jesus.

HOW TO BE A HERO

Convinced? Then let's marry courage to our conviction and move out.

- **Commit to praying the Bible.** If you need help, visit bea-hero.org for resources such as *Praying the Bible: The Book of Prayers*.
- **Invest in the life of a child—Sponsor one.** Among many worthy options we've include some in the appendix.
- **Start/support a children's home or project working with "children at risk."** Again, you can do this on your own, but we're happy to hook you up through beahero.org.
- **Advocate on behalf of the marginalized.** There are all kinds of wonderful ways to make this happen. One group in Australia was so inspired by the Be a Hero challenge that at the end of the conference they started **The Salvation Army Justice Wing**, an online means of disseminating information and mobilizing demonstrators, letter-writers, and prayers. To get connected in your region, visit beahero.org.
- **Go see it for yourself—go on a Hero Holiday.** There are many options for this challenge. If it is going to take you awhile to save up to travel a long distance, make an effort to go to a slum area in your region for a week or two, living among the people there. If you need some direction, visit beahero.org.

We're mobilizing mercy and justice for end-time harvest. God can morph invisible people into *People* people. Truly, the face of the earth will change as the hearts of its people are transformed. We want to track this whole movement, so we would love for you to sign up today at beahero.org.

CHAPTER TWELVE

A PARADIGM FOR END-TIME HARVEST

As terrible as things are, there is much to celebrate. Despite the senses-pummeling report of the Seven Deadlies (Chapter 9) you might still recall the breath-gasping recounting of the acceleration of Great Commission expansion from "Who Are They and Where Do They Come From?" (Chapter 8).

God covenanted with Abraham to bless all the nations of the earth through him (see Gen. 12:3). Some opine that God is fulfilling His covenant faster than you can shake a stick at it.[1]

As God's people everywhere move into the breach, billions can be saved. From where will they come? The poor, the dying, and the dispossessed.[2]

How old will they be? They will be young, many just children.[3]

We've thought strategically about how to leverage ourselves to reach the bulk of the two-thirds world in which the seven deadly sins are norm. We are uniquely positioned to mobilize mercy and justice and wed venture philanthropy with power evangelism to win the world for Jesus.

We have everything we need. We've got the best technology, the best means of travel, the best methods, and the most resources in history.

What stops us?

The short answers come on two levels: personal and corporate.

PERSONAL

On the personal level they include ignorance, information, practical help to mobilize us, and, most importantly, personal revival. After reading this book, the first three hindrances have been removed. You must deal with the personal revival on your own.[4]

Jesus did prophesy that we'd do even greater things than He did (see John 14:12). Let's see. He preached that the kingdom of God was at hand. He healed the sick, raised the dead, cleansed lepers, and dislocated demons. He demonstrated authority over the sky (calming the storm), the water (walking on it), and the land (cursing a fig tree). He exercised mastery over social prejudices, over religious intolerance, over racial discrimination. He epitomized mercy and compassion. And He prophesied that His Church would arise to do even greater things.

Jesus initiated a revolution that has not yet been fully realized. We are His strategy. He is putting it all on the line. He is counting on us. A great crowd of witnesses joins Him up in heaven, watching and cheering us on. Jesus has dreamt up a ruthless, reckless, mobile, radical army of heroes who cannot be bought by the world, because we belong to Jesus...who cannot be enticed by temptations because our natural inclination to sin has been crucified (see Rom. 6:5-6)...who go for souls like they are their own children, for whom to live is Christ and to die is gain...who die every day...who are covenanted, passionate warriors devoted to world conquest.

Justice is not only a means of accomplishing the mission, not merely an avenue for the expression of the compassion that naturally overflows a surrendered heart. It is also a measure of the status of the revolution. *Rice Christians in the two-thirds world plus carnal Christians in the developed world do not add up to revolution.* A deficient gospel does not change the face of the earth. Only a gospel of the Kingdom brings transformation. We can measure the revolution by the reduction and ultimate obsolescence of our seven deadly sins: gross poverty, orphans of the street, slavery and child labor, sex and the city, AIDS and plagues, the effects of war, and religious persecution.

When we've effectively treated, decimated, or eradicated these scourges, we'll know that the revolution is reaching a climax. When the invisible people of the world, the poor, the alien, the sick, the needy, the widow, and the orphan, regain the dignity for which they were created and become People people, we have joined the saints who famously turned the world upside down. When we see the kingdom of God established ubiquitously around the world, peace, joy, and love, we can begin to write the victory reports for the Hero Army.

Granted, there are trends that indicate the emergence of another set of deadly sins, such as terrorism, raping the earth, tribalism, the (dis)information explosion, globalization,[5] and the disintegration of the family.[6] But if we can experience a revival along the lines of Josiah, according to the charter of Job, on the scale of David, the ramifications in terms of social justice should encompass these as well.

We must never underestimate the dynamic potential of even a small but committed group. Indeed, the days of the slave trade were numbered when the members of the Clapham sect first met in William Wilberforce's living room.

"Are the motives of Christianity so unnecessary to its practice, that one may be spared its principles, and still have the former—the motives—with undiminished force?"[7] Of course not. The motive is to win an end-time harvest that will reflect enormous glory to Jesus. To accomplish it, our hearts must be in tune with Him. *And the face of the earth will change as the hearts of its people are transformed.*

As Mother Teresa used to say, "We're just pebbles being thrown into the sea and causing ripples."[8] Let's make ripples that expand through the agony of the world to reach each single person for Jesus.

Corporate

That's enough to get you started personally. Ezekiel found that the river gets deeper. Wade in angle deep with a child sponsorship. Get in up to your knees with a children's home. Soon you will get deep enough that your bowels are swamped. You'll be moved to weeping and your tears will mingle with the river until you're in over your head. And while you're wading in, you'll find, like Ezekiel, that there are oceans to swim in.[9]

"YOU DIDN'T GIVE AT THE OFFICE"

The Western worldview encourages the mental fallacy that plays like this: "I gave at the office." Giving your tithe is not enough. Statistics confirm that about 5 percent of North American church tithes go to missions.[10] But even that 5 percent doesn't usually go to the invisible people whose cause the heroes champion. It is stretched to cover infrastructure, missionaries, evangelism, discipleship, and, maybe, the invisible people. You did not "give at the office."

Terms have blurred our vision. The words are not true. "Poor" is not poor. The biblical poor includes more than just the homeless addicts washing windows on major city street intersections in the West. Our aperture must expand to include the world poor. Right now the common Western perspective sees only a tiny piece of the enormous world puzzle. Swell the aperture to see what God sees—He sees the whole world, not just a single city in the West. It must enlarge to include the invisible people, "their" poor. *Their* poor have no social net, have no access to government services, and so have no recourse other than slavery and prostitution or other crime. We cannot presume that we have the whole picture.

We're not burdened because we think the job is already done. We think that if the guy would just stop drinking and walk down the street then The Salvation Army will feed him. The poor child in Sudan, in Bangladesh, in Nicaragua, cannot. The job is not done.

Watch this perspective:

> I am not a hippie. I'm not even idealistic. I came from punk rock; I was never a hippie with flowers in my hair. It was always about the deal—getting the record deal, going with the band and getting it done. In the business that I'm doing now with DATA, it's to get checks out of governments. It's hard-headed. It's not about dreaming, it's about doing. You start with your imagination like John Lennon did, but then you have to walk out onto the street and actually make it happen. You can't fix every problem, but the ones you can, you must if you're the overdog.[11]

"NUMB"

One of the pastors from Rwanda at a World Intercessors Conference recounted his experience. He and his two friends, all pastors, grew concerned of the growing ugliness in their society. They realized that they had to do something about the ethnic hatred. So together they wrote a paper to distribute to pastors throughout the country. The night before it was to go to press, the genocide began. Both of his co-authors were hacked to death with machetes.

He described the genocide, during which 800,000 people were killed in a month and a half: "The evil dehumanized the people so that they could tolerate incredible atrocities and not be moved." Conversely, as you gaze into the face of God and pray that the attributes of God get internalized, Paul teaches that you are being transformed in God's image. The more you gaze at God the more human you become.

COMMUNISM—CAPTURING HEARTS

A century ago, when the injustice to the worker was reaching its zenith, people around the world were agitating for change, because justice touches the heart of people. Justice comes from God's heart, and we're made in His image. In central Europe and Russia, the Church, instead of acting wholesale—which includes the rights of the worker,[12] the rights of women, and the poor, and the alien—sided with the rich.

A false reformation emerged that, though intended to right injustice, only enslaved them. The Church lost the war. Two generations went into the wilderness. Stalin butchered 51 million of his own people in order to enforce his version of utopia. Mao slayed 44 million Chinese in order to impose his utopia. Hitler slaughtered 25 million.

Why did the masses sign up? They wanted honest pay for honest work. They wanted to feed their child and educate them. They wanted the end of discrimination and class systems. Communism said, "We'll all do this for the common good of everyone and achieve our utopia." "Heaven on earth without God." This single idea fueled the hearts of a third of the earth. Unfortunately they got hell!

Here's the question? Where was the Church? Why wasn't the Church leading the justice movement? And winning the higher ground like the early Church?

If the righteous do not take on this global mandate, which is nothing more than the words of the gospel and the justice of God, an illegitimate taskmaster will (secular society). And while they give out the food they will take the authority.

The United Nations Millennium Development Goals[13] for 2015 reflect the world's consensus on this issue. The goals are:

- Eradicate extreme poverty and hunger by half
- Achieve universal primary education

- Promote gender equality and empower women
- Reduce child mortality
- Improve maternal health
- Combat HIV/AIDS, malaria, and other diseases
- Ensure environmental sustainability
- Develop a global partnership development.[14]

Do these sound familiar? They look similar to our "seven deadlies." And 191 countries in the United Nations know the problems.

We're in a critical hour. The whole world knows that this is wrong and it must be changed. And they are bound and determined to do something about it. If the Church doesn't do anything, then it won't be done in Jesus' name. If the collectives of the Hero Army go out like Mother Teresa and win the higher ground, the contracts for dispensing money, the resources, and the authority will be given to us.

SPIRITUALITY IN THE MODERN WORLD

In global arenas such as the UN, World Bank, G-8 and G-20 summits, etc., there is an increasing understanding that the world cannot be changed without giving attention to spiritual matters. In the past century, religion was virtually ignored at these levels, while those in power sought to improve the state of world affairs through education and wealth. However, when billions of dollars and Harvard educations were thrown at the problems of nations, they proved insufficient to solve the deep-seated causes of the problems, because money and teaching alone did not reach the roots that grew the fruits of genocide, poverty, and plagues like AIDS. However, this myopic view is beginning to change. As Peter Gardener states in his book, *Praying at the Global Gates*:

> Political and economic leaders today are drawing religious leaders into the debate at a global level. They realize that religious belief, embedded for centuries, goes deeper than changing political theory and policy. Since it is thought that 80-90% of the world's population holds some religious affiliation, significant changes at the global level will need to involve religious leaders.[15]

As a result of this growing understanding of the importance of religion on world affairs, World Faith leaders are "gaining unprecedented access into the heart of powerful global gates."[16] The World Economic Forum has even brought religious leaders, such as Buddhist Zen Leader Thich Nhat Hanh, into their deliberations. In 2001, this Buddhist teacher taught all the WEF participants for 70 minutes on "mindfulness," and led participants in a "silent minute" so they could "become aware of [their] breathing so that mind may return to body."[17] While it may be disconcerting for Christians to discover that this type of philosophy is having such direct access to the world's most powerful influencers, it should also make us realize that this could be a season of great opportunity. After all, if the world is asking for spirituality, we have the most powerful spirit, the Holy Spirit, indwelling us and leading us. In other words, we have the most to offer.

> As we enter a new millennium, the spiritual factor in the global equation is being considered like never before. Those in leadership positions are seeking stronger religious connections, to the point where they are even setting up plans to invite and involve religious and spiritual guidance to global political and economic institutions.[18]

This could well be the Church's finest hour—if we become strategic in our thinking and planning. However, if we abdicate the global arenas to the cults, then the solutions that world leaders come up with will be demonically influenced, causing even more death and destruction. It is time for the Esthers, Daniels, and Josephs to take their places in the courts of power until, like Nebuchadnezzar, the world acknowledges that "Heaven rules" (see Dan. 4:26).

What is at stake here is global authority as the Church is positioning for the great end-time harvest.

Mercy and justice are what move people. For too long we've been pushing a message devoid of the guts of the Kingdom. For too long we've been giving them thoughts and theories to get them saved, and then let them die.

The world disdains the empty message. If we will only do the works of Jesus, we won't have to speak much.

It is easy to throw in the towel and see our individual insignificance in the shadow of the mammoth problem. But together we become dangerous to the enemy.

Heroes in every generation, as the revivalists in Thoreau's day, "were seized by a vision that faithful people are called to extraordinary lives of kindness and service, and they were not ashamed to announce to people that God calls them not to blandness but to heroics."[19]

And we need to see that we can be obedient to God and fulfill His purposes for His world. In His strength we can crush an army (see Ps. 18:29). In His strength we can break the fangs of the wicked (see Job 29:17). In His strength the heroic end-time Army can be deployed to see multitudes saved. Surely, the face of the earth changes as the hearts of its people are transformed. Be a hero. And may God accelerate the transformation!

A BLUEPRINT FOR ACTION

By Patrick McDonald[1]

Strategy and Strength: Battles are won on strategy not just strength. Wesley and Stephen asked me to write a "strategy for global action." This is a short overview of *"what needs to happen"* to *eradicate child poverty* and do so in a way that gives Jesus due credit for His provision for, and pleasure in, that cause.

First off, I firmly believe we can be the generation that eradicates child poverty! Is this utopian optimism or urbane naivety? No. James Grant, late executive of UNICEF is famously quoted for stating: **"It is not that we have tried to solve the challenge of poverty and failed, it is that we have never tried at all."**

We have today—perhaps for the first time in history—the resources, technology, and the broad political will to protect and provide for the needs of our children. All of our children! Someone once told me that "A point of view is only ever a view from a point," and unless we have that "point of view"—that we can eradicate child poverty in our generation—I suspect we will fail yet another generation of hungry, homeless, and hurting children.

"The average European cow receives $2.20 a day, whereas half the world's population of nearly three billion people struggle to survive on less than $2 a day." This is much more than we give in aid… "Unfair trade rules rob poor countries of an export income of £2 billion every day—that's 14 times what they receive in aid."[2]

India alone spends 30 percent of its budget on its military and 3 percent on its education. What is the cost of sending a spaceship to Mars? Let's stop buying the line that "this is impossible to really change" or that "its just the way it is" and realize that this type of thinking allows for our own apathy and mediocrity. It can be done. It must be done.

The Key: Secondly, there is probably no better way to help children than by mobilizing and equipping the Christian movement to concerted action. Regardless of whom people think Jesus is there is no other movement better able to achieve that goal.

Why?

- Because the Church is present nigh on everywhere. Fully 28 percent of the global population, organized into more than 3 million congregations worldwide, provide an unprecedented platform for current and future action.[3]
- Because poverty bothers us. No other movement has such clear and consistent mandate for action with and for the poor. "Pure religion" is to help the orphan, and wherever you have Christians and children at risk you have a response.
- Because we care and are hugely involved personally and through our programs. In Britain, churches operate 144,000 social action programs[4] up and down the land. The church is the single largest provider of care in existence.
- Because there is a clear link between poverty and morality. If you drink it all away, the kids won't get breakfast. Sin is expensive. Greed and injustice are linked. You cannot feed a child for very long without also asking why it's hungry and nigh on nobody has better access to "the powers" nor more moral weight than the Church.

Poverty Goals: The international community has established ambitious poverty eradication goals but they rely on the participation of what is called "civil society" or "faith-based organizations" including churches. The opportunities are as huge as they are real. The challenge is down to us, down to the Christian community, to you and me. I believe no generation of Christians has ever been presented with such tangible opportunity to achieve our vision on such a massive scale. So let's take a look at what needs to happen. What then is our job?

As people we need to realize that:

Charity Starts at Home: What is the point in winning the world and yet losing one's soul? Christians in particular have every encouragement to ensure the well-being of our own children. To pass on not only wealth but wisdom. Childhood lasts around 6,000 days, make sure every day counts and that those kids grow up knowing full well that you are there for them. Be excited about what excites them. Study them, know them, bless them, and help them become all that God intended.

Besides, a "justice lifestyle" is key. An average consumer in the UK will spend £1 million pounds (about USD $1.8m)[5] on consumables during a lifetime; that represents power. Where we seek to shop and what we seek to buy directly affect the lives of those who produced those goods. Seek out fair-traded products; invest ethically. Be an advocate. Speak out when porn moves in and, as you do, make sure your kids are always part of your mission. They will be great colleagues and will soon do greater things than you ever did. It's fun to watch!

As Churches we Need to: As churches we need to invest massively in children. Our budgets should show our knowledge of their strategic significance and numeric majority. Our missions efforts at home and abroad should be geared at the "4-14" (years of age) window. Have we got a full-time children's pastor? Are the kids in our congregation part of the outreach or simply recipients of our attention? We have huge scope to do a lot with a little, especially as we realize that children themselves are a great resource for ministry.

Envision: People perish without vision. Vision is the catalyst for greatness, the fuel for courage, the energy for the extraordinary. We have a huge job on our hands simply bringing the needs of children and their importance to the attention of the masses. Millions must know. But more so, we need to generate a significant commitment for action. Through our time, treasure, and talent we must throw ourselves into the challenge of reaching and raising a generation of children.

This is the stuff of mass marketing—marketing a cause not merely a product.

Entry: Vision is only sustained by hope; hope that this works. People need easy access to lots of options of what to do with their newfound passion. Awareness must be translated into commitment sustained through results. God has provided wonderful tools of E-mail and web sites and although www.viva.org is a good beginning, we need a more beefy elaborate information portal that is able to harness the commitments made. In time, consultants could use the same information, add to it but present people or institutions with more personalized response to their aspirations.

Equipping: Hundreds of thousands of Christians work with children and yet we have no system of training the workers through courses, journals, or rewarding demonstrable skills with coherent global licensing. If we want to "up the game" we need training that starts where people are and then build capacity, competence, and ongoing dependence on God. This has to involve extensive licensing of good service-providing programs and capacity building for programs "almost there." In a world of ever higher standards, the Church will be left behind—or worse our programs will be legislated out of business—unless we impose high standards on our own work.

Networks: Individual action and local churches doing their bit is essential but becomes transformational when tied together in local networks—35 to 50 churches committing to coordinate and collaborate around city strategies developed between them would be powerful.

God's mandate for our communities is transformation and nothing less. He has not thrown us three shoes and asked us to put one on each foot. We need to embrace the size and complexity of the challenge and then get to work making the difference.

Starting by understanding the needs of our communities and the resources—secular and Christian—employed in the response, we can set ambitious goals between us and begin resourcing the solution. This will move the church from a club singing songs once a week to a meaningful stakeholder transforming our communities—from a fringe group of "those guys" to a respected community player able to negotiate block grants on behalf of whole communities of projects and able to address systemic issues of injustice.

As a movement we need to offer:

Advocacy: Similarly we need global coalitions to tackle the major systemic issues of injustice imbedded in our legislation and practices. Europeans give more subsidies to our cows than we provide hungry Africans in aid, and in doing so, deprive the very same Africans the opportunity to raise commercially viable cattle. Then we complain that there is no hope for Africa! God have mercy. Debt and trade remain root causes of poverty and they are far from dealt with.

Provision: I have touched on this already but to detail my call for action we need to take action in regard to:

- Foster kids: Open our homes to children needing residential care. Orphans exist in every society and their care is always fraught with trouble. Whilst some institutional care is inevitable it is clear that the lower the ratio between the number of children to the number of caring long-term committed adults the better. That places fostering high on the agenda and as well as small family group homes.

- Child survival: Child survival, especially from preventable disease, remains a huge priority. Pre-natal, post-natal, basic healthcare programs in the slum (teaching kids to brush their teeth, providing basic vaccines and vitamin supplements) are of great value. I believe real benefit could be rendered if such programs could be tied together in more elaborate networks offering a type of "triage community healthcare" referring more complex problems "up the chain" to better (but fewer) health clinics. We should see tens of thousands of churches set up basic pharmacies and community health clinics.

- Nutrition: Food security, especially for under fives is prerequisite for healthy development. Portals for delivery usually include schools but often programs operate in isolation from local area development plans. The delivery of food is not combined with local production and technical assistance to parents.

- Education: The provision of basic and/or primary education for all children is achievable and essential. Better trained and more motivated teachers and integration between school programs and other programs are essential but often rely on the provision of development coordinators that are hard to find. We must see tens of thousands of new schools set up in elaborate private-public partnerships effectively funded and properly managed.

- Refugees: Millions of children are losing vital years "between places" or reared in "unsuitable places" because they are displaced from wars. Their rights are ignored, their needs overlooked. Partnerships amongst refugee programs must deliver more and better results but require competent staff that are very hard to fund due to the intangible nature of their work (peace building, negotiation, multilateral talks, talks about talks).

- Exploitation: The internet-based child porn needs regulating, as does the growing trade in children. Whilst legislation is being enforced we are dealing with an out of control moral revolution that permits sex with children. With AIDS in the picture the need for virgins in the brothel industry has gone through the roof and even though she has been sewn up multiple times, a child's claim to virginity appears more legitimate than that of an adult. Much harder enforcement is one route. Revival another. Pray for both!

- Investment: At the end of the day far too much of all of the above relies on volunteerism, which, although good, is hard to count on. Children deserve better than our hopeful optimistic maybe. They deserve our investment and our solid commitment. We need to see more tax dollars raised and dedicated not just to wars against illusive terrorists with exciting habits in beards, but against the plight of a whole generation dying on our doorsteps.

Governments are being called on by the OECD to commit 0.7 percent of GNP on their development/aid budget, yet only a fraction of countries comply (mostly the Scandinavian countries). The U.S. alone spends $370 billion on the military whilst just $6 billion could eradicate world hunger. We talk a lot about poverty but do little. Hear me…we do little! In the end game it remains a convenient extra for the few, not a core commitment for the many. This must change.

Framework: The Christian movement badly needs a global framework for action: a framework for movement-wide action that would benchmark current work and set goals for our individual and collaborative achievement. This framework will be hugely influential in mobilizing more Christian action for children and in raising our sights to what God desires. The global framework could be adopted by organizations, churches, denominations, and families, encouraging them to establish their strategy for implementing godly goals for children.

Such a framework of action would establish a set of godly ideals for children ensuring that every child should have the opportunity to, for example: know God; live in safety; be loved by at least one adult; eat enough; drink enough; grow up healthy; learn to read and write; participate in shaping their future, etc.

The Framework would seek to compliment not duplicate the UN Convention of the Rights of the Child (CRC). The Framework would intend to amplify and accelerate Christian participation in the execution of CRC objectives.

Brokering: The Christian movement must develop intermediary bodies able to handle large-scale community-wide contracts of service provision. Whilst I call for more investment, especially from governmental bodies, I recognize the real obstacles of spending those resources effectively. To work with a multitude of small entities with varying qualities is impossible for big officialdoms. We need better, more flexible, intermediary bodies able to broker the difficult tension between budget deadlines and effective sustainable service delivery.

New Financial Paradigms: Sustainability, not handouts, is the name of the game. We need to intentionalize the set up of "Kingdom businesses," which can generate income for the Kingdom and its causes. Kingdom venture capital groups can provide the capital and consultancy required to start and support new and growing businesses to become sufficiently successful to render an ongoing percentage of profit to a selected charitable cause. Children can hardly be asked to pay for the services they require. They are expensive and require investment, which is why we cannot look at how to help children at risk without also looking at every way of resourcing their needs. The stable base of good business is in many places a lifeline for Christian ministry, and its historic record is good. It is a struggle to scale but remains an active priority to implement and scale.

Prayer Precedes Power! Last but not least—none of this will happen without a massive mobilization of prayer. It precedes power! Around the World-Wide Day of Prayer for Children at Risk millions of man-hours of prayer are mobilized and new initiatives of "children praying for children" continue to mobilize and fuel people's interest and action in children at risk.

God's Heart for Children: God's purpose in making and redeeming man is life in all its fullness. Millions of children growing up stunted and destroyed by poverty clash with that aim and God will always seek to raise children to become all that He intended—that involves a life of love, health, safety, with marketable skills, and opportunities to serve, as well as the chance to be part of a worshiping community and through that know God.

God's vision of child poverty is not merely a socioeconomic game of welfare provision and security. Man does not live on bread alone and life without purpose or meaning is not a life at all. God's declared goal is always life, liberty, and love—lots of it. Let's follow hard on His heels and make it our goal too.

APPENDIX ONE

FIVE ORGANIZATIONS

Having read the book, we hope that you are primed and ready to act. There are many good Christian organizations out there to mobilize your warm feelings and direct your passion. We've done up brief bios on five of them.

There is a mix of large and small, new and old, east and west. This is intended as a taste of what is out there, much of it accessible from the Internet.

They are not the final word on their respective areas of concern. But we believe that they are living out the mandate that we have, and we heartily endorse them to you.

1. HOPE FOR THE NATIONS

Today's Orphans... Tomorrow's Leaders

Hope for the Nations (HFTN) was created by a coalition of visionary leaders from New Life Church (founded by Wesley and Stacey Campbell) who had a deep conviction to address the needs of children in destitute situations around the world. Over the course of its existence, HFTN has broadened its scope while sharpening its focus. HFTN now engages in community development, poverty reduction, and gender equity in areas where these issues intersect with children. Through their system of healthy partnerships, they have established projects in Liberia, India, Kenya, Nepal, Mexico, Myanmar, Thailand, Russia and Indonesia. HFTN is continuing to develop their partnerships and international networks in order to increase the efficiency of efforts directed toward the helping of children at risk around the world.

HFTN has three objectives: Children, community, and self-sufficency.

COALITION

HFTN believes that the only way to tackle the daunting problems facing today's developing nations is through coalition. For each location we bring together a variety of participants and resources that we refer to as the coalition.

For more information, contact:
CanadaTel (250) 712-2007
Fax (250) 862-2942
admin@hopeforthenations.com

2. THE SALVATION ARMY IN BANGLADESH

The Salvation Army in this desperately poor country is waging the war in primitive Salvationist style. Social justice in this context includes a hand up as well as a hand out. Several programs, including education, health, and economic development, are aimed at empowering people.

HASINA'S STORY

When Hasina's family grew to 9 members it became difficult for her husband to support them. They sold all their valuables and mortgaged the small piece of land their home was built on. One day she met the Development Supervisor from The Salvation Army who listened to her story and encouraged Hasina to join the sewing project in Daitala. At the project Hasina received sewing training, learnt how to handle the family money, and how to save for the future. After a month of training Hasina received her first sewing assignment, and when she had completed it, received her first earnings. She has worked hard to earn as much as she can for her family. Within 10 months it was possible

for her family to buy back their land and to purchase a goat.
"Now we are happy!" says Hasina.

For more information, contact:

Territorial Headquarters House: 40B Road 11 Dhanmondi Dhaka

Postal Address: GPO Box 985 Dhaka 1000

Tel: [880] (2) 813 817

Fax: [880] (2) 882 3568

E-mail: bangladesh@ban.salvationarmy.org

http://www.salvationarmy.org.bd/Banweb.nsf/fm_homepage?openform

3. HopeHIV

HopeHIV was founded due to the vision of Phil and Wendy Wall. In 1997 they attempted to adopt a little girl called Zodwa from Ethembeni ("Place of Hope"), an AIDS Care orphanage in Johannesburg. After nine months of legal constraints and frustrations, Phil and Wendy were unsuccessful in their attempt. Consequently, they decided that as they could not adopt one child physically, they would instead work for the financial adoption of the AIDS orphans of Africa. HopeHIV is part of the response to that vision.

HopeHIV aims to financially adopt the AIDS orphan generation and raise awareness about the issue of HIV/AIDS. HopeHIV aims to raise funds to provide finances for projects that care for these children.

HopeHIV initiates village-based life-skills programs for teenaged orphans, like the Chikombola Youth Project in Zambia and the Masiye Camp in Zimbabwe for 1,000 community-based AIDS orphans, designed to enable them to generate income and economic capacity. HopeHIV is also involved in "Best-Practice" transfer programs that enable local community leaders to implement community-based orphan care projects.

For more information, contact:

HopeHIV

PO Box 1190, Kingston and Surbiton KT2 6LB

Tel: 02 8288 1196

E-mail: info@hopehiv.org

Web site: hopehiv.org

4. Viva Network

Some people work directly with children at risk, doing work such as running drop-in centers for street children, counseling children of war, and fostering orphans. Others work on their behalf, giving money, praying, influencing people and supporting those working directly with the children. The Viva Network facilitation team helps both these groups build relationships. This enables them to work together more effectively for children at risk.

AIMS

In service and with humility, Viva Network aims to:

1. **Increase Effectiveness**: increase the sense of community and the combined effectiveness of the existing Christian response to children at risk.
2. **Mobilize New Initiatives**: amongst children at risk, equipping individuals, groups and churches to launch effective ministries.
3. **Speak Out**: challenge the community at large by raising awareness of children at risk and encouraging an effective response.
4. **Influence Policy**: influence decision-makers and change social structures in order to make a difference to the lives of children at risk.

For more information, see the Viva Network web site: http://viva.org/

5. BE A HERO
THE GOAL

Founded by Wesley and Stacey Campbell, Be a Hero's goal is to educate, inspire, equip, and facilitate people of all ages through conferences, books, magazines, and living examples in order to challenge them to "Be A Hero" in the lives of those around them—especially the poor, the exploited, the oppressed, and 'children at risk.'

The mandate of "Be a Hero" is three-fold:

1. Assist children at risk,
2. Promote advocacy for the poor and oppressed, particularily 'children at risk,' and,
3. Create a vehicle for crisis events.

"Be A Hero" is presently accomplishing this goal by calling for heroes everywhere who will take action by the five characteristics outlined in the WHAT IS A HERO chapter.

THE PLAN

"Be a Hero" was conceived to meet the need for a strategy to connect thousands of people who have a heart for 'children at risk' to the ground-level organizations who are actually doing the work—building orphanages and schools, rescuing children from slavery, feeding the poor. Many times, people have a desire to do something to help needy children, but have no idea how to go about it. "Be a Hero" provides the compassionate with step-by-step directions on how to gather those in their sphere of influence, and together, do something life-saving and life-changing!

"Be a Hero" does not, of itself, build orphanages, or sponsor orphans. We partner with organizations that: are seasoned and proven; are experienced and efficient; have a close personal relationship with us, and are good stewards of the finances. Our function is to research and examine organizations and projects to make sure they meet our standards before we promote their projects. We then "match" interested 'heroes' with a project that fits their vision of what they would like to do to save 'children at risk.'

Be a Hero mobilizes conference speakers, pastors, and those with a platform (artists, preachers, musicians, writers, etc.) to recruit thousands of people who have a heart for children at risk. Join the Be a Hero Army today (beahero.org).

ORGANIZATIONS ATTACKING THE SEVEN DEADLY SINS

By now, more than your sense of justice has been piqued. You'll want to explore other avenues of service to be a hero. To save you from trying to "re-invent the wheel" and from randomly surfing the Internet, here is a short list of representative organizations involved in attacking the seven deadly sins.

DEADLY SIN #1—DIRT POOR

Feed the Children
http://www.christianity.com/feedthechildren

Childcare International
www.childcare-intl.org

Children's Hunger Relief Fund
www.chrf.org

Mission Aviation Fellowship
www.maf.org

Enterprise Development International
www.endpoverty.org

Venture International (Venture Middle East, Inc.)
www.ventureftf.org

DEADLY SIN #2—CHILDREN IN CHAINS
Children's HopeChest
www.gospelcom.net/chc

Salvation Army World Service Office (SAWSO)
http://www.salvationarmyusa.org

Youth With A Mission
http://www.ywam.org/mercy.html

Campolo Ministries
www.tonycampolo.com

DEADLY SIN #3—ORPHANS OF THE STREET
World Vision
http://www.wvi.org/home.shtml

DEADLY SIN #4—SEX AND THE CITY
Interserve
http://www.interserve.org/

The Future Group
Youwillbecaught.com

DEADLY SIN #5—AIDS AND PLAGUES
Tear Fund
www.tearfund.org

Compassion International
www.compasssion.com

Christian Children's Fund
http://www.christianchildrensfund.org/

Medical Missionary Association
http://www.mmahealthserve.org.uk/mma/home.htm

Heal The Nations
http://www.healthenations.com/index.htm

F.A.M.E.
medicalmissions@fameworld.org

DEADLY SIN #6—THE EXIGENCIES OF WAR? WAR-AFFECTED CHILDREN
Children's Survival Fund
(888) 544-9348

Samaritan's Purse
www.samaritan.org

Center for Bio-Ethical Reform
Abortionno.org

DEADLY SIN #7—RELIGIOUS PERSECUTION
Barnabas Fund
http://www.barnabasfund.org/

Christian Solidarity International
http://www.csi-int.ch/

International Christian Concern
http://www.persecution.org/

Voice of the Martyrs
http://www.persecution.com/

APPENDIX THREE

CHILD SPONSORSHIPS

There are many great child sponsorship organizations. Be a Hero will either facilitate your sponsorship, or put you in contact with your favorite group. Costs range, depending on country, but traditionally $30 (USD) a month or a dollar a day covers food and shelter, and another $30 (USD) a month or a dollar a day covers basic health care, schooling, books, and uniform. Various agencies mix and match these various components depending on their program. For instance, Compassion International does not start children's homes or take orphans, but they work through the local church to assist very poor families by providing one meal a day at the church for a child, coupled with schooling, Christian training, and job training.

Traditionally, upon receiving your reply, organizations send you a sponsorship package, which includes a brief case history and photograph of a child in the country of your choice. Many sponsorship organizations also endeavor to maintain a periodic link through reports or brief letters.

MULTIPLY SPONSORSHIPS

Do you want a great idea to multiply sponsorships? Watch this! Let's put Phil Wall's 10/10 Challenge to work for BE A HERO.

Emphasize this theme at your church. Set up a table outside the sanctuary. Make the books available. Buy 50 copies at an author's 50% discount and sell them for retail ($15.99 USD). The first 25 books sold pay for all of the books. The rest pay for the support costs of one child for one whole year! And, 50 more readers have the opportunity to jump on board!

This will work with your church, your cell groups, your Christian friends, even your work mates. Contact BE A HERO (www.beahero.org) for more details.

END NOTES

CHAPTER 1: BE A HERO

1. Rolland and Heidi Baker, *There Is Always Enough* (2003), p. 15.

2. James Allan Francis, "One Solitary Life" (adapted), (1926), retrieved from the Internet January 5, 2004, from http://home.att.net/~jrd/one_solitary_life.htm.

3. Rolland and Heidi Baker, *There Is Always Enough* (2003), pp. 16-17.

4. Rolland and Heidi Baker, *There Is Always Enough* (2003), p. 34.

5. Rolland and Heidi Baker, *There Is Always Enough* (2003), p. 44.

6. Taken from various sources such as Rolland and Heidi Baker, *There Is Always Enough* (2003); *Mama Heidi* (video) 2003; personal meetings, January 14-16, 2004.

7. Retrieved from the Internet January 3, 2004, from http://www.nostalgiacentral.com/pop/liveaid.htm. It is interesting that the most popular evangelists in the West in 2004 are Mel Gibson and Bono.

8. Retrieved from the Internet January 15, 2004, from http://www.nostalgiacentral.com/pop/liveaid.htm.

9. "Bono's Mission," *TIME*. February 23, 2002.

10. Retrieved from the Internet February 23, 2002, from http://www.time.com/time/sampler/article/0,8599,212605,00.html.

11. David Waters, "Commercial Appeal: Bono Hopes You, Too, Will Care," retrieved from the Internet December 13, 2003, from *U2 World* at http://www.u2world.com/news/article.php3?id_article=20255.

12. Retrieved from the Internet, March 2001, from http://www.findarticles.com/cf_dls/m2548/2001_March/73411097/p2/article.jhtml?term=.

13. Jubilee 2000 Press Release. Retrieved from the Internet May 2, 2000, from http://www.jubileeplus.org/jubilee2000/jubilee2000_archive/uganda020500.htm.

14. DATA web site. Retrieved from the Internet January 4, 2004, from http://www.data.org/whyafrica/.

15. David Waters, "Commercial Appeal: Bono Hopes You, Too, Will Care," retrieved from the Internet December 13, 2003, from *U2 World* at http://www.u2world.com/news/article.php3?id_article=20255.

16. Cathleen Falsani, "Bono Credits Church," *Chicago-Sun Times*, retrieved from the Internet April 22, 2004, from *U2 World* at http://www.u2world.com/news/article.php3?id_article=20240.

17. David Waters, "Commercial Appeal: Bono Hopes You, Too, Will Care," retrieved from the Internet December 13, 2003, from *U2 World* at http://www.u2world.com/news/article.php3?id_article=20255.

18. Cathleen Falsani, "Bono Credits Church," *Chicago-Sun Times*, retrieved from the Internet April 22, 2004, from U2 World at http://www.u2world.com/news/article.php3?idarticle=20240.

19. Cathleen Falsani, "Bono Credits Church," *Chicago-Sun Times*, retrieved from the Internet April 22, 2004, from U2 World at http://www.u2world.com/news/article.php3?id_arti cle=20240.

20. Cathleen Falsani, "Bono Credits Church," *Chicago-Sun Times*, retrieved from the Internet on April 22, 2004, from U2 World at http://www.u2world.com/news/article.php3?id_article=20240.

21. Retrieved from the Internet January 15, 2004, from http://wfn.org/2002/12/msg00088.html.

22. Cathleen Falsani, "Bono Credits Church," Chicago-Sun Times, retrieved from the Internet on April 22, 2004, from U2 World at http://www.u2world.com/news/article.php3?id_article=20240.

23. Personal communication, April 2, 2004.

24. Retrieved from the Internet January 15, 2004, from http://www.ijm.org/ijm_case_Sridhar.html.

25. Personal communication, April 4, 2004.

26. Personal communication, April 4, 2004.

27. ABC Radio Australia. Retrieved from the Internet January 8, 2004, from http://www.abc.net.au/ra/asiapac/programs/s635703.htm.

28. ABC Radio Australia. Retrieved from the Internet January 8, 2004, from http://www.abc.net.au/ra/asiapac/programs/s635703.htm.

29. Susan McClelland, "Sad Little Girls," *Maclean's Magazine*, November 24, 2003.

30. Retrieved from the Internet January 8, 2004, from www.thefuturegroup.org.

31. Poem by Yasmin M. Wahid, from the Preface of: Joyce Ellery and Ivor Telfer, *A Task Accomplished*, 1992.

32. Personal communication, April 12, 2004.

33. Personal communication, April 4, 2004.

34. Personal communication, April 4, 2004.

35. "Jim" represents the people of IJM, International Justice Mission, IJM web site. http://www.ijm.org/ijm_case_radha.html. Retrieved January 15, 2004.

36. Voice of the Martyrs web site: http://www.persecution.com/about/index.cfm?action=vom. Retrieved January 15, 2004.

CHAPTER 2: FACES AND HEARTS

1. Although some testify, "by my God I can scale a wall" (Ps. 18:29).

2. *Vine's Expository Dictionary of Biblical Words*, 1985.

3. *Strong's Concordance*, 1368, *gibbowr*.

4. *Vine's Expository Dictionary of Biblical Words*, 1985.

5. Tony Campolo, "The Triumph of the Religion of Main Street," *Partly Right* (1995), p. 13.

6. John 16:8.

7. James Kennedy and Jerry Newcombe, *What If Jesus Had Never Been Born?* (1994), pp. 3-4.

8. Tony Campolo, "The Triumph of the Religion of Main Street," *Partly Right* (1995), p. 13.

9. David S. Landes, *The Wealth and Poverty of Nations* (1999), p. 174.

10. The *Wall Street Journal* Editorial Page, "Spiritual Capital," October 31, 2003. Retrieved from http://opinionjournal.com/taste/?id=110004237. Despite the cynicism of post-modern Western intellectuals, who can dismiss altruism—the unselfish concern for the welfare of others as, "the ultimate genetic selfishness." In Pierre Van Der Berghe, in James Dale Davidson and William Rees-Mogg. *The Sovereign Individual* (1997), p. 266.

11. " 'Heroe's Telethon Raises $150 Million," Associated Press. September 26, 2001.

12. Music News All Music News, September 26, 2001. Retrieved from the Internet from http://music.yahoo.com/music/news/launch/story.html?a=n/music/news/launch/urban/20010926/20/p1&b=n/music/news/launch/urban/20010926/20/p2.

13. Tony Campolo, "The Triumph of the Religion of Main Street," *Partly Right* (1995), p. 19.

14. James Kennedy and Jerry Newcombe, *What If Jesus Had Never Been Born?* (1994), p. 34.

15. "Christian History, The Monkey Trial & the Rise of Fundamental- ism," *Christianity Today*, (Issue 55, Vol. XVI, No. 3), 1997, p. 20.

16. James Martineau, cited in James Kennedy and Jerry Newcombe. *What If Jesus Had Never Been Born?* (1994), p. 29.

17. Kenneth Scott Latourette, *A History of Christianity*, volume 1, 1975. Retrieved from the Internet from http://www.religion-online.org/cgi-bin/relsearchd.dll/showbook?item_id=532.

18. Henry Chadwick, "Early Christian Community," in John McManners (ed.), *The Illustrated History of Christianity* (1990).

19. As cited in Patrick Johnstone, *The Church Is Bigger Than You Think* (1998), p. 60.

20. Patrick McDonald, *Reaching Children in Need* (2000), p. 58.

21. "Christian History, Women in the Medieval Church," *Christianity Today*, (Issue 30, Vol. X, No. 2) 1991, p. 14.

22. Earle E. Cairns, *An Endless Line of Splendor* (1986), p. 275.

23. J. Edwin Orr, *The Flaming Tongue* (1973) p. ix-xiv.

24. Earle E. Cairns, *An Endless Line of Splendor*, (1986), p. 277-284.

25. Earle E. Cairns, *An Endless Line of Splendor*, (1986), p. 305.

26. Earle E. Cairns, *An Endless Line of Splendor*, (1986), p. 290.

27. Earle E. Cairns, *An Endless Line of Splendor*, (1986), p. 303.

28. See Section Three of this book.

29. "In the Wake of the Second Great Awakening," *Christian History* (Vol. VIII, No. 3,23), 1989, p. 31.

30. "In the Wake of the Second Great Awakening," *Christian History* (Vol.VIII, No. 3,23) 1989, p. 31.

31. "In the Wake of the Second Great Awakening," *Christian History* (Vol.VIII, No. 3,23) 1989, p. 31.

32. "Spiritual Awakening in North America," *Christianity Today* (Vol. VIII, No. 3, Issue 23), 1983, p. 31.

33. J. Stanley Oakes Jr., "The Last Hope for the University," in Roy Abraham Varghese, ed., *The Intellectuals Speak Out About God* (1984), p. xxii.

34. Tony Campolo, "The Triumph of the Religion of Main Street," *Partly Right* (1995), p. 20.

35. Donald G. Tewkesbury, *The Founding of American Colleges and Universities Before the Civil War* (1969), p. 84.

36. Donald G. Tewkesbury, *The Founding of American Colleges and Universities Before the Civil War* (1969), p. 84.

37. J. Stanley Oakes Jr., "The Last Hope for the University," in Roy Abraham Varghese, ed., *The Intellectuals Speak Out About God* (1984), p. xxii.

38. Jeffrey Shultz and John G. West, Jr., eds., *The C.S. Lewis Reader's Encyclopedia* (1998).

39. Karen Norton, *One Burning Heart* (1991), pp. 18-19,32.

40. Karen Norton, *One Burning Heart* (1991), p. 32.

41. Patrick McDonald, *Reaching Children in Need*, (2000), p. 62.

42. Shi Mai'an and Lao Guanzhong, in James Dale Davidson and William Rees-Mogg, *The Sovereign Individual* (1997), p. 145.

43. 2 Peter 3:9; Repentance and faith are necessary to salvation.

44. President Dwight D. Eisenhower. April 16, 1953, cited in www.costofwar.com. Retrieved January 30, 2004.

45. costofwar.com. Retrieved from the Internet on December 16, 2003.

46. Retrieved from the Internet January 6, 2004 from http://www.war resisters.org/piechart.htm.

47. $12 billion for Afghanistan. Retrieved from the Cost of War web site January 12, 2004 from http://www.nationalpriorities.org/Issues/Military/ Iraq/CostOfWar.html.

48. Richard Norton-Taylor, "Cost of Afghan Operation Soars," *The Guardian*, December 20, 2002.

49. "Britain Counts Cost of Iraq War," *ABC News Online*, December 9, 2003.

50. Extrapolated from costofwar.com. Retrieved from the Internet December 17, 2003.

51. "Found What He's Looking For," *TIME Europe*, April 20, 2003.

52. Bart Pierce, *Seeking Our Brothers* (2000), p. 9.

53. *Newsweek*, April 16, 2001.

54. Philip Jenkins, *The Next Christendom* (2002).

55. Paul Marshall, *Their Blood Cries Out* (1997), p. 8.

56. Mother Teresa, *A Simple Path* (1995), p. 152-153.

57. James Dale Davidson and William Rees-Mogg, *The Sovereign Individual* (1997), p. 374.

58. James Wolfensohn, in "What the World Needs Now," *TIME*, January 26, 2004.

59. Patrick Johnstone, *The Church Is Bigger Than You Think* (1998), p. 58.

60. As cited in Patrick Johnstone, *The Church Is Bigger Than You Think* (1998), p. 59. The following chapters should help on this front.

61. We intend to help galvanize a theological framework for mercy and social justice in these pages.

62. Geoff Ryan, "To Be or Not to Be," in *Sowing Dragons*, 2000.

63. Ernest Becker, cited in Thomas Long, "Beavis And Butt-Head Get Saved," *Theology Today* (Vol. 51, No.2.), July 1994. Retrieved from the Internet from http://theologytoday. ptsem.edu/search/index-browse.htm.

CHAPTER 3: GOD'S BIG IDEA

1. Ambedkar Centre for Justice and Peace. Retrieved from the Internet from http:// www.saxakali.com/CommunityLinkups/dalit3.htm.

2. *Human Rights in India Today*, 1992 edition, NCPHR, p. 17.

3. Carla Power, *Newsweek*, June 25, 2000.

4. There are numerous examples throughout the Old Testament of the Holy Spirit coming upon God's people. **Gideon:** Judges 6:34: "Then the Spirit of the Lord came upon Gideon"; Judges 14:6, 19; 15:14; **Samson:** "The Spirit of the Lord came upon him in power"; First Samuel 10:9, Saul: "the Spirit of God came upon him in power, and he joined in their prophesying;" First Samuel 16:13; **David:** "and from that day, the Spirit of the Lord came upon David in power"; First Samuel 19:20: "the Spirit of God came upon Saul's men and they also prophesied"; Second Kings 3:15: "While the harpist was playing, the hand of the Lord came upon Elisha and he said…." This is brief sampling of this teaching.

5. Numbers 11:29; Jeremiah 31:31-34; Hosea 2:16; Joel 2:28-29.

6. Martyrs—Greek—Acts 1:8.

7. 2 Kings. 3:15-16; see also Isaiah 8:11 and Ezekiel 8:1; 33:21-22.

8. Luke 11:20.

9. Dallas Willard, *The Divine Conspiracy* (1998), p. 116-117.

10. Ralph Neighbour Jr., *The Arrival Kit* (1993).

11. Dave Andrews, *Not Religion But Love* (2001), p. 61-62.

12. *Strong's Hebrew/Greek Dictionary*, #4941.

13. Spiros Zodhiates, *The Hebrew-Greek Key Word Study Bible* (1990), p. 1746.

14. Spiros Zodhiates, *The Hebrew-Greek Key Word Study Bible* (1990), p. 1746.

15. Exodus 21:1; Leviticus 18:5.

16. Numbers 27:5; Job 23:4.

17. As in Exodus 21:9.

18. Isaiah 59:15. God sees.

19. *Strong's Hebrew/Greek Dictionary*, #6666.

20. Spiros Zodhiates, *The Hebrew-Greek Key Word Study Bible* (1990), p. 1768.

21. Spiros Zodhiates, *The Hebrew-Greek Key Word Study Bible* (1990), p. 1768.

22. For example, see Jesus in John 14 for several instances.

23. e.g. John 3:36; Acts 14:1,2.

24. Ex-Lion Tamer. http://surreally.net/fullbleed/exliontamer/archives/000585.html. Retrieved January 24, 2004.

25. http://www.nmmle.org/Essay.html.

26. http://web.ukonline.co.uk/ddlg.uk/story1.htm. Retrieved January 15, 2004.

27. *Strong's Hebrew/Greek Dictionary*, #7355.

28. *Seattle Post-Intelligencer*. May 24, 2000. Retrieved from the Internet from http://seat tlepi.nwsource.com/honduras/page01.shtml.

29. *Strong's Greek/Hebrew Dictionary*, New Testament, from *ptosso*.

30. e.g. Psalm 74:21;86:1.

31. *Strong's Hebrew/Greek Dictionary*, #6041.

32. BBC News. No date. http://news.bbc.co.uk/hi/english/static/in depth/world/2001/ road to refuge/persecution/story.stm. Retrieved January 15, 2004.

33. How many Americans will agree that the Twin Towers tragedy drew out exceedingly more passion and action than myriads of numerically worse disasters in other parts of the world?

34. See also Jeremiah 7:6-7.

35. Operation Blessing web site. Retrieved from the Internet on January 15, 2004 from http://www.ob.org/programs/disaster relief/news/2002/dr 2002 0125 afghan widows.asp.

36. "An Orphan's Story," BBC News. November 27, 2002.

37. "The "Y" Factor," retrieved from the Internet January 27, 2004 from http://www. neveh.org/winston/yfactor/y-10.html.

38. Luke 3:10-14, Ephesians 4:28.

CHAPTER 4: HEROES OF THE WARS OF THE LORD

1. Patrick Johnstone, *The Church Is Bigger Than You Think*, (1998), p. 78-79.

2. Patrick Johnstone, *The Church Is Bigger Than You Think*, (1998), p. 76.

3. Dom Jean Leclercq, *Spirituality of the Middle Ages* (1978), p. 61. In the 21st century, the conditions of heroism are different. Read on.

4. Patrick Johnstone, *The Church Is Bigger Than You Think*, (1998), p. 71-72.

5. Patrick Johnstone, *The Church Is Bigger Than You Think*, (1998), p.73.

6. Dom Jean Leclercq, *Spirituality of the Middle Ages* (1978), p. 61.

7. Dom Jean Laurie, *Spirituality of the Middle Ages* (1978), p. 61-62.

8. Who did Walfroy 30 years better on that pole—http://www.echnyc.com/~panman/ simeon.html.

9. Retrieved January 15, 2004, from http://www.newadvent.org/cathen/06453a.htm and http://myhero.com/hero.asp?hero=mkolbe.

10. An elaboration of Job 29:7-17.

11. William Sanford LaSor, David Allan Hubbard, Frederic William Bush, *Old Testament Survey* (1982), p. 118.

12. Exodus 12:29,31—Seriously, this was a direct power encounter that Yahweh won, "going away."

13. Henry H. Halley, *Halley's Bible Handbook* (1965), p. 111.

14. In the classic movie adaptation of the biblical story, *The Ten Commandments*.

15. Thomas Cahill, *The Gifts of the Jews* (1998), p. 114-115.

16. "Evil"—not because it was Egypt, but because it oppressed an innocent people for generations.

17. *Strong's Concordance*, #2204.

18. Numbers 5:21-31. *Vine's Expository Dictionary of Biblical Words* (1995).

19. For example: Exodus 20:5; 34:14; Deuteronomy 5:9. *International Standard Bible Encyclopedia* (1996), Biblesoft.

20. It is so important that it made the Ten Commandments. See Exodus 20:5; Exodus 34:14 (KJV): "For thou shalt worship no other god: for the Lord, **whose name is Jealous**, is a jealous God." See also Deuteronomy 4:24 (NASB): "For the Lord your God is a consuming fire, **a jealous God**. See also Deuteronomy 6:5 (NIV): "**For the Lord your God, who is among you, is a jealous God and His anger will burn against you**, and He will destroy you from the face of the land."

21. Thomas Cahill, *The Gifts of the Jews* (1998), p. 105ff.

22. And Yahweh has a Messiah. So Christianity is the oldest religion extent.

23. Because we're created in the image of God. This comes from a teaching by Paul Cox, Campus Crusade for Christ, USA. 1989.

24. Eugene Peterson, "The Pastor's Sabbath," *Leadership* (Spring Quarter,1985), p. 54. The exile was God's response to their disobedience, a forced rest for the land. See also Leviticus 26:34-35.

25. 1 Samuel 1:3; *Unger's Bible Dictionary*.

26. Charles Spurgeon, *Spurgeon's Expository Encyclopedia* (1988), p. 14.

27. William Sanford LaSor, David Allan Hubbard, Frederic William Bush, *Old Testament Survey* (1982), p. 232-234.

28. 1 Samuel 5:9, Septuagint.

29. 1 Samuel 5:6, Septuagint.

30. 1 Samuel 6:19, Septuagint.

31. Dr. Lightfoot, in *Matthew Henry's Commentary*.

32. Chaldee reading of 1 Samuel 7:6.

33. David was all about intimacy with God. See Jason Upton, *The Key of David*, retrieved on January 26, 2004 from Jasonupton.com. We're singing this melody through the first step that makes a hero. Read on for details.

34. The beauty of God is that Amos's prophecy (see Amos 9:11) is expanded here to include the Gentiles. So as we connect with God in the Key of David—intimacy—we are preparing an evangelistic environment that will ultimately draw the nations to Jesus' feet. See Mike Bickle, International House of Prayer, on the Internet at www.Fotb.com.

35. Michael L. Brown, *Revolution* (2000), p. 59-60.

36. Of course, he left the influence of Zechariah, grew as proud as he was famous, and crashed, personally. See the rest of Second Chronicles 26 for his pathetic end. The lesson is that his success depended on accountable intimacy. While he remained accountable to Zechariah and intimate with God, he was heroic.

37. *Christian Debater* (R), P.O. Box 144441, Austin, TX 79714. Phone: (512) 218-8022. www.BibleQuery.org.

38. Taken from *Timeframe* 1500-600 BC, (Time-Life Books), and *The Bible Knowledge Commentary: Old Testament*, p. 1494. Source-*Christian Debater* (R), P.O. Box 144441, Austin, TX 79714. Phone: (512) 218-8022. www.BibleQuery.org.

39. Spiros Zodhiates, ed., *The Hebrew-Greek Key Study Bible* (1990).

40. In real terms, you need to compare Nineveh with someplace like Salem, Oregon.

41. That's four years of pressing in.

42. The locust devours the harvest. John devoured the devourer of the harvest. He prepared the way for a great harvest. Properly, prophets do that. I heard this teaching from evangelist Andrew Shearman, now based in Mobile. For more information go to the following Internet web site: http://www.abundantlifeministry.org/roundtable/membersandministry.htm.

CHAPTER 5: VICTORIAN ENGLAND

1. Well, he was, but you get the point.

2. Grace Kelley, "Nineteenth Century Medicine," in http://www.gober.net/victorian/time.html. Retrieved January 15, 2004.

3. Mary Johnston, "Irish Emigration," in http://www.gober.net/vic torian/time.html. Retrieved January 15, 2004.

4. Charles Booth, *Life and Labour of the People of London*, 1886. Cited in http://www.gober.net/victorian/time.html. Retrieved January 15, 2004.

5. http://www.gober.net/victorian/time.html. Retrieved January 15, 2004.

6. Robert F. Haggard, "Jack the Ripper As the Threat of Outcast London," in the University of Virginia, *Essays in History* (Vol. 35), 1993, p. 1.

7. Robert F. Haggard, "Jack the Ripper As the Threat of Outcast London," in the University of Virginia, *Essays in History* (Vol. 35), 1993, p. 6.

8. Robert F. Haggard, "Jack the Ripper As the Threat of Outcast London," in the University of Virginia, *Essays in History* (Vol. 35), 1993, p. 2.

9. Robert F. Haggard, "Jack the Ripper As the Threat of Outcast London," in the University of Virginia, *Essays in History* (Vol. 35), 1993, p. 4.

10. Judith Walkowitz, *Prostitution and Victorian Society* (Cambridge University Press, 1980).

11. Anthony S. Wohl, *Sanitation and Disease in Rich And Poor*. Retrieved on January 15, 2004, from the Internet on the Victorian Web.

12. Father and daughter died of sewage-induced typhoid.

13. Son almost died.

14. We're talking about Queen Victoria. Anthony S. Wohl, *Sanitation and Disease in Rich and Poor*. Retrieved January 15, 2004, from the Internet on the Victorian Web.

15. Dale H. Porter, *The Thames Embankment: Environment, Technology, and Society in Victorian London*, 1998. Retrieved on the Victorian Web GPL.

16. Edwin Chadwick, *Report From the Poor Law Commissioners on an Inquiry Into the Sanitary Conditions of the Labouring Population of Great Britain* (1842), p. 370.

17. Walter Besant, *All Sorts and Conditions of Men—An Impossible Story*, 1882. Cited by Deborah McDonald on the Victorian Web. Retrieved June 6, 2002, from http://landow.stg.brown.edu/victorian/.

18. The quandary existed because legislators were apparently at a loss to explain to Queen Victoria what homosexual acts existed between women. See *Bloomsbury Dictionary of English Literature* (1997).

19. Megara Bell, *The Fallen Woman in Fiction and Legislation*. See Cathy Edgar at http://www.gober.net/victorian/reports/prostit.html. Victorian Web. Retrieved January 15, 2004.

20. Judith Walkowitz, cited in Megara Bell, *The Fallen Woman in Fiction and Legislation*, http://www.gober.net/victorian/reports/prostit.html. Retrieved January 15, 2004.

21. Megara Bell, *The Fallen Woman in Fiction and Legislation*. See Cathy Edgar at http://www.gober.net/victorian/reports/prostit.html. Victorian Web. Retrieved January 15, 2004.

22. "Everyone Did It," *The Economist*, November 24, 2001.

23. The preceding section comes from Anthony S. Wohl, *Opium and Infant Mortality*, p. 35-36. Victorian Web. Retrieved January 15, 2004.

24. "Everyone Did It," *The Economist*, November 24, 2001.

25. Eric Hobsbawm, *Industry and Empire: The Birth of the Industrial Revolution* (1999), p. 133.

26. *Hansard's Parliamentary Debates* (3rd Series, Vol. XIX), July 18, 1833, p. 912. Reprinted from an old history textbook, Jonathan F. Scott and Alexander Baltzly, eds., *Readings in European History Since 1814* (Appleton-Century-Crofts, Inc., 1930), and is included in an unpublished paper by Laura Del Col, "The Life of the Industrial Worker in Nineteenth-Century England," West Virginia University.

27. There were 63 brothels in Whitechapel. There were also a huge number of "casual prostitutes." Robert F. Haggard, "Jack the Ripper As the Threat of Outcast London," in the University of Virginia, *Essays in History*, (Vol. 35) 1993, p. 4.

28. John Burnett, *The Annals of Labour: Autobiographies of British Working Class People*, 1820-1920, (1974), from the introduction.

29. Taken from the *Report From His Majesty's Commissioners for Inquiring Into the Administration and Practical Operation of the Poor Laws (1834)*, pp. 306-14. Transcribed and added by Marjie Bloy. Victorian Web. Retrieved January 28, 2004.

30. David Cody, "Child Labor," The Victorian Web at http://www.victorianweb.org/. Retrieved January 15, 2004.

31. Retrieved from the Internet April 15, 2004, from http://www.rootsweb.com/~belghist/Flanders/Pages/childLabor.htm. Also on the Victorian Web. Retrieved on January 28, 2004, from *Parliamentary Papers*, 1842 (Vols. XV-XVII), Appendix I, pp. 252, 258, 439, 461; Appendix II, pp. 107, 122, 205. "The second of the three great reports embodies the results of the investigation into the conditions of labor in the mines made by Lord Ashley's Mines Commission of

1842. The Mines Act of 1842 that resulted prohibited the employment in the mines of all women and of boys under thirteen."

32. Penelope Davies, *Children of the Industrial Revolution* (1972), p. 27.

33. "The Benefit of the Factory Legislation," from Hansard's Parliamen- tary Debates, Apr. 4, 1879 (3rd Series, Vol. CCXLV), pp. 355-356. Retrieved January 28, 2004, from the Victorian Web. The material was reprinted in an old history textbook, *Readings in European History Since 1814*, edited by Jonathan F. Scott and Alexander Baltzly, 1930. "Any man who has stood at twelve o'clock at the single narrow door-way, which serves as the place of exit for the hands employed in the great cotton-mills, must acknowledge, that an uglier set of men and women, of boys and girls, taking them in the mass, it would be impossible to congregate in a smaller compass. Their complexion is sallow and pallid—with a peculiar flatness of fea- ture, caused by the want of a proper quantity of adipose substance to cushion out the cheeks. Their stature low—the average height of four hundred men, measured at different times, and different places, being five feet six inches. Their limbs slender, and playing badly and ungracefully. A very general bowing of the legs. Great numbers of girls and women walking lamely or awkwardly, with raised chests and spinal flexures. Nearly all have flat feet, accom- panied with a down-tread, differing very widely from the elasticity of action in the foot and ankle, attendant upon perfect formation. Hair thin and straight—many of the men having but little beard, and that in patches of a few hairs, much resembling its growth among the red men of America. A spiritless and dejected air, a sprawling and wide action of the legs, and an appearance, taken as a whole, giving the world but 'little assurance of a man,' or if so, 'most sadly cheated of his fair proportions'...." Laura Del Col, "The Life of the Industrial Worker in Nineteenth-Century England," Victorian Web. Retrieved January 28, 2004. *The Physical Deterioration of the Textile Workers* [P. Gaskell, *The Manufacturing Population of England* (London: 1833), pp.161-162, 202-203.]

34. The Victorian Web. Retrieved on January 27, 2004, from http://www.victorian web.org/history/hist8.html.

35. *Parliamentary Papers*, 1831-1832 (Vol. XV), pp. 44, 95-97, 115, 195, 197, 339, 341-342.

36. Jonathan F. Scott and Alexander Baltzly, eds., *Readings in European History Since 1814* (Appleton-Century-Crofts, Inc., 1930), included in an unpublished paper by Laura Del Col, "The Life of the Industrial Worker in Nineteenth-Century England," West Virginia University.

37. David Cody, "Child Labour," retrieved January 15, 2004, from the Victorian Web at http://www.victorianweb.org/. That said, Christians played a key role in children's rights. "After radical agitation, notably in 1831, when "Short Time Committees" organized largely by Evangelicals began to demand a ten hour day, a royal commission established by the Whig gov- ernment recommended in 1833 that children aged 11-18 be permitted to work a maximum of twelve hours per day; children 9-11 were allowed to work 8 hour days; and children under 9 were no longer permitted to work at all (children as young as 3 had been put to work previ- ously). This act applied only to the textile industry, where children were put to work at the age of 5, and not to a host of other industries and occupations. Iron and coal mines (where chil- dren, again, both boys and girls, began work at age 5, and generally died before they were 25), gas works, shipyards, construction, match factories, nail factories, and the business of chimney sweeping, for example (which Blake would use as an emblem of the destruction of the inno- cent), where the exploitation of child labor was more extensive, was to be enforced in all of England by a total of four inspectors." Retrieved January 27, 2004 from the Victorian Web at http://www.victorianweb.org/history/hist8.html. Taken from the *Report From His Majesty's Commissioners for Inquiring Into the Administration and Practical Operation of the Poor Laws* (1834), pp. 306-14. Transcribed and added by Marjie Bloy.

38. G. Bernard Shaw. *Major Barbara: With an Essay As First Aid to Critics by Bernard Shaw* (1907).

39. Italics added for emphasis. G. Bernard Shaw, *Major Barbara: With an Essay as First Aid to Critics by Bernard Shaw* (1907).

40. The "Blood and Fire" is The Salvation Army tricolor standard. The "Blood and Fire" war cry proclaims Salvation through the Blood of Jesus and holiness through the power of the Holy Spirit.

41. G. Bernard Shaw, *Major Barbara: With an Essay As First Aid to Critics by Bernard Shaw* (1907).

42. Reference to Greek drama and mythology—Euripides' play, *The Bacchae*-is made by Fiona Macintosh, comparing the effect of worship of the Greek god Dionysus to that of The Salvation Army. See Fiona Macintosh, "The Shavian Murray and the Euripidean Shaw: Major Barbara and the Bacchae," *Classics Ireland* (Vol. 5), 1988. Retrieved January 15, 2004, from http://www.ucd.ie/classics/98/Macintosh98.html.

43. *Dionysus, God of Joy & His Cult*, retrieved January 27, 2004, from http://www.archaeonia.com/religion/cults/dionysian.htm.

44. Fiona Macintosh, "The Shavian Murray and the Euripidean Shaw: Major Barbara and the Bacchae," *Classics Ireland* (Vol. 5), 1988. Retrieved January 15, 2004, from http://www.ucd.ie/classics/98/Macintosh98.html.

CHAPTER 6: REVOLUTION

1. George Scott Railton, in G.S.R., compiled by John D. Waldron. Originally appeared in the *Christian Mission Magazine*, January 1873.

2. Catherine Booth, in J. Rhemick, *A New People of God* (1984), pp. 202-203.

3. J. Edwin Orr, *The Second Great Awakening* (1964), p. 62.

4. J. Edwin Orr, *The Second Great Awakening* (1964), p. 68.

5. Geoff Ryan, "To Be or Not to Be," in *Sowing Dragons* (2000).

6. Catherine Booth, in St. John Ervine, *God's Soldier: General William Booth* (1934), Vol. 1, p. 461.

7. Cited in Brian Tuck, *Salvation Safari* (1993), p. 21.

8. Flora Larsson, *My Best Men Are Women* (1974), p. 47.

9. R.G. Moyles, *The Blood And Fire In Canada*, (1977), p. 9.

10. From 251 to 1,552 Corps.

11. Notes from Major Ray Herron, Australia School For Youth Leadership, January 23, 2004.

12. Geoff Ryan, "To Be or Not to Be," in *Sowing Dragons* (2000).

13. "100 Great British Heroes," *BBC News, World Edition*, August 21, 2002. "BBC Two Reveals the Nation's 100 Greatest Britons of All Time," *BBC Press Release*, August 21, 2002.

14. "Charity Case," *CPA Online*, December 2001. CPA reports that The Salvation Army received about double the closest charity in donation in 2001 from Australians. http://www.cpaaustralia.com.au/03 publications/02 aust cpa magazine/2001/35 dec/3 2 35 12 charitycase.asp. The Salvation Army received the largest donations in 9 of the last 10 years in America. "Buddy, We're Sparing Fewer Dimes," *CBS News*. Retrieved from the Internet October 27, 2003, from www.cbsnewsonline. The Salvation Army received the largest donation ever to a Christian organization from the estate of Joan Kroc: $1.5 billion. *USA Today*. Retrieved January 20, 2004, from www.usatoday.com. It is commonly known as "America's Favorite Charity."

15. PM Arthur Meighan, in Stephen Court and Danielle Strickland, *Salvationism 101* (2000), p. 29.

16. Cyril Barnes, *Words of William Booth* (1975).

17. Catherine Booth, *The Salvation Army in Relation to the Churches* (1883), p. 31-32.

18. William Booth, *Orders and Regulations* (1879) from the Introduction.

19. Catherine Booth, *Aggressive Christianity* (1881), p. 190.

20. William Booth, in answer to his own question, "Are all to be officers?" in Norman Murdoch, *The Origins of the Salvation Army* (1996), p. 141.

21. William Booth, in Bramwell Booth, *Talks With Officers* (1921), p. 102.

22. George Scott Railton, *Heathen England* (1880), p. 83.

23. *Orders And Regulations* (1879), Section 1:17.

24. Major Wells, California, *The War Cry*, in John Rhemick, *A New People Of God* (1984), p. 79.

25. R.G. Moyles, *The Blood and Fire in Canada* (1977), p. 58.

26. William Booth, 1878.

27. Catherine Booth, *Papers on Godliness* (1882), p. 62.

28. Italics added for emphasis. Isak Dinesan, *Letters From Africa 1914-1931*, Phoenix Fiction Services, translated by Anne Born, (Chicago: University of Chicago Press, 1984), cited in Geoff Ryan, "To Be or Not to Be," in *Sowing Dragons*, (2000).

29. George Scott Railton, *Heathen England*, (1887), p. 145.

30. *Newcastle Daily Chronicle*, May 22, 1879.

31. *Newcastle Daily Chronicle*, May 22, 1879.

32. Catherine Booth, *The Salvation Army in Relation to the Churches* (1883), pp. 47-48.

33. Catherine Booth, with reference to First Corinthians 14, *Aggressive Christianity* (1881), p. 55.

34. Catherine Booth, *Papers on Godliness* (1882), p. 124.

35. Catherine Booth, *Papers on Aggressive Christianity* (1881), p. 32.

36. *Newcastle Daily Chronicle*, May 21, 1879.

37. Source: The Salvation Army International Heritage Centre. Retrieved January 15, 2004.

38. Sallie Chesham, *Preaching Ladies*, (1983), pp. 6-8.

39. Sallie Chesham, *Preaching Ladies*, (1983), p. 15.

40. R.G. Moyles, *The Blood and Fire in Canada* (1977), p. 44.

41. R.G. Moyles, *The Blood and Fire in Canada* (1977), p. 59.

42. Cited in Brian Tuck, *Salvation Safari* (1993), pp. 18-19.

43. Caps in original, in R.G. Moyles, *The Blood and Fire in Canada* (1977), pp. 50-51.

44. Source: The Salvation Army International Heritage Centre. Retrieved January 15, 2004.

45. Cited by John Rhemick, *A New People of God* (1984), p. 205.

46. Frances Power Cobbe, "The Last Revival," *The Contemporary Review*, 1882.

47. "Rowdy Religion," *The Saturday Review*, May 31, 1884.

48. *Crime* Magazine web site. http://crimemagazine.com/PrisonsParole/devilsisland.htm. Retrieved January 10, 2004.

49. *Crime* Magazine web site. http://crimemagazine.com/PrisonsParole/devilsisland.htm. Retrieved January 10, 2004.

50. David P. Nolte, "A Heart for What Is Right," retrieved January 11, 2004, from http://www.kfalls.net/~dnol/aheartforright.html.

51. *Crime* Magazine web site. http://crimemagazine.com/PrisonsParole/devilsisland.htm. Retrieved January 10, 2004.

52. *Crime* Magazine web site. http://crimemagazine.com/PrisonsParole/devilsisland.htm. Retrieved January 10, 2004.

53. Charles Pean, *The Conquest of Devil's Island* (1953).

CHAPTER 7: IN DARKEST ENGLAND AND THE WAY OUT

1. The Salvation Army International Heritage Centre. Retrieved January 15, 2004.

2. J. Evan Smith, *Booth the Beloved* (1949), pp. 123-124.

3. William Booth, *In Darkest England and the Way Out* (1890), p. 13.

4. Source: The Salvation Army International Heritage Centre. Retrieved January 15, 2004.

5. E. Cobham Brewer, *Dictionary of Phrase and Fable* (1898). *The Submerged Tenth*—"The lowest of the proletariat class. A phrase much popularized in the last quarter of the nineteenth century by General Booth's book, *In Darkest England*." General John Gowans, "Poverty and The Salvation Army—The Call to the Excluded," *Journal of Aggressive Christianity*, December 2003. www.armybarmy.com/JAC. Gowans notes, "They were The Impoverished. They were 'Les Miserables' of his time. William felt called to The Excluded. He named them 'The Submerged Tenth.' Their poverty was the agent of their exclusion, the source of much of their misery, the nourishment of a great deal of their godlessness."

6. Brackets added. Dallas Salvation Army web site. http://www.salvationarmydallas. org/aboutus_poverty.asp. January 27, 2004.

7. W.T. Stead. *Catherine Booth* (1891), pp.10-11.

8. Caughey Gauntlett, *Today in Darkest Britain* (1990), p. 14.

9. Economic History Resources web site. http://www.eh.net/hmit/ppowerbp/. http://www. xe.com/ucc/convert.cgi. Retrieved January 28, 2004.

10. Source: The Salvation Army International Heritage Centre. Retrieved January 15, 2004.

11. Economic History Resources web site. Retrieved January 28, 2004, from http://www.eh.net/hmit/ppowerbp/ and http://www.xe.com/ucc/convert.cgi.

12. Economic History Resources web site. Retrieved January 28, 2004, from http://www.eh.net/hmit/ppowerbp/ and http://www.xe.com/ucc/convert.cgi.

13. Source: The Salvation Army International Heritage Centre. Things have picked up. In the first week after the Twin Towers Tragedy, September 11, 2001, The Salvation Army served relief workers 485,000 meals. Source 20/20 television show—"The Salvation Army assisted more than 121,000 people in the almost one year since the September 11 terrorist attacks, providing grief and mental health counseling, financial assistance, and other basic social services. In addition, Salvation Army officers, staff, and 107,169 volunteers—clocking more than 1.6 million volunteer hours—served almost 5 million meals to relief workers and victims." Retrieved August 22, 2002, from http://www.nwarmy.org/news/articles.asp?Story ID=552.

14. Chapter 4.

15. Part 2, Chapter 1.

16. Caughey Gauntlett. *Today in Darkest Britain* (1990), p. 28.

17. Caughey Gauntlett. *Today in Darkest Britain* (1990), pp. 158-169

18. Caughey Gauntlett. *Today in Darkest Britain* (1990), p. 45.

19. Caughey Gauntlett. *Today in Darkest Britain* (1990), p. 21.

20. Salvationists don't die. They are promoted to Glory.

21. The Salvation Army preaches the gospel in 175 languages in 109 countries, and, in 2001:
- operated 37 hospitals;
- operated nearly 550 health clinics;
- served more than 1.2 million patients;
- operated more than 6,000 schools;
- operated more than 700 colleges, universities, and distance learning centers;
- operated more than 12,000 general hostels and shelters;
- operated more than 960 special homes (children, elderly, blind, street children, etc.);
- operated almost 300 drug rehabilitation centers;
- operated more than 1,450 daycare centers;
- visited almost 250,000 prisoners;
- helped more than 137,000 people through courts;
- helped more than 52,000 prisoners upon release;
- traced more than 8,000 missing persons;
- operated more than 1,000 feeding centers;

- served more than 20,000,000 people;
- and so on. The Salvation Army, *Year Book*, 2003.

22. The money was earmarked for community centers, not happy meals! The Salvation Army received $1.5 billion from the estate of Joan Kroc. *USA Today*. www.usato day.com. Retrieved on January 20, 2004. Shawna Richer, "Big Mac give Sally Ann $1.5 billion," *Globe and Mail*. Retrieved January 21, 2004.

23. "Great Nottinghamians: William Booth," BBC News web site. Retrieved October 2002, from http://www.bbc.co.uk/nottingham/features/2002/10/william_booth_great_briton. shtml.

24. The Salvation Army. International Headquarters Heritage Center. Retrieved January 28, 2004, from http://www1.salvationarmy.org/heritage.nsf/36c107e27b0ba 7a98025692e0032abaa/e875c5b6377a3ba68025694b004a1202?OpenDocument.

25. The Salvation Army. International Headquarters Heritage Center. Retrieved January 28, 2004, from http://www1.salvationarmy.org/heritage.nsf/36c107e27b0ba7a98025 692e0032abaa/e875c5b6377a3ba68025694b004a1202?OpenDocument. And "Great Men of God," at Christians in Touch web site. Retrieved January 28, 2004, from http://www.chris tiansintouch.com/greatMen_WB.cfm.

26. "Great Men of God," at Christians in Touch web site. Retrieved on January 28, 2004, from http://www.christiansintouch.com/greatMen_WB.cfm.

CHAPTER 8: WHO ARE THEY AND WHERE DO THEY COME FROM?

1. Patrick Johnstone, *The Church Is Bigger Than You Think*, (1998), pp. 67-68.

2. Until the 1800s. Patrick Johnstone, *The Church Is Bigger Than You Think*, (1998), pp. 67-68.

3. The U.S. Center for World Mission, in Pasadena, CA, released global mission statistics for 2001: Fully one third of the world's population is Christian (2.02 billion). While the world population growth rate sits at 1.6 percent, the overall Christian growth rate is 2.6 percent. Notably, the growth rate of smaller groups within Christianity are significantly higher. Evangelicals are growing at 4.7 percent and Charismatics are growing at 7.3 percent. Other groups agree with these statistics: Global Evangelization Movement web site: http://www.gem werc.org/index.htm and http://www.pastornet.net.au/jmm/aame/aame0081.htm 2000.

4. Retrieved March 7, 2004, from http://www.pastornet.net.au/jmm/aame/aame0049.htm.

5. Retrieved October 29, 2003, from www.missionfrontiers.org/newslinks/statewe.htm.

6. Meanwhile, Pentecostals and Charismatics are exploding at a growth rate of 7.3 percent, more than four and a half times as fast as the total population (this is well more than 2 times the growth rate of Islam)! Evangelicals aren't far behind, at 5.7 percent, more than three and a half times as fast as the total population (more than double the growth rate of Islam). Other Protestants are growing at almost double the rate of the world population, 2.9 percent. Roman Catholics are growing at about 1.2 percent (Retrieved March 7, 2004 from www.mis sionfrontiers.org/newslinks/statewe.htm.).

7. Philip Jenkins, *The Next Christendom* (2002), p. 4.

8. Philip Jenkins, *The Next Christendom* (2002), p. 4.

9. CMI-Worlds Stats. Retrieved March 9, 2004, from http://glowministriesinterna tional.com/cmi/pages/stats.htm.

10. Ralph D. Winter and Bruce A. Koch, "Finishing the Task: The Unreached Peoples Challenge," *Mission Frontiers* (June 2000), p. 33.

11. Representing about 5 percent of the world's population, similar to Buddhism.

12. Wycliffe International. Retrieved March 7, 2004, from www.wycliffe.net.

13. Global Recordings Network. Retrieved March 7, 2004 from http://www.gospel recordings.com.

14. Patrick Johnstone, *The Church Is Bigger Than You Think*, (1998), p. 232.

15. Patrick Johnstone, *The Church Is Bigger Than You Think*, (1998), p. 232.

16. The Jesus Film Project. Retrieved March 7, 2004, from http://www.jesusfilm.org /progress/translations.html.

17. The Jesus Film Project. Retrieved March 7, 2004, from http://www.jesusfilm.org /progress/statistics.html.

18. The Jesus Film Project. Retrieved March 7, 2004, from http://www.jesusfilm.org /progress/statistics.html.

19. The Jesus Film Project. Retrieved March 7, 2004, from http://www.jesusfilm.com /progress/statistics.html.

20. Patrick Johnstone, *The Church Is Bigger Than You Think*, (1998), p. 230.

21. Wycliffe International. Retrieved March 7, 2004, from www.wycliffe.net.

22. "Status of Global Mission, 2003," at World Evangelization Research Center. Retrieved March 9, 2004, from http://www.gem-werc.org/resources.htm.

23. Retrieved March 9, 2004, from http://backtojerusalem.com.

24. Lecture of David Aikman at University of the Nations, Kona Hawaii, February 25, 2004; also, http://www.americandaily.com/item/3999. Retrieved December 18, 2003.

25. http://backtojerusalem.com/history1.htm. Retrieved on March 10, 2004.

26. Public lectures of both Loren Cunningham, and Peter Wagner respectively, September 19, 2003, NLC, Kelowna, and March 5, 2004, Red Deer, Alberta.

27. http://backtojerusalem.com/vision.htm. Retrieved March 10, 2004.

28. Josephus, *The Works of Josephus*, translated by William Whiston (Hendrickson Publishers, 1987). Retrieved March 12, 2004, from http://www.pbs.org/wgbh/pages/front line/shows/religion/maps/primary/josephus sack.html.

29. Josephus, *The Works of Josephus*, translated by William Whiston (Hendrickson Publishers, 1987). Retrieved March 12, 2004, from http://www.pbs.org/wgbh/pages/front line/shows/religion/maps/primary/josephus sack.html.

30. *Strong's Concordance*, words: 2347, 3173.

31. "World Bank Global Economic Prospects and the Developing Countries, 2002," World Development Bank web site. Retrieved January 2, 2004.

32. Dan Brewster, "The 4/14 Window: Child Ministries and Mission Resources" in Phyllis Kilbourn, ed., *Children in Crisis*, 1996, p. 127.

33. Sources: ILO Child Labour Statistics; UNICEF, The State of the World's Children, 2002; UN Population Division. The *style* of presentation of this information is the author's-added emphasis and paragraph breaks for clarity.

CHAPTER 9: SEVEN DEADLY SINS

1. George Grant, *The Micah Mandate* (2001), p. 29.

2. Cited in George Grant, *The Micah Mandate* (2001), p. 221.

3. Bryant L. Myers, "Strategic Trends Affecting Children," in Glenn Miles and Josephine-Joy Wright, ed., *Celebrating Children* (2003), p. 110.

4. "Listen to the Children Crying," *Charisma* (June 2000).

5. Bryant L. Myers, "Strategic Trends Affecting Children," in Glenn Miles and Josephine-Joy Wright, ed., *Celebrating Children* (2003), p. 110.

6. *The Economist* (March 31, 2001).

7. World Vision, at Viva Network web site. Retrieved October 1, 2003, from http://www.viva.org/frontline/reference/statistics/health.htm.

8. Retrieved January 15, 2004, from http://www.staytruetolife.org/seven.asp.

9. Art Beals, *Beyond Hunger* (1985), p. 29.

10. *TIME* (August 6, 2001).

11. UNICEF, "The State of the World's Children 2001," United Nations Development Program, *Poverty Report 2000*, http://www.undp.org/povertyreport/chapters/chapter 1.

12. *The Officer Magazine*, (April 2000).

13. UNICEF study finds one billion children in poverty, October 21, 2003. http://www.un.org/apps/news/story.asp?NewsID=8622&Cr=child&Cr1=poverty.

14. Bryant L. Myers, "Strategic Trends Affecting Children," in Glenn Miles and Josephine-Joy Wright, ed., *Celebrating Children* (2003), p. 110.

15. *The Officer Magazine*, (April 2000).

16. *The Officer Magazine*, (April 2000).

17. *The Officer Magazine*, (April 2000).

18. *The Officer Magazine*, (April 2000).

19. *The Officer Magazine*, (April 2000).

20. *The Officer Magazine*, (April 2000).

21. World Vision, at Viva Network web site. Retrieved July 3. 2003, from http://www.viva.org/frontline/reference/statistics/health.htm.

22. *The Officer Magazine*, (April 2000).

23. World Vision, at Viva Network web site. Retrieved July 3. 2003, from http://www.viva.org/frontline/reference/statistics/health.htm.

24. Press Summary, "The State of the World's Children 2001," UNICEF.

25. In 1998, the top five child killers were: perinatal conditions 20%, respiratory infections 18%, diarrhea diseases 17%, vaccine-preventable diseases 15%, and malaria 7%. Press Summary, "The State of the World's Children 2001," UNICEF.

26. World Population Profile 1998, Thomas McDewitt, International Program Center, U.S. Census Bureau 1999, web site, in Patrick McDonald, *Reaching Children in Need* (2000), p. 21.

27. United Nations Population Fund, at Viva Network web site. Retrieved July 3. 2003, from http://www.viva.org/frontline/reference/statistics/health.htm.

28. "Provincial authorities in Guangdong (formerly Canton), China, recently ordered that 20,000 abortions and sterilizations be performed in the impoverished region of Huaiji before year's end. Census officials had reported the average family in Huaiji to include five or more children, giving Communist authorities an excuse to crack down on residents for flagrantly flouting the nation's official one-child policy," in *The New American*, Alert Network (Vol. 17, No. 19), September 10, 2001.

29. *The New American*, Alert Network (Vol. 17, No. 19), Septem-ber 10, 2001.

30. Robert Stearns, *Prepare the Way* (1999), p. 154.

31. Centers for Disease Control and Prevention, UNAIDS and the World Health Organization. May 17, 2000. The Kids AIDS Site. http://www.kidsaidssite.com/cgi-bin/Web Ob.../6.0.17.1.1.3.0.1.0.17.0.CustomContentLinkDisplayComponent.0.

32. Every day 7,000 people between 10 and 24 years of age worldwide acquire the virus. This translates into five young people every minute. Report from UNAIDS, April 22, 1998. The Kids AIDS Site. http://www.kidsaidssite.com/cgi-bin/WebOb.../6.0.17.1.1.3.0.1.0.17.0.CustomContentLinkDisplayComponent.0.

33. HIV/AIDS Epidemic Update: December 1999 UN/AIDS Joint United Nations Program on HIV/AIDS. The Kids AIDS Site. http://www.kidsaidssite.com/cgi-bin/WebOb.../6.0.17.1.1.3.0.1.0.17.0.CustomContentLinkDisplayComponent.0.

34. "World Pulse," *Action International Ministries* (October 3, 1995), p. 6.

35. http://appnetaid.netlojix.com/programs/HIV/about_hiv.html. Retrieved July 4, 2001.

36. "Orphans of AIDS," *TIME*, December 13, 1999.

37. UNAIDS Security Council Session on AIDS Crisis, *New York Times* (January 10, 2000).

38. The Hunger Site, 2000. http://www.thehungersite.com/cgi-bin/WebObjects/CTDSites.

39. Viva Network web site. Retrieved July 3, 2003, from www.viva.org.

40. Food and Agriculture Organization of the United Nations, at The Hunger Site. Retrieved July 3, 2003, from http://www.thehungersite.com/cgi-bin/WebObjects/CTDSites.

41. United Nations Development Program *Poverty Report 2000*. Retrieved July 24, 2003, from http://www.undp.org/povertyreport/chapters/chapter 10.

42. Stuart Hart, "Strategies for a Sustainable World," *Harvard Business Review* (January-February 1997), pp. 68-69, cited in Tom Sine, *Mustard Seed vs. McWorld* (1999), pp. 64-65.

43. Viva Network web site. Retrieved July 3, 2003, from www.viva.org.

44. U.S. Department of Agriculture, Economic Research Service, 1999. Retrieved from http://www.thehungersite.com/cgi-bin/WebObjects/CTDSites.

45. United Nations Development Program *Poverty Report 2000*. Retrieved from http://www.undp.org/povertyreport/chapters/ chapter 7.

46. *The Officer Magazine*, (April 2000).

47. Press Summary, "The State of the World's Children 2001," UNICEF.

48. *The State of the World's Children 1999*: Education, UNICEF, as quoted from *Facts and Figures 1998*, UNICEF, in Patrick McDonald, *Reaching Children in Need*, (2000), p. 21.

49. *The Officer Magazine*, (April 2000).

50. *Pravda* (English version). http://english.pravda.ru/usa/2001/05/03/4589.html. May 3, 2001.

51. About 177 million children are stunted mainly because of malnutrition in pregnant women. Press Summary, "The State of the World's Children 2001," UNICEF. Close to 15 million girls aged 15-19 give birth every year. Press Summary, "The State of the World's Children 2001," UNICEF.

52. Rachael Combe, not a religious person, was transformed by her trip to India and wrote about it in *Elle*, January 2002.

53. November 3, 2003. "The Working World of Children" by Child Workers in Asia (CWA); cited in http://www.freethechildren.org/youthinaction/child labour personal stories.htm.

54. Marshall McLuhan.

55. This is his real name. For details, read on.

56. Quentin Hardy, "Hitting Slavery Where It Hurts," Forbes.com. Retrieved January 12, 2004.

57. Bryant L. Myers, "Strategic Trends Affecting Children," in Glenn Miles and Josephine-Joy Wright, ed., *Celebrating Children* (2003), p. 110.

58. UNICEF Information Sheet, "All Work and No Play: The Scourge of Child Labour," in Patrick McDonald, *Reaching Children in Need* (2000), pp. 31-32.

59. Child Hope, Fact Sheet on Working Children, at Viva Network web site. Retrieved July 3. 2003, from http://www.viva.org/frontline/reference/statistics/health.htm.

60. Quentin Hardy, "Hitting Slavery Where It Hurts," Forbes.com. Retrieved January 12, 2004.

61. Quentin Hardy, "Hitting Slavery Where It Hurts," Forbes.com. Retrieved January 12, 2004.

62. Gary Haugen. "Christians, Violence, and Injustice—Understanding God's Character Is Critical in Our Response" *Discernment* (Winter 2000, Vol. 7, No. 1), retrieved from http://ijm.org/article vol7.html.

63. Quentin Hardy, "Hitting Slavery Where It Hurts," Forbes.com. Retrieved January 12, 2004.

64. Marjorie McDermid, "Sexually Exploited Children" in Phyllis Kilbourn, ed., *Children in Crisis*, (1996), p. 35.

65. International Labour Organization, at Viva Network web site. Retrieved July 3. 2003, from http://www.viva.org/frontline/reference/statistics/health.htm.

66. International Labour Organization, World Vision, at Viva Network web site. Retrieved July 3. 2003, from http://www.viva.org/frontline/reference/statistics/health.htm.

67. World Vision, "Children At Risk" Development Education Brochure, at Viva Network web site. Retrieved July 3. 2003, from http://www.viva.org/frontline/reference/statistics/health.htm.

68. International Labour Organization, at Viva Network web site. Retrieved July 3. 2003, from http://www.viva.org/frontline/reference/statistics/health.htm.

69. United Nations Children's Fund—Information Sheet, March 29, 1994, at Viva Network web site. Retrieved July 3. 2003, from http://www.viva.org/frontline/reference/statis tics/health.htm.

70. International Labour Organization, at Viva Network web site. http://www.worldvi sion.org/worldvision/mag.nst/stable/WVT_girls_exploitation_0398. Retrieved July 3, 2003.

71. Viva Network web site. Retrieved July 3, 2003, from www.viva.org.

72. November 3, 2003. "The Working World of Children" by Child Workers in Asia (CWA); cited in Free The Children web site. http://www.freethechildren.org/youthinac tion/child_labour_personal_stories.htm. Retrieved July 17, 2003.

73. Viva Network web site. Retrieved July 3, 2003, from www.viva.org.

74. Source: Global march against child labor—July 11, 2001, at Viva Network web site at http://www.viva.org.

75. Source: Global march against child labor—July 11, 2001, at Viva Network web site at http://www.viva.org.

76. *Newsweek*, (April 2, 2001).

77. UNICEF web site, 2001.

78. CNN web site. http://www.cnn.com/2001/WORLD/africa/04/16/child.slavery /index.html. April 16, 2001.

79. CNN web site. http://www.cnn.com/2001/WORLD/africa/04/16/child.slavery/ index.html. April 16, 2001.

80. CBS News web site. http://cbsnews.com/now/story/0%2C1597%2C71386- 412%2C00.shtml. July 3, 2003.

81. "Chocolate Companies Blamed for Slave Labour," *BBC News*, http://www.anti-slav erysociety.org/ May 4, 2001.

82. "Bitter Pill," ABC News. http://more.abcnews.go.com/sections/world/dailynews/ cotedivoire010504_choco.html. May 4, 2001.

83. "African Children Used As 'Chocolate Slaves'," *The Province*, (April 2001).

84. Bryant L. Myers, "Strategic Trends Affecting Children," in Glenn Miles and Josephine-Joy Wright, ed., *Celebrating Children* (2003), p. 110.

85. World Population Profile 1998, Thomas McDewitt, International Program Center, U.S. Census Bureau 1999, web site, Patrick McDonald, *Reaching Children in Need* (2000), p. 21.

86. *Relay*; second quarter, 1998, as quoted in *Statistics Concerning the Needs of Underprivileged and Street Children Worldwide*, October 1998—Street Children Ministries, in Patrick McDonald, *Reaching Children in Need* (2000), p. 21.

87. Dan Brewster, " 'Children At Risk' Because They Have Not Heard the Good News: The 4/14 Window," in Glenn Miles and Josephine-Joy Wright, ed., *Celebrating Children* (2003), p. 176.

88. UNICEF, March 29, 1994, http://viva.org/frontline/reference/statis tics/street.htm.

89. *New York Times*, February 5, 1990, http://viva.org/frontline/reference/statistics/ street.htm.

90. *Encyclopedia of World Problems and Human Potential*. Union of International Associations, 1994, in Patrick McDonald, *Reaching Children in Need* (2000), p. 23.

91. Viva Network web site. Retrieved July 3, 2003, from www.viva.org.

92. World Vision web site. http://mongolia.worldvision.org.nz/lightstories.html. Retrieved January 15, 2004.

93. Phyllis Kilbourn, "Street Children: Who Are They? Where Are They?" in Phyllis Kilbourn, ed., *Street Children: A Guide to Effective Ministry* (1997), p. 13.

94. Child Hope, as quoted in *Children at Risk*: A Global Education curriculum series, Street Children. The Office on Global Education, USA, in Patrick McDonald, *Reaching Children in Need* (2000), p. 26.

95. *Growing Up on the Rough Side*. The Gospel Message. 1998, in Patrick McDonald, *Reaching Children in Need* (2000), p. 36.

96. Viva Network web site. Retrieved July 3, 2003, from www.viva.org.

97. Viva Network web site. Retrieved July 3, 2003, from www.viva.org.

98. Bhopal Medical Appeal, December 3, 1994. Retrieved November 3, 2003, in http://www.bhopal.net/oldsite/sunil.html.

99. Action International Ministries, in Patrick McDonald, *Reaching Children in Need* (2000), p. 27.

100. CNN web site. http://edition.cnn.com/2001/BUSINESS/asia/10/02/worldbank. biz/index.html. Retrieved October 2, 2001.

101. "Virgin Ruse," *The Straits Times* (Singapore) Interactive, Sunday, July 16, 2000. Cited in http://www.bigpond.com.kh/users/ngoforum/child_prostitution.htm.

102. "Child-Porn Ring Ends With 100 Arrests," *Reuters News Agency*, August 8, 2001.

103. *New York Times*, July 17, 1996, p. A8, cited in a quote from Tom Sine, *Mustard Seed vs. McWorld* (1999), pp. 73-74.

104. U.N.: "Child Sex Trade 'a Form of Terrorism'," CNN web site. Retrieved December 21, 2001, from http://edition.cnn.com/2001/WORLD/asiapcf/east/12/17/childsex.confer ence/index.html.

105. *Globe and Mail*. June 27, 2001.

106. Colin Powell, "Powell Responds to Cambodia Investigation," NBC News on msnbc.com. January 23, 2004.

107. Colin Powell, in "Children for Sale," NBC News on msnbc.com. January 30, 2004.

108. ChildHope, Fact Sheets on Street Girls, March 1990, in Patrick McDonald, *Reaching Children in Need* (2000), pp. 38-39.

109. Tony Culmane, "Why Are Children on the Streets" in Phyllis Kilbourn, ed., *Street Children: A Guide to Effective Ministry* (1997), p. 27.

110. USA Today web site. http://www.usatoday.com/graphics/census2000/usdem/ usdem.htm.

111. Census web site. http://www.census.gov/population/cen2000/phc-t3/tab03.pdf.

112. World Vision, "Children at Risk"-No.4, Development Education Publication, at Viva Network web site. http://www.viva.org/frontline/referene/statistics/sexploit.htm.

113. UNICEF, at Viva Network web site. Retrieved on July 3, 2003, from http://www. viva.org/frontline/referene/statistics/sexploit.htm.

114. Quentin Hardy, "Hitting Slavery Where It Hurts," Forbes.com. Retrieved on January 12, 2004.

115. Ross A. MacInnes, *Children in the Game: Child Prostitution-Strategies for Recovery*, (1998).

116. Quentin Hardy, "Hitting Slavery Where It Hurts," Forbes.com. Retrieved on January 12, 2004.

117. P. Green estimates that 80 percent of the girls rescued from Thailand brothels are HIV-positive. In *Prostitution: The Victims*, unpublished paper, 1994, in Patrick McDonald, *Reaching Children in Need* (2000), p. 39.

118. Phyllis Kilbourn, "Street Children: Who Are They? Where Are They?" in Phyllis Kilbourn, ed., *Street Children: A Guide to Effective Ministry* (1997), p. 13.

119. *Sexually Victimized Children*, New York: Free Press 1979, in Patrick McDonald, *Reaching Children in Need* (2000), p. 41.

120. "The Prevalence and Nature of Child Sexual Abuse in Australia," *Australian Journal of Sex, Marriage, and the Family* (Vol. 9, 1988), p. 4, in Patrick McDonald, *Reaching Children in Need* (2000), p. 41.

121. Viva Network web site. Retrieved July 3, 2003, from www.viva.org.

122. "Children for Sale," NBC News on msnbc.com. January 30, 2004.

123. Porn accounts for 7 percent of Google's Index. Pamela Paul, "The Porn Factor," *TIME* (February 12, 2004).

124. Pamela Paul, "The Porn Factor," *TIME* (February 12, 2004).

125. Marjorie McDermid, "Sexually Exploited Children" in Phyllis Kilbourn, ed., *Children in Crisis* (1996), p. 34.

126. Pamela Paul, "The Porn Factor," *TIME* (February 12, 2004).

127. Viva Network web site. Retrieved July 3, 2003, from www.viva.org.

128. Viva Network web site. Retrieved July 3, 2003, from www.viva.org.

129. Viva Network web site. Retrieved July 3, 2003, from www.viva.org.

130. Marjorie McDermid, "Sexually Exploited Children" in Phyllis Kilbourn, ed., *Children in Crisis* (1996), p. 37.

131. *TIME*, February 18, 2002: "The Taliban often argued that the brutal restrictions they placed on women were actually a way of revering and protecting the opposite sex. The behavior of the Taliban during the six years they expanded their rule in Afghanistan made a mockery of the claim."

132. Patrick Dixon, *The Rising Price of Love* (1995), p. 124.

133. "CDC Admits Public Misled On Condoms, 'Safe Sex,'" *The New American* (August 8, 2001).

134. "CDC Admits Public Misled On Condoms, 'Safe Sex,'" *The New American* (August 8, 2001).

135. "CDC Admits Public Misled On Condoms, 'Safe Sex,'" *The New American* (August 8, 2001).

136. Laurie Garrett, *The Coming Plague* (1994), p. 5.

137. "AIDS Researchers See Rise of Drug-Resistant HIV 'Superbug,'" *National Post* (September 2, 2001).

138. "AIDS Researchers See Rise of Drug-Resistant HIV 'Superbug,'" *National Post* (September 2, 2001).

139. Eric Ram, "Preventing And Treating HIV And STDs" in Phyllis Kilbourn, ed., *Street Children: A Guide to Effective Ministry* (1997), p. 111.

140. Patrick Dixon, *The Rising Price of Love* (1995), p. 72.

141. "Gates Makes $100M Donation to Fight AIDS," *The Globe and Mail* (June 19, 2001).

142. Two million children die annually because they have not been immunized. Source: "State of the World's Vaccines and Immunization," WHO/UNICEF, 1996, in Patrick McDonald, *Reaching Children in Need* (2000), p. 43.

143. *The State of the World's Children*, UNICEF, 1998. Patrick McDonald, *Reaching Children in Need* (2000).

144. "World Pulse," Action International Ministries, October 3, 1995, in Patrick McDonald, *Reaching Children in Need* (2000), p. 47.

145. United Nations, in Patrick McDonald, *Reaching Children in Need* (2000), p. 45.

146. Rachel Hurst, Disabled Peoples International. Submission to the Committee on the rights of the child: thematic day on disabled children, October 6, 1997, p. 3, in Patrick McDonald, *Reaching Children in Need* (2000), pp. 46-47. This is our book in a nutshell. Someone whose heart has been transformed by the gospel has gone and reached the marginalized and forgotten, and in so doing, has changed social, physical, professional, relational, and spiritual aspects of and quality of life. When a whole lot of people follow the example, the face of the earth changes.

147. Viva Network web site. Retrieved July 3, 2003, from www.viva.org.

148. Viva Network web site. Retrieved July 3, 2003, from www.viva.org.

149. http://www.christianchildrensfund.org/working_for_children/health/_hiv_aids/irenes_hand.cfm. January 15, 2004.

150. Tim Jakes and Susan Jakes, "Stalking a Killer," *TIME Asia* (September 30, 2002).

151. Report on the global HIV/AIDS epidemic: December 2000 UNAIDS Joint United Nations Programme on HIV/AIDS, http://www.egpaf.org/facts.html. March 14, 2003.

152. Report on the global HIV/AIDS epidemic: December 2000 UNAIDS Joint United Nations Programme on HIV/AIDS, http://www.egpaf.org/facts.html. March 14, 2003.

153. Youth Report 2000- White Office of National AIDS Policy, http://www.egpaf.org/facts.html. March 14, 2003.

154. Anthony C. LoBaido, "Child-Rape Epidemic in South Africa," World Net Daily. December 26, 2001. http://www.worldnetdaily.com/news/article.asp?ARTICLE_ID=25806> http://www.worldnetdaily.com/news/article.asp?ARTICLE_ID=25806.

155. Anthony C. LoBaido, "Child-Rape Epidemic in South Africa," World Net Daily. December 26, 2001. http://www.worldnetdaily.com/news/article.asp?ARTICLE_ID=25806> http://www.worldnetdaily.com/news/article.asp?ARTICLE_ID=25806.

156. Anthony C. LoBaido, 'Little Angels' Rescue Victims Of Baby Rape,' World Net Daily, worldnetdaily.com. April 17, 2002.

157. Anthony C. LoBaido, 'Little Angels' Rescue Victims Of Baby Rape,' World Net Daily, worldnetdaily.com. April 17, 2002.

158. Anthony C. LoBaido, "Child-Rape Epidemic in South Africa," World Net Daily. December 26, 2001. http://www.worldnetdaily.com/news/article.asp?ARTICLE_ID=25806> http://www.worldnetdaily.com/news/article.asp?ARTICLE_ID=25806.

159. Anthony C. LoBaido, "Child-Rape Epidemic in South Africa," World Net Daily. December 26, 2001. http://www.worldnetdaily.com/ news/article.asp?ARTICLE_ID=25806> http://www.worldnetdaily.com/news/article.asp?ARTICLE_ID=25806.

160. Anthony C. LoBaido, ''Little Angels' Rescue Victims Of Baby Rape,' World Net Daily, worldnetdaily.com. April 17, 2002.

161. You may want to send some money to them at littleangels.co.za/.

162. Anthony C. LoBaido, "Searching For Throw-Away Babies," World Net Daily. worldnetdaily.com. May 8, 2002.

163. Anthony C. LoBaido, "Searching For Throw-Away Babies," World Net Daily. worldnetdaily.com. May 8, 2002.

164. Anthony C. LoBaido, "Searching For Throw-Away Babies," World Net Daily. worldnetdaily.com. May 8, 2002.

165. Alison Rader, "Children with HIV/AIDS," in Phyllis Kilbourn, ed., *Children in Crisis* (1996), p. 44.

166. Viva Network web site. Retrieved July 3, 2003, from www.viva.org.

167. Viva Network web site. Retrieved July 3, 2003, from www.viva.org.

168. 70% of those living with HIV/AIDS reside in sub-Saharan Africa. "Death Stalks a Continent," *TIME* (February 12, 2001).

169. "UN: 70 Million Will Die of AIDS by 2022," cnn.com. July 2, 2002.

170. Tim Jakes and Susan Jakes, "Stalking a Killer," *TIME Asia*. September 30, 2002.

171. Patrick Dixon, *The Rising Price of Love* (1995), p. 170.

172. Patrick Dixon, *The Rising Price of Love* (1995), p. 171.

173. Patrick Dixon, *The Rising Price of Love* (1995), p. 171.

174. George W. Bush, "State of the Union Address." http://www.nationalreview.com/document/document012903.asp. January 20, 2004.

175. "Found What He's Looking For," *TIMEurope Magazine*. April 20, 2003.

176. UPI. April 27, 2001.

177. "The Health Of Nations," *The Economist* (December 20, 2001).

178. George W. Bush, "State of the Union Address." http://www.nationalreview.com/document/document012903.asp. January 20, 2004.

179. The Commission on Macroeconomics and Health released findings at the end of 2001 indicating that a mere 0.01% of GDP from 'rich countries' to "save 8 million souls a year from untimely death." In "The Health of Nations," *The Economist* (December 20, 2001).

180. Tim Jakes and Susan Jakes, "Stalking a Killer," *TIME Asia* (September 30, 2002).

181. Mike Cohen, "A Noble Custom?" *Associated Press* (February 27, 2000).

182. The Seize the Day Foundation. https://www.nhf.org/applications/donate.htm?FDN=Seize%2Bthe%2BDay%2BFoundation&ProjNum=F11700. January 10, 2004.

183. Minister Essop Pahad, "Opening Remarks: UN Committee on the Rights of the Child," Geneva, Switzerland. Presentation of the South Africa Country Progress Report on the Implementation of the Convention on the Rights of the Child. January 25, 2000.

184. Aziz Hartley, "Botched Circumcisions Get the Chop," *The Daily News* (January 7, 2004).

185. Seize The Day Foundation. https://www.nhf.org/applications/donate.htm?FDN=Seize%2Bthe%2BDay%2BFoundation&ProjNum=F11700. January 10, 2004.

186. Patrick McDonald, Reaching *Children in Need* (2000), p. 29.

187. Seren Boyd, *Tear Times*, 1999, 21, in Patrick McDonald, *Reaching Children in Need* (2000), p. 28.

188. *Microsoft Word Dictionary*, PowerBook.

189. Retrieved November 3, 2003, from http://www.freethechildren.org/youthinaction/war affected children.htm.

190. "Girls Under Guns: The Special Situation of Girl Children Affected by Armed Conflict—A Case Study of Girls Abducted by Joseph Kony's Lord's Resistance Army (LRA) in Northern Uganda," a report for World Vision International, December 1995, in Patrick McDonald, *Reaching Children in Need* (2000), p. 28.

191. *Warchild* web site at warchild.ca. July 3, 2003.

192. "Sex Slavery Awaits Ugandan Schoolgirls," *BBC News online*, June 25, 2003.

193. "Sex Slavery Awaits Ugandan Schoolgirls," *BBC News online*, June 25, 2003.

194. Child Soldiers web site at http://www.child-soldiers.org/, July 3, 2003.

195. They were age 12 a few years ago when they gained near-legend status for some startling victories against mainstream guerrilla armies. "Twin Terrors Tamed Boy Leaders of Myanmar Rebel Group Surrender to Thai Authorities," *The Associated Press*, January 16, 2001.

196. "Twin Terrors of Burma: A Look at the 12-Year-Olds Behind God's Army," ABC News web site, *The Associated Press*, January 24, 2000.

197. "Mama's Boys: God's Army Twins Reunited With Mother in Thailand," ABC News web site, *The Associated Press*, March 15, 2001.

198. "Mama's Boys: God's Army Twins Reunited With Mother in Thailand," ABC News web site, *The Associated Press*, March 15, 2001.

199. "Mama's Boys: God's Army Twins Reunited With Mother in Thailand," ABC News web site, *The Associated Press*, March 15, 2001.

200. Viva Network web site. Retrieved from www.viva.org.

201. Viva Network web site. Retrieved from www.viva.org.

202. United Nations Office for the Coordination of Humanitarian Affairs (OCHA), December 12, 2003.

203. Frances Harrison, "Sri Lanka's Child Soldiers," *BBC News* UK Edition, January 31, 2003.

204. Retrieved on January 15, 2004, from http://www.unicef.org/children conflict /past.htm.

205. Viva Network web site. Retrieved July 3, 2003, from www.viva.org.

206. United Nations Office for the Coordination of Humanitarian Affairs (OCHA), December 12, 2003.

207. Fergal Keane, "Africa's Forgotten and Ignored War," *BBC News* UK Edition, October 18, 2003.

208. http://www.unicef.org/children conflict/past.htm.

209. A Peruvian woman, recruited by the Shining Path, a guerrilla group, at age 11. November 3, 2003. http://www.freethechildren.org/youthinaction/war affected children.htm.

210. Retrieved January 15, 2004, from http://www.unicef.org/children conflict/past.htm.

211. *State of the World's Children*, UNICEF 1995, in Patrick McDonald, *Reaching Children in Need* (2000), p. 29.

212. Retrieved July 3, 2003, from http://unicef.org/voy/meeting/war/war-exp2.htm.

213. Retrieved July 3, 2003, from http://unicef.org/voy/meeting/war/war-exp2.htm.

214. Viva Network web site. Retrieved July 3, 2003, from http://www.viva.org/front line/reference/statistics.htm.

215. Viva Network web site. Retrieved July 3, 2003, from www.viva.org.

216. Viva Network web site. Retrieved July 3, 2003, from www.viva.org.

217. *The Economist* (March 31, 2001).

218. *TIME* (January 7, 2002), p. 116.

219. *The Economist* (March 31, 2001).

220. Quentin Hardy, "Hitting Slavery Where It Hurts," Forbes.com. January 12, 2004.

221. *TIME* (June 12, 2001).

222. *The Economist* (March 31, 2001).

223. "Uganda Kids' Scary Flight From Night," *Vancouver Sun* (Friday, February 13, 2004).

224. United Nations Office for the Coordination of Humanitarian Affairs (OCHA), December 12, 2003.

225. Retrieved July 3, 2003, from http://unicef.org/voy/meeting/war/war-exp2.htm.

226. Retrieved July 3, 2003, from http://unicef.org/voy/meeting/war/war-exp2.htm.

227. Retrieved July 3, 2003, from http://unicef.org/voy/meeting/war/war-exp2.htm.

228. Retrieved November 3, 2003, from http://www.freethechildren.org/youthinac tion/war_affected_children.htm.

229. Danyun, *Lilies Amongst Thorns* (1991), p. 50.

230. David Hunt, *The Heavenly Man* (1999), p. 37.

231. David Hunt, *The Heavenly Man* (1999), p. 37.

232. David Hunt, *The Heavenly Man* (1999), p. 45.

233. Chapter on Asia and the Pacific from http://web.amnesty.org/web/ar2001.nsf/reg ASA/regASA?OpenDocument, February 2, 2002.

234. Philip P. Pan, *Washington Post* Foreign Service, February 13, 2002.

235. Does the token coverage of AI concerning the plight of Chinese Christians belie anti-Christian discrimination on the part of anti-discrimination organizations?

236. November 2000 to April 2001.

237. *Newsweek* (April 16, 2001).

238. *USA Today* (October 29, 2001).

239. Philip P. Pan, *Washington Post* Foreign Service, February 13, 2002. "Robin Munro, a China specialist at the School of Oriental and African Studies in London…said…they could be among the most significant internal documents on religious persecution in China seen in the West. 'I've never seen anything like it in such quantity,' he said. 'These documents are from all around the country, all consistent, all quite draconian, and all expressing implacable hostility toward these groups and determination to eradicate them. The party sees these groups as a mortal threat, and it's really going into overdrive now.' The papers were published this week as part of a 141-page report outlining the results of an unusually extensive study on Christians in China. The committee said it identified more than 23,000 people arrested since 1983 for unauthorized religious activity and collected statements from 5,000 victims of torture and persecution in 22 provinces and 200 cities."

240. Sammy Tippit, *The Gathering Storm* (1996), p. 151.

241. http://www.urban-ministries.net/trends.htm. January 15, 2004.

242. In Sammy Tippit, *The Gathering Storm* (1996), p. 152. We can expect 165,000 to be martyred this year alone. Retrieved on November 5, 2003, from http://www.pastornet. net.au/jmm/aame/aame0045.htm.

243. Richard John Neuhaus, editor of *First Things*, says this in the August/September 2001 issue, in the "While We're At It" section:

> You may recall that a few years ago there was much media hype about a rash of burnings of black churches across the South. It turned out to be just that, hype. But the National Council of Churches and others raised about a million dollars for rebuilding churches that were not burned. The money was spent, of course, on "fighting racism." Now in Canada, the federal Multiculturalism Minister (yes, they have such an office), Hedy Fry, raised an alarm about racist cross-burnings. That, too, turned out to be fictional. But Lorne Gunter of the *Edmonton Journal* notes there really was an instance of cross-burning a year earlier in Montreal, when feminists stormed the Catholic cathedral on International Women's Day, an observance much encouraged by Multiculturalism Minister Fry. "The feminists, hiding behind ski masks, set alight homemade crosses, then stormed the cathedral. They vandalized the walls and altar with spray paint proclaiming 'No God, no masters.' They knocked down elderly nuns, destroyed hymnals and prayer books, smeared the walls with used sanitary napkins, and strewed condoms around, all in the name of tolerance. It seems these protesters could not bear any views on abortion or women's rights that disagreed with their own. And since the Catholic Church believes all abortion is sin and chooses not to ordain women as priests, well then, its cathedrals

were fair game for a good ransacking." You will probably not be surprised to learn that the Ministry of Multiculturalism had nothing, as in absolutely nothing, to say about what happened in Montreal.

244. Cited in *The Politics of Religious Freedom*. Retrieved January 14, 2004, from http://www.web.net/~wifeaont/di2po.html.

245. Cited in http://gem-werc.org/gd/gd16.pdf; http://users.erols.com/mwhite28/warstat0.htm#Martyrs. 2001.

246. Barrett et al., *World Christian Trends*, cited in *20th Century Atlas*, retrieved January 13, 2004, from http://users.erols.com/mwhite28/warstat0.htm#Martyrs.

247. *20th Century Atlas*, retrieved January 15, 2004, from http://users.erols.com/mwhite28/warstat0.htm#Martyrs.

248. Retrieved January 12, 2004, from http://users.erols.com/mwhite28/warstat1.htm#Hitler; http://users.erols.com/mwhite28/warstat1.htm#Mao; http://users.erols.com/mwhite28/warstat1.htm#Stalin.

249. *20th Century Atlas*, retrieved January 12, 2004, from http://users.erols.com/mwhite28/warstats.htm.

250. Philip Jenkins, *The Next Christendom* (2002), pp. 73-74,93,212.

251. Philip Jenkins, *The Next Christendom* (2002), pp. 73,84,93,212.

252. The Islamic portions of the country have successfully instituted *Sharia* law in their states. For a recent well-noted example of some of the strife this has caused, see http://www.news24.com/News24/Africa/News/0,,2-11-1447_1420315,00.html. Retrieved on September 23, 2003.

253. 1998—1-2 million at Redeemed Christian Church of God campaign; 2000—1.6 million at one meeting with Reinhard Bonnke. See, for example, paragraph 9 of http://www.christianitytoday.com/ct/2001/002/5.40.html. Retrieved February 5, 2001.

254. Paul Marshall, *Their Blood Cries Out* (1997), pp. 10-11.

255. Paul Marshall, *Their Blood Cries Out* (1997), p. 17.

256. "The Horrors of Jihad," *Charisma*. June, 2001.

257. "The Horrors of Jihad," *Charisma*. June, 2001.

258. Paul Marshall, *Their Blood Cries Out* (1997), p. 31.

259. Paul Marshall, *Their Blood Cries Out* (1997), p. 116.

260. Possibly in anticipation, the U.S. Commission on International Religious Freedom is taking a heightened interest in what is happening to the largest group of Christians in the Middle East, the Copts of Egypt, who are the object of relentless persecution by militant Muslims, with little or no response from the Mubarak government. Freedom House has published a 130-page meticulously documented book, *Massacre at the Millennium*, on one aspect of the persecution, the murder of 21 Christians in Al-Kosheh. For more information, write Freedom House at Center for Religious Freedom, 1319 18th Street, NW, Washington, D.C. 20036. Source: *First Things* (August/September 2001).

261. *International Herald Tribune* (April 12, 2001).

262. Lee Soon Ok, in *International Herald Tribune* (April 12, 2001).

263. "Suffering for Christ in a Land of Slavery," *Charisma* (June 2001).

264. "Hiding From the Dragon," *Charisma* (June, 2001).

CHAPTER 10: THIS BUD'S FOR YOU

1. The Bill and Melinda Gates Foundation has already given or committed $4.9 billion, with a war chest of $24 billion, according to *TIME* (November 5, 2001).

2. *TIME* (October 22, 2001).

Chapter 11: What Is A Hero?

1. See the epilogue Blueprint for Global Action.

2. "Bono's Mission," *TIME* Magazine. February 23, 2002.

3. If you are not connected with a local manifestation of the Army of God (i.e. some sort of church) then you are a renegade, who cannot be fully trusted and whose impact will necessarily be limited. So sign up. As Billy Graham says, "Join the church of your choice."

4. What we're saying is that you must be actively involved in a local expression of the Body of Christ. Catherine Booth Jr. defined Christianity as heroism. If you are attempting to exercise your heroism alone your Christianity is not legitimate. Get plugged into an orthodox, authentic, Christian community.

5. See Wesley Campbell and Stacey Campbell. *Praying the Bible: The Book of Prayers* (2002).

6. For more teaching, see Stacey Campbell and Wesley Campbell, *Praying the Bible: The Book of Prayers* (2002).

7. See Stacey Campbell and Wesley Campbell. *Praying the Bible: The Book of Prayers* (2002).

8. *The Economist*, Vol. 369 (November 29 to December 5, 2003), p. 79.

9. *Giving USA 2003*, the Annual Report on Philanthropy. published by the AAFRC Trust for Philanthropy. Retrieved February 23, 2004. http://www.charitynavigator.orgindex.cfm/bay/content.view/catid/3/cpid/42.htm.

10. "Charity Holds Its Own In Tough Times," *Giving USA 2003*, The Annual Report on Philanthropy for the Year 2002.

11. Most by tithing. *Giving USA 2003*, the Annual Report on Philanthropy. Retrieved February 23, 2004. Published by the AAFRC Trust for Philanthropy. http://www.charitynavigator.org/index.cfm/bay/content.view/catid/3/cpid/42.htm February 23, 2004.

12. *Giving USA 2003*, the Annual Report on Philanthropy. published by the AAFRC Trust for Philanthropy. Retrieved February 23, 2004. http://www.charitynavigator.org/index.cfm/bay/content.view/catid/3/cpid/42.htm.

13. "Charity Holds Its Own In Tough Times." *Giving USA 2003*, The Annual Report on Philanthropy for the Year 2002.

14. *Current Population Reports*—Projections of the Number of Households and Families in the United States: 1995 to 2010. Texas A & M Universities Libraries. Retrieved March 8, 2004.

15. "Giving and volunteering in five countries." January 15, 1997; *Canadian Fund Raiser* http://www.charityvillage.com/cv/research/rsta19.html.

16. http://religionworld.org/dd/archiv10/3401.htm.

17. George Whitefield, *George Whitefield's Journals*. (1989). p 88.

18. George Whitefield, *George Whitefield's Journals*. (1989). p 92.

19. Economic History Resources web site. http://www.eh.net/hmit/ppowerbp/. http://www.xe.com/ucc/convert.cgi. Retrieved January 28, 2004.

20. George Whitefield, *George Whitefield's Journals*. (1989), October 1740 notes.

21. To read the inspiring story of Phil and Wendy Wall go to Appendix One, HopeHIV.

22. See web site: HopeForTheNations.com; Heroesofthenation.com.

23. See viva.org for an excellent resource on advocacy.

24. http://www.fh.org/ministryindex/index.shtml. January 3, 2004.

25 http://watermattersaustralia.org/take-action/index.htm. January 4, 2004.

26. http://watermattersaustralia.org/take-action/polliepush-ideas.htm. January 4, 2004.

27. http://www.tear.org.au/advocacy/refugees/taking-action.htm#d. January 2, 2004.

28. viva.org.

29. http://www.viva.org/tellme/events/. January 5, 2004.

30. *The Catholic Encyclopedia*, Volume XII. (Robert Appleton Company, 1911). Online Edition Copyright © 2003 by K. Knight.

31. Steven Gertz "Christian History Corner: Hajj, Feasts and Pilgrimage," christianitytoday.com. December 21, 2003.

32. Miranda Althouse Green. "On The Road," *British Archaeology*. (Issue No 52) April 2000. http://www.britarch.ac.uk/ba/ba52/ba52feat.htm. January 4, 2003.

33. *The Catholic Encyclopedia*, (Volume XII.by Robert Appleton Company, 1911). Online Edition Copyright © 2003 by K. Knight.

34. Steven Gertz "Christian History Corner: Hajj, Feasts and Pilgrimage," christianity today.com. December 21, 2003.

35. "Not by journeying but by loving we draw nigh unto God. To Him who is every-where present and everywhere entire we approach not by our feet but by our hearts," in *The Catholic Encyclopedia*, (Volume XII.by Robert Appleton Company, 1911). Online Edition Copyright © 2003 by K. Knight. Compare with Jerome's, "it is not the fact of living in Jerusalem, but of living there well, that is worthy of praise." Same source.

CHAPTER 12: A PARADIGM FOR END-TIME HARVEST

1. See Ralph Winter and Bruce Koch, *Finishing the Task*, cited in October 29, 2003. www.missionfrontiers.org/newslinks/statewe.htm.

2. Check out our maps in Chapter 8. "Who Are They and Where Do They Come From?" For example, many will come from South Asia. South Asia is one of the world's poor-est regions. Forty-five percent of the population lives below the international poverty line of $1 a day, comprising about 40 percent of the world's poor. http://lnweb18.worldbank.org/sar/sa.nsf, October 23, 2003.

3. Nearly 2.158 billion, according to October 29, 2003, UNICEF statistics; http://www.unicef.org/sowc03/tables/table5.htm.

4. We urge you to repent of every sin that God reveals in your life. Though painful, this is essential to every revival. God is a compassionate Father just dying to be in love with you. Let Him. Seek His face. Let Him sit in His throne in your life. It will transform you. Contact us or see the appendix for resources to help.

5. See Tom Sine's *Mustard Seed vs. McWorld* for a penetrating consideration of the global economic forces and the gospel potential in the 21st century, 1999, and "Globalisation and Its Critics," *The Economist*, September 27, 2001, for a contrary perspective.

6. 750,000 British children have no contact with their fathers following the breakdown of marital relationships. 1,300,000 lone parents are bringing up children in Britain. Viva Network web site. Retrieved July 3, 2003, from www.viva.org.

7. William Wilberforce, *Real Christianity* (1882), p. 44.

8. Mother Teresa, *A Simple Path* (1995), p. 159.

9. Patrick McDonald tackles the corporate challenges of a global strategy specifically in the epilogue of this book, "A Blueprint for Action."

10. http://www.uscwm.org/mobilization_division/pastors_web_folder/global_mission_statistics.html. Retrieved on March 22, 2004.

11. Bono quoted in The *Hollywood Reporter* (February 21, 2003). http://www.hollywoodreporter.com/thr/article_display.jsp?vnu_content_id=1821629.

12. See James 5.

13. September 2000.

14. **1. Eradicate extreme poverty and hunger**
Target for 2015: Halve the proportion of people living on less than a dollar a day and those who suffer from hunger.
More than a billion people still live on less than US $1 a day: sub-Saharan Africa, Latin America and the Caribbean, and parts of Europe and Central Asia are falling short of the poverty target.
2. Achieve universal primary education
Target for 2015: Ensure that all boys and girls complete primary school.

As many as 113 million children do not attend school, but the target is within reach. India, for example, should have 95 percent of its children in school by 2005.

3. Promote gender equality and empower women

Targets for 2005 and 2015: Eliminate gender disparities in primary and secondary education preferably by 2005, and at all levels by 2015.

Two-thirds of illiterates are women, and the rate of employment among women is two-thirds that of men. The proportion of seats in parliaments held by women is increasing, reaching about one-third in Argentina, Mozambique and South Africa.

4. Reduce child mortality

Target for 2015: Reduce by two thirds the mortality rate among children under five.

Every year nearly 11 million young children die before their fifth birthday, mainly from preventable illnesses, but that number is down from 15 million in 1980.

5. Improve maternal health

Target for 2015: Reduce by three-quarters the ratio of women dying in childbirth.

In the developing world, the risk of dying in childbirth is one in 48, but virtually all countries now have safe motherhood programs.

6. Combat HIV/AIDS, malaria, and other diseases

Target for 2015: Halt and begin to reverse the spread of HIV/AIDS and the incidence of malaria and other major diseases.

Forty million people are living with HIV, including five million newly infected in 2001. Countries like Brazil, Senegal, Thailand and Uganda have shown that the spread of HIV can be stemmed.

7. Ensure environmental sustainability

Targets:

- *Integrate the principles of sustainable development into country policies and programs and reverse the loss of environmental resources.*
- *By 2015, reduce by half the proportion of people without access to safe drinking water.*
- *By 2020 achieve significant improvement in the lives of at least 100 million slum dwellers.*

More than one billion people lack access to safe drinking water and more than two billion lack sanitation. During the 1990s, however, nearly one billion people gained access to safe water and the same number to sanitation.

8. Develop a global partnership for development

Targets:

- *Develop further an open trading and financial system that includes a commitment to good governance, development and poverty reduction—nationally and internationally.*
- *Address the least—developed countries' special needs, and the special needs of landlocked and small—island developing States.*
- *Deal comprehensively with developing countries' debt problems.*
- *Develop decent and productive work for youth.*
- *In cooperation with pharmaceutical companies, provide access to affordable essential drugs in developing countries.*
- *In cooperation with the private sector, make available the benefits of new technologies-especially information and communications technologies.*

Many developing countries spend more on debt service than on social services. New aid commitments made in the first half of 2002 could mean an additional $12 billion per year by 2006. http://www.undp.org/mdg/

15. Peter Gardener, *Praying At The Global Gates*, p. 19.

16. Peter Gardener, *Praying At The Global Gates*, p. 19.

17. Peter Gardener, *Praying At The Global Gates*, p. 19.

18. Peter Gardener, *Praying At The Global Gates*, pp. 19-20.

19. Henry David Thoreau, *Walden* (1854). http://xroads.virginia.edu/~HYPER/WALDEN/toc.html.

EPILOGUE: BLUEPRINT FOR GLOBAL ACTION

1. This is an extract of *Child Poverty—Your Challenge* by Patrick McDonald, watch website for details.

2. http://www.cafod.org.uk/get_involved/campaigning/campaign_issues/trade. March 18, 2004.

3. Source: Peter Brierley, Christian Research Association.

4. Source: faithworks.info research 2003.

5. £406 a week x 52 weeks in the year x 50 years (a low average for lifetime of family expenditure) = £1,055,600. http://www.statistics.gov.uk/cci/nugget.asp?id=284. March 18, 2004.

OTHER BOOKS BY WESLEY CAMPBELL

Praying the Bible: The Book of Prayers
Praying The Bible Out Loud Will Transform Your Life!

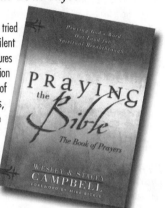

If you want to focus your prayers to get results, use the method that's as tried and true as the Bible itself: Pray the Bible out loud, before moving into silent communion with God. From Jesus' example, we know that praying the Scriptures aloud brings powerful results. Wesley & Stacey Campbell take an ancient tradition - the prayer book - and give it a modern twist: Praying The Bible: The Book of Prayers presents complete passages of 88 prayers in 8 distinct prayer genres, with introductions on how to pray each genre, including The Theophanies, The Psalms, Prayers of Wisdom, The Song of Songs, Prayers of the Prophets, The Prayers of Jesus, Apostolic Prayers and The Hymns of the Revelation.

The results? A unique and long-overdue prayer tool for novice and seasoned intercessors alike and for everyone who seeks a more consistent, sustained prayer life and a pathway to a deeper life with God.

Praying the Bible: The Pathway To Spirituality
How to Increase your Love for God by Praying the Bible

The Bible emphasizes the importance of prayer in our day-to-day relationship with God and tells us how to pray for proven effectiveness. Building upon this biblical truth, Wesley and Stacey Campbell lead us on a pathway to spirituality that runs continually upward and gains momentum with each of the seven steps.

Praying the Bible: Pathway to Spirituality takes you on a life-changing journey - from walking, to running, to being directly connected with God's presence!

Along the pathway, you will learn the importance of prayer and how to go about it - and why God's Word is the one and only source of true prayer power.

The 'Pathway To Spirituality' is a concise presentation of the oldest model of prayer, spanning over two thousand years. Everyone who engages in this proven method of prayer will experience a marked improvement in their own prayer life.

The authors share their own exciting personal prayer experiences as they guide you through the seven steps - how to pray, what to pray, when to pray, and more - to a deeper connection with God. This book is practical and revelational, historical and educational - an invaluable tool for novice prayers and seasoned intercessors alike. Bound to be a classic!

The "Supernatural Heroes" Series
Historical, biographical, inspirational and supernatural! Read about God's heroes of the past as they brought God's rule to the earth.

* St. Patrick of Ireland (*Currently in Progress*)

PRAYING THE BIBLE CD SERIES
Produced by Wesley & Stacey Campbell

PTB 01 - "Prayers from the Desert : Praying the Psalms"
with Wesley Campbell
"Prayers from the Desert" focuses specifically on praying the Psalms. And, like the Psalms in the Bible, these prayers are set to original musical arrangements and accompaniment.

PTB 02 - "The Fire of Love : Praying the Song of Songs"
with Mike Bickle
"Many waters cannot quench love...it burns like a blazing fire, the very flame of the LORD." This prophetic love song is also accompanied by an original soundtrack.

PTB 04 - "Apostolic Prayers"
with Mike Bickle
For years, Mike has prayed the "Apostolic Prayers". With revival bursting upon us, this album will help you pray the way the apostles did - so we get the same results!

PTB 05 - "Prayers for the Harvest"
with Ken Gott
Pastoring a church situated in one of the roughest neighborhoods of England, Revivalist Ken Gott, knows what it's like to pray for the poor, the criminals and the oppressed.

PTB 06 - "The Bride's Anthem
with Mike Bickle
In "The Bride's Anthem," Mike Bickle prays the visions of the Apostle John from the perspective of the adoring Bride waiting for her soon coming Bridegroom.

PTB 07 - "Prayers for X-treme Disciples"
with Lou Engle & Stacey Campbell
Praying with the passion of a modern-day John the Baptist, Lou Engle cries out for a new generation of "X-treme Disciples." This CD will break every prayer stereotype ever heard.

PTB 10 - "The Voice of Healing"
with Todd Bentley
The passion of Todd Bentley's life and ministry is to see others set free through the anointing of the Holy Spirit and to see them come to the reality of an intimate relationship with Jesus. Come and drink of the Healing Waters.

PTB 11 - "Prayers For Israel"
with Jim Goll

Jesus told us to "pray for the peace of Israel." Since becoming a nation in 1948, thus fulfilling biblical predictions, Israel has been the site of ongoing conflict. Join Jim Goll as he prays with special passion for the ancient people of God - the Jews.

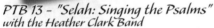

PTB 12 - "Prayers for the Elijah Revolution"
with Lou Engle & Stacey Campbell

In his day, Elijah brought about a revolution through his prayers. Hear Lou Engle pray through the life of Elijah, as he prays for another Elijah Revolution in our own day. Lou passionately intercedes, calling men and women to unite in gatherings of fasting and prayer.

PTB 13 - "Selah: Singing the Psalms"
with the Heather Clark Band

After writing the music for "X-treme Disciples" and "The Elijah Revolution", Heather became hooked on Praying The Bible. Taking it a step further, she began to sing/pray the Psalms with catchy rhythms and lyrics straight from the Word of God.

PTB 15 - "Children's Prayers Vol. 1"
with Caleb, Judah, Joab, Simeon & Vashti Campbell

Wesley and Stacey's five children (ages 4-12) pray bible prayers set to children's music and vocals, with the intent to model, instruct, and draw your children into prayer and is suitable at night for your children to listen as they go to sleep, in the morning as they start their day, in the car, or at play. P.S. . . . moms & dads like it too!

PTB 16 - "Psalms & Hymns Vol. 1"
with Wesley Campbell

"How Majestic Is Your Name"...the beauty of the Hebrew Psalms. Set to all new arrangements of the great Hymns. Join Wesley Campbell as he prays the Word of God as it is written.

PTB 17 - "Dark Yet Lovely"
with Heather Clark

"Dark am I...yet lovely." This album tells the story of the Song of Songs. These intimate and passionate songs display the love relationship between the Bride & Bridegroom.

PTB 19 - "Selah 11: Like Men Who Dreamed"
with Heather Clark

This is the third Scripture CD done by Heather, and it is a unique combination of celebration, worship and Scripture.

TOLL FREE ORDERING: 1-888-738-4832
resources@prayingthebible.com
www.prayingthebible.com

NEW CDS FROM PRAYING THE BIBLE

Produced by Wesley and Stacey Campbell

Open Heavens Vol. I
with Bob Jones, Todd Bentley, Lou Engle & Stacey Campbell

Bob Jones, Todd Bentley, Lou Engle & Stacey Campbell, relate their stories, visions, experiences and encounters with God and his angels. Listen as contemporary prophets and visionaries reveal what the Spirit is saying to us today.

Open Heavens Vol. II
with Todd Bentley, Bob Jones & Stacey Campbell

These stories of the supernatural will encourage you to receive an impartation for yourself, so that you too can participate in what God is doing all over the earth.

Prayers of Intimacy
with Tabitha

"Prayers of Intimacy" charts a new path in personal devotion with a unique blend of prayer and worship - the texts are taken directly from the "Psalms" and the "Song of Solomon" and are mostly prayed as they are written, while still allowing for Spirit led spontaneity.

REVIVAL NOW! WORSHIP CD SERIES

Produced by Wesley & Stacey Campbell

RNW 02 - "Fireland: Cry of the Celts"
with Liz Fitzgibbons & Wesley Campbell

This CD was recorded live at famous Bangor, Ireland, which was the site of the longest running 24-hour house of prayer since the Tabernacle of David. Prophetic song, wild drummers from Balyclare, and Irish jigs makes this an authentic firey Celtic worship CD.

RNW 03 - "Temple Dance"
with JoAnn McFatter

JoAnn McFatter has become renowned for her unique style and spontaneous song. Enjoy an entire album of pure prophetic song, set to the haunting sounds of middle eastern music.

RNW 05 - "Cry Mercy"
with David Ruis & Heather Clark

Hear David Ruis like you've never heard him before. Recorded live at Avalanche 2000 in Kelowna, BC. Canada. All proceeds from this project, go to "Hope For The Nations", for 'children at risk' around the world.

TOLL FREE ORDERING: 1-888-738-4832
resources@prayingthebible.com
www.prayingthebible.com

PRAYING THE BIBLE : TEACHING SERIES

Pathway to Spirituality: Teaching Series
with Wesley and Stacey Campbell

Wesley and Stacey Campbell lead us on a pathway to spirituality that runs continually upward and gains momentum at each of the seven steps. The authors share their own exciting personal prayer experiences as they guide you through the seven steps to a deeper connection with God. This teaching series is practical and educational, enriching and inspiring - an invaluable tool for both novice and seasoned intercessors alike. Available in Cassette, Video, Compact Disc & DVD.

Be A Hero! Mobilizing Mercy & Social Justice for the End-Time Harvest
with Wesley Campbell

Be a Hero! The charge makes our blood run cold. Like a Gideon, we protest - "who me?" Yet this is the cry resonating throughout the earth. God is challenging you to enlist in the noblest of all battles - the battle for mercy and justice. 1.2 billion 'children at risk' cannot be ignored. Dying kids on our doorstep is what loving our neighbor is all about!

Wesley Campbell makes a compelling case for you to be a hero in the life of 'children at risk' by praying, sponsoring an orphan, advocacy, starting a children's home or project and going on a 'hero' holiday. Loaded with facts and stats, this message is a convincing call to "Be A HERO!" by mobilizing for mercy and social justice. 4 Part Series available in Cassette, Video, Compact Disc & DVD.

◆ ◆ ◆ ◆ ◆ ◆ ◆ ◆ ◆

CONTACT INFORMATION

Bookings for Wesley & Stacey Campbell:

Please contact Be A HERO!
c/o 2041 Harvey Avenue, Kelowna, B.C. V1Y 6G7
Phone: (250) 717-1003 Fax: (250) 717-1013
E-mail: info@prayingthebible.com

Conferences & Schools:

Be A HERO! along with New Life Church in beautiful Kelowna, BC., Canada, host 4-6 conferences per year, including the Eyes & Wings Prophetic Conference and 1 - 2 training & equipping schools per year, including the "Be A Hero! Schoo and the "Go School". If you would like to join us for any or all of these events, please contact us at the above address or check out our website at www.beahero.org for more details.

Resources:

TOLL FREE ORDERING: 1-888-738-4832
resources@prayingthebible.com
www.prayingthebible.com

WORSHIP CDS FROM GLOBALIFT

BOUNDLESS VOL. 1
A worldwide compilation of worship songs featuring musicians Nathan Rowe, Michelle Kay, Tony Baso, Phil Laeger, Street Corner Medix, Mark Hood, Tom Freeman, and Danielle Strickland.

SOUL CANDY
DA compilation of worship songs from Canada- Tom Freeman, Danielle Strickland, Tanis, and Wattershed.

SoZo
Live Salvation Army worship from Canada, featuring worship leader Tim Bartsch.

PRAYER CDS FROM GLOBALIFT

AND CAN IT BE?
Featuring prayers based on ROOTS by Tony Campolo, Phil Wall, and more. Original soundtrack is by Mark Hood and Tom Freeman

SALVO P.O.P.
Prayers of Praise by Chick Yuill, Janet Munn, Robert Marshall, Stacey Campbell, Wesley Campbell and more.

ARMY OF THE LORD
Revivalist Nolan Clark preaches on the Commander of the Lord's Army with original soundtrack by Tom Freeman and Danielle Strickland.

To Order Resources:
info@thewarcollege.com
www.armybarmy.com

BOOKS FROM GLOBALIFT

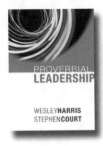

PROVERBIAL LEADERSHIP
Stephen Court & Wesley Harris

THE SIREN CALL OF A DANGEROUS GOD:
ESSAYS IN EVANGELICAL DIALECTIC
Geoff Ryan

· ♦ · ♦ · ♦ · ♦ · ♦ · ♦ ·

CONTACT INFORMATION

For Bookings, Resources and Event Information for
Stephen Court & Danielle Strickland:
Please contact GlobaLift
info@thewarcollege.com
www.armybarmy.com

614 Salvation Army hosts the following schools in Vancouver, BC. Canada:

Booth Tucker Institute: Short term leadership training for those interested in catching the heart of God for Incarnational urban missions.

War College: A one year residential school to train warriors to win the world for Jesus in Canada's poorest postal code (Vancouver - Downtown Eastside).

For more details, please contact us at our website: www.armybarmy.com

Additional copies of this book and other
book titles from DESTINY IMAGE are
available at your local bookstore.

For a bookstore near you, call 1-800-722-6774.

Send a request for a catalog to:

Destiny Image® Publishers, Inc.

P.O. Box 310
Shippensburg, PA 17257-0310

*"Speaking to the Purposes of God for This
Generation and for the Generations to Come"*

**For a complete list of our titles,
visit us at www.destinyimage.com**